Beth Moore

BELOVED DISCIPLE

The Life and Ministry of John

LifeWay Press®
Nashville, Tennessee

ISBN 0-6330-1851-1

This book is the text for course CG-0707 in the subject area
Personal Life in the Christian Growth Study Plan.

Dewey Decimal Classification Number: 225.92
Subject Headings: JOHN, APOSTLE
BIBLE.N.T. JOHN—STUDY
DISCIPLESHIP TRAINING—WOMEN

Unless otherwise indicated, Scripture quotations are from the Holy Bible,
New International Version, copyright © 1973, 1978, 1984 by International Bible Society.

Scripture quotations identified KJV are from the *King James Version*.

Scripture quotations identified AMP are from *The Amplified New Testament*
© The Lockman Foundation 1954, 1958, 1987. Used by permission.

Scripture quotations identified NASB are from the NEW AMERICAN STANDARD BIBLE,
© Copyright The Lockman Foundation, 1960, 1962, 1963, 1968, 1971, 1972, 1973, 1975, 1977, 1995.
Used by permission.

Scripture quotations identified CEV are from the *Contemporary English Version*
Copyright © 1991, 1992, 1995 American Bible Society. Used by permission.

To order additional copies of this resource, write to LifeWay Church Resources Customer Service;
One LifeWay Plaza; Nashville, TN 37234-0013; fax (615) 251-5933;
phone toll free (800) 458-2772; e-mail *customerservice@lifeway.com;* order online at *www.lifeway.com;*
or visit the LifeWay Christian Store serving you.

Printed in the United States of America

Leadership and Adult Publishing
LifeWay Church Resources
One LifeWay Plaza
Nashville, TN 37234-0175

To my new son, Curt—

If I could have looked the world over for a life partner for my firstborn,
I would have chosen you. No need. God already had. My dear Curt,
as I wrote this study, I often thought how very much you favor the apostle John.
You are a true man of vision, driven to the *Logos* by godly affection.
You are the essence of a deeply beloved disciple.

I love you.

Beth Moore

$\mathcal{B}$eth Moore realized at the age of 18 that God was claiming her future for full-time ministry. While she was sponsoring a cabin of sixth-graders at a missions camp, God unmistakably acknowledged that she would work for Him. There Beth conceded all rights to the Lord she had loved since childhood. However, she encountered a problem: although she knew she was "wonderfully made," she was "fearfully" without talent.

Beth hid behind closed doors to discover whether a beautiful singing voice had miraculously developed, but the results were tragic. She returned to the piano from which years of fruitless practice had streamed but found the noise to be joyless. Finally accepting that the only remaining alternative was missions work in a foreign country, she struck a martyr's pose and waited. Yet nothing happened.

Still confident of God's calling, Beth finished her degree at Southwest Texas State University, where she fell in love with Keith. After they married in December 1978, God added daughters Amanda and Melissa to their household.

As if putting together puzzle pieces one at a time, God filled Beth's path with supportive persons who saw something in her she could not. God used individuals like Marge Caldwell, John Bisagno, and Jeannette Cliff George to help Beth discover gifts of speaking, teaching, and writing. Seventeen years after her first speaking engagement, those gifts have spread all over the nation. Her joy and excitement in Christ are contagious; her deep love for the Savior, obvious; her style of speaking, electric.

Beth's ministry is grounded in and fueled by her service at her home fellowship, First Baptist Church, Houston, Texas, where she serves on the pastor's council and teaches a large Sunday School class. Beth believes that her calling is Bible literacy: guiding believers to love and live God's Word.

Beth loves the Lord, loves to laugh, and loves to be with His people. Her life is full of activity, but one commitment remains constant: counting all things but loss for the excellence of knowing Christ Jesus, the Lord (see Phil. 3:8).

Beth's previous Bible studies have explored the lives of Moses, David, Paul, Isaiah, and Jesus. In *Beloved Disciple: The Life and Ministry of John* she invites you along to learn from the long life and incomparable writings of "the disciple whom Jesus loved" (John 21:20). May you be blessed by your journey, as were those who traveled to Greece for the videotaping and those who worked with Beth to bring you *Beloved Disciple*.

Contents

Introduction

I have the privilege of writing this introduction only days after my husband escorted our firstborn down the aisle and into the arms of her handsome groom. My heart is moved by the tenderness of God's personal affections, which He demonstrates to each of us in His divine timing. How like Him to choose this precious time in my life to plan a wedding while writing a study that culminates with joyous anticipation of the wedding supper of the Lamb!

John the apostle had no idea that the events, experiences, and transitions in his life experience were all etched on a divine map to move him toward an unparalleled destiny. He alone was positioned to receive the Revelation. I wonder whether after the final vision John realized that he had been getting ready for a wedding from the start. He had first learned of Christ through the faithful tutelage of a Baptizer who was also called "the friend of the bridegroom" (John 3:29, KJV). Then Christ chose a wedding in Cana to first reveal His glory to His small band of followers by turning water to wine. Christ also chose wedding themes for several of His most powerful parables. No doubt, Christ meant to make a point, and I believe the point of His arrow pierced its way into the heart of the youngest disciple.

Every disciple and early follower of Christ left a legacy for future believers. John's legacy was love. After all, what is a wedding without love? Perhaps like no other disciple, John understood that relationship is the point. Every command of Christ and call to obedience is to enhance relationship and place the recipient in a posture the Giver can bless. All else is law. I may as well warn you. You won't find much law in this study. It just wasn't John's style. This study is about finding our way to the heart of Jesus and reclining so closely that our pulse begins to throb in tandem, loving what He loves and hating what He hates.

If John were here, I believe he would tell us, above all, to sell out to love. Legalists tend to get a little nervous when we talk about surrendering to love over service, but Scripture proves that those who loved most lavishly served most sacrificially. John was only one among good company. Mary of Bethany, Peter, and Paul were each compelled by holy passion. Affection will forever be the most efficient energy a believer can burn in her labors.

Allow me to give you the bottom line before we turn the first page in hopes that you might adopt John's attitude from the very beginning: John was free to love because he was so utterly convinced that he was loved. He called himself the beloved disciple. How differently would each follower live if we characterized ourselves above all else as the beloved disciple of Jesus Christ? This is the goal of our journey.

God is planning a wedding. Every moment of our believing lives is meant to prepare us for that day. John was like the wise virgins in Matthew 25, who did not know when the bridegroom would come but kept their lamps filled with oil. As you will discover in the last third of the study, even in exile when no one was looking, John kept his heart-lamp full with the oil of the Holy Spirit. No wonder Christ chose him to receive the final revelation. May John's legacy become oil in each of our lamps, preparing each of us for our Bridegroom.

I'll soon be turning in my mother-of-the-bride dress for fine white linen. Glory! But while I've still got another wedding on my mind, allow me to say that I was in no hurry for Amanda to make her final flight out of our nest. In fact, I really could have gotten in a bad mood about it … except for our groom. I awakened on the morning of the wedding with indescribable gladness—even laughter—in my heart. I sat down and wrote Curt a letter to tell him why, for God had used him to make our joy complete. The profound passage in our family's life was not only bearable but also celebratory because I was totally convinced of our groom's love for his bride.

Dear One, you and I can celebrate our profound passage through this life because we can "know and rely on the love God has for us" (1 John 4:16). Leave it to John to pen those words. Our water is turned to wine and our joy is complete because our Bridegroom is Jesus the Christ, the living, breathing Son of God. Oh, for the day we'll see Him face-to-face!

As surely as God loved me and timed this study for me, He will do the same for you. My reasons happened to surround a wedding. Yours will be entirely unique to you. In whatever way Christ applies the truths of these pages to your precious life, let Him romance you along the way. No matter what may be going on in your life, never forget that you are a bride.

Introductory Group Session

As we begin a journey that will take us throughout Galilee into Samaria, to Jerusalem, to Ephesus, and to Patmos, let's consider adopting the same invitations for embarkation that John encountered.

Read John 1:35-51.

1. Let's sense Christ asking us the same question: "_____, My child, what do you want?
   [Your name]

   What are you seeking here and now in this _____ _____ of your life?"

2. Let's be willing to "_____ _____ _____."

3. Consider the unfathomable grace of God that we sometimes "find" Christ when we didn't even know

   _____ was the_____ we were _____ _____.

4. We will miss untold treasures if we confuse "_____ ____ _____"

   with "_____ _____ _____."

5. Let's begin our journey as a true seeker "in whom there is _____ _____."

6. Wherever we've recently _____, Jesus has _____ ____ _____.

7. As Christ reveals how He has "_____" _____, our eyes are somehow

   _____ to "see" _____.

FRESH WINDS OVER GALILEE

Day 1
Since That Time

Day 2
The Identity of Family

Day 3
They Were Fishermen

Day 4
Old Ties and New Ties

Day 5
A Hard Act to Follow

I love new beginnings, don't you? I am honored to embark on this new beginning with you. Let's count on God to take us places with Him we've never been and to accomplish a work we didn't know He could. As James and John cast their nets on the sun-kissed waters of the Sea of Galilee, they had no idea that the Son of God was casting His net for them. Soon they would find themselves captured by His call and compelled by His love. Let's allow the same divine affection to catch us as we too are called to be disciples of Jesus Christ.

I hope you take part in weekly small-group gatherings, video presentations, and discussions. If not, you can work through this study by yourself. However, the accountability, encouragement, and shared experiences of a small group create an ideal learning process.

The Principal Questions will guide your discovery in the Word each week. Each day also provides a Personal Discussion Question (🖋) that you will apply to your life and discuss with your group.

Principal Questions

Day 1: What was John the Baptist's purpose for preaching?
Day 2: How was John identified in his family?
Day 3: What name did Simon call Jesus in Luke 5:5?
Day 4: How did Christ build His new followers?
Day 5: According to Mark 1:25-26, what happened when Jesus commanded the demons to come out of the man?

Day 1 SINCE THAT TIME

TODAY'S TREASURE

" 'The Law and the Prophets were proclaimed until John. Since that time, the good news of the kingdom of God is being preached.' "—Luke 16:16

The year was A.D. 28—give or take a few years. For a chosen people who hadn't heard a word from God in four centuries, life was pretty good west of the Jordan. They had covered their insecurities with a blanket of sameness. The absence of a fresh encounter with God had them clutching to what they had left: the law.

Interesting, isn't it? The Hebrew people climbed to the summit of legalism during the silent years that fell between Malachi and Matthew. That's what really religious people do who don't have much of a relationship.

Can you relate? On the scales in the margin draw an arrow where your balance lies between relationship and legalism.

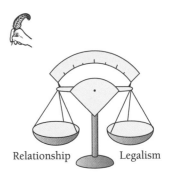

Relationship   Legalism

The Hebrew people wanted to know what they could expect from life, so they formed an expectation and enforced it with a vengeance. They got life as they wanted it, threw it over their heads like a security blanket, and hid from change. If anyone questioned the status quo, the committed acted as if the blanket had always been there. No doubt, many ascribed to the prevailing attitude described in 2 Peter 3:4. " 'Ever since our fathers died, everything goes on as it has since the beginning of creation.' "

But they were wrong. Since creation everything has never simply gone on. God has been carefully executing a plan of inconceivable perfection. Even in the silent years of Israel's history, God was never inactive. We have no idea how hard His hands may work even when His mouth seems closed. God's silence never equals slumber.

For those of us trying to grasp what the God of the universe is doing with planet Earth, few titles of Christ are more significant than those that issued from His own mouth in Revelation 22:13. What are they?
❏ **Alpha and Omega**   ❏ **First and Last**
❏ **Lion of the tribe of Judah**   ❏ **Beginning and End**

I cannot describe how impressed I am with the manifold perfections and consistencies of Scripture. A book that unfolds with the words "In the beginning" concludes with One who declares Himself both as that very Beginning and as the End. Life on this planet had a precisely executed beginning, and it will have a certain end. He who planned them both to perfection does not just leave everything in between to go on as it would—or as it always had.

God has a will for earth. Before He uttered, " 'Let there be light' " (Gen. 1:3), every day of His kingdom calendar was filled from beginning to end. We can refuse to cooperate, but we cannot keep God from executing the critical events on His own schedule. Thankfully, no amount of tradition can stop God when He has a mind to change things.

God has a will for earth.

Just as the establishment got things the way they wanted and swore they had always been, someone had the gall to stick his head out from under the security blanket. Sooner or later, he'd lose his head for it, but in the meantime, he'd shake up a few things.

Read Luke 3:1-9. In what ways did John the Baptizer seem to stick his head out from under the security blanket of sameness?
❑ Preached repentance to forgiveness
❑ Demanded faithfulness to the sacrificial system
❑ Demanded fruit in keeping with repentance
❑ Warned of impending judgment

I don't want you to miss the inference of a very deliberate God keeping a precise schedule on the kingdom calendar. Luke 3:1 says,

"In the _____ of the reign of Tiberius Caesar."

Luke 3:2 then says "during the high priesthood of Annas and Caiaphas" something very critical happened. What was it?
❑ John the Baptist came. ❑ The Word of God came. ❑ Jesus Christ came.

Today's Treasure quotes Christ Himself. Please reread it. How does this verse pinpoint John's life as a point of change on the kingdom calendar?

_____

_____

_____

After four hundred years of silence, suddenly the Word of God came. After such a long wait to see God reveal Himself afresh to mortal creatures, I wonder if all of heaven hushed to hear it. Of course, those on earth didn't have to hush. The Baptizer talked nice and loud. And when he was not nice, he was still loud. Loud enough, in fact, that Pharisees and Sadducees from Jerusalem went to the fringe of the security blanket on the banks of the Jordan to see what all the commotion was about (see Matt. 3:5,7). Theirs were among the few heads that stayed dry that day. They held their security blanket over their heads to keep from getting doused in change.

Always one to swim against the current, John the Baptist delivered a message that traveled the Jordan upstream into the waters of a handful of fishermen in a village called Bethsaida. Drawn like fish to bait, several of them trekked to hear him and hung on his every word. In fact, John 1:35 refers to them as disciples of John the Baptist. Don't let the term seem heretical to you. The label *disciple* seems almost sacred to many of us, but keep in mind the only thing that made the twelve disciples of Jesus sacred was the One they followed. *Disciple* simply indicates a pupil and follower of someone's teaching.

Thankfully, John the Baptist was a man worth following, precisely because he led straight to Jesus. Let's read a personal testimony about the teaching of the Baptizer from the quill of the man we have committed to study for the next 10 weeks.

> John the Baptist was a man worth following, because he led straight to Jesus.

Read John 1:19-31, focusing on the question in verse 22, " 'What do you say about yourself?' " In what two ways did John the Baptist define himself?

Who he was not: _____

Who he was: _____

I don't think that's a bad question for us to ask ourselves as we launch this boat together. So what about you? What do you say about yourself? What we don't say in words, we ultimately say in deeds. Daily we say all sorts of things about ourselves. Sometimes what we say about ourselves is not necessarily accurate, but it's what we believe. Trust me. I know about this one. I lived much of my life with a highly inaccurate estimation of who I wasn't and who I was. As a young person, I dizzily swung between feelings of *I am a victim, and I'm not as good as anybody else* and *I'm no one's victim, and I'm going to be better than everyone else*. As I stare at that brief testimony, I sigh at the recollection of it all. Believing and living a lie was so exhausting. What finally got me off the swing? Learning to see myself in relationship to Jesus Christ.

Don't get the idea that I've arrived or that whatever I've learned so far hasn't been a process. I struggled with my identity even as I grew healthier, and I still do at times. In my first years of ministry I tried so hard to *be* my mentor that I tried to do everything just as she did it. Has anyone besides me ever discovered that trying to be someone else is exhausting?

Because of Jesus, John knew who he was and who he wasn't. Who wasn't he? "He did not fail to confess, but confessed freely, 'I am not the Christ' " (John 1:20). Much of his public was plenty willing to hail him as the Christ, had John let them. He didn't.

According to John 1:27, how differently did John see himself from Christ?

_____

_____

So who was John the Baptist, according to his own definition? " 'I am the voice of one calling in the desert, "Make straight the way for the Lord" ' " (v. 23). I find what he said about himself very refreshing. He understood Christ's greatness and how unworthy he was in comparison, but he didn't see himself as having the value of an inchworm under a rock. His life had value through its connection to Christ.

John the Baptist has just introduced a concept that another John will carry on for us throughout our 10-week travel together. Among many other things, we're going to learn how to define ourselves by our relationship to Jesus Christ. We'll arrive at an important place of maturity when we can say who we are—and who we are not.

As we try to compare ourselves to John the Baptist, we might be tempted to think: *Well, one thing is certain. No one's going to get me confused with Christ.* To the contrary, some people will try to make anyone with a semblance of spiritual maturity their personal savior. Have you ever had anyone try to make you their savior of sorts? Our most convenient response might be shifting all responsibility to the poor, confused person. After all, can we help it if someone mistakes us for more than we are?

John the Baptist's example might suggest that we can and must "help it" whenever possible. Like him, we need to confess freely things like: "I'm so sorry if I've led you to believe otherwise, but I am not your salvation. I have no power to deliver you." "I can't be our entire family's rock. If you're all standing on me for stability, we're all about to have a sinking spell." Or "I don't have all the answers. I'm still trying to figure out what the questions are."

So do we just let everyone down? No, we ask them to let us down, right off that man-made pedestal of toothpicks. Our role in the lives of those God sends our way for help is not unlike John the Baptist's. We become a voice in their desert helping them prepare a way for the Lord.

> What we don't say in words, we ultimately say in deeds.

I can't wait to see why God has invited me along on this journey. I have no preconceived notions, no idea where this study is going. An unknown adventure lies ahead of me as surely as it does for you. I dearly love an adventure! I can't wait to see all the stops we'll make and all the keepsakes we'll pick up along the way, but when all is said and done, I have a feeling we will learn much about identity. Whose? Christ's and two of His very important disciples. One we'll meet tomorrow. The other you can meet in the nearest mirror.

As we conclude today, let's form a baseline for our present perceived identity so that we can draw comparisons after our journey. Don't give the answers you think you should. Instead, please be completely honest. You won't be asked to share your responses in your small group. They are just between God and you.

As clearly as you can presently see, please list the following.

Who you've discovered you aren't: _____

_____

Who you've discovered you are: _____

_____

I'm so glad you've joined me on this journey. Let's see where the Lord takes us as we explore His Word together.

$Day\ 2$ THE IDENTITY OF FAMILY

TODAY'S TREASURE
"Going on from there, he saw two other brothers, James son of Zebedee and his brother John."—Matthew 4:21

Family. Only the divine can be more essential. The devout Jew could not detach the familial from the spiritual. God Himself wove the two together from the beginning: "The Lord God caused the man to fall into a deep sleep; and while he was sleeping, he took one of the man's ribs and closed up the place with flesh. Then the Lord God made a woman from the rib he had taken out of the man, and he brought her to the man" (Gen. 2:21-22). A spiritual act if you'll ever find one.

Then in Genesis 4:1 "Adam lay with his wife Eve, and she became pregnant and gave birth to Cain. She said, 'With the help of the Lord I have brought forth a man.' Later she gave birth to his brother Abel."

God never abandoned the concept of family.

Family life became synonymous with family problems almost from the start, but God never abandoned the concept. Indeed, family was a very good idea and became a powerful medium through which God has worked throughout history. In Genesis 28:13 God formally introduced Himself to Jacob like this: " 'I am the Lord, the God of your father Abraham and the God of Isaac. I will give you and your descendants the land on which you are lying.' "

God emphasized the meshing of the familial and spiritual so strongly in the Old Testament that space permits me only a few of many references: Exodus 12:25-27 says, " 'When you enter the land that the Lord will give you as he promised, observe this ceremony. And when your children ask you, "What does this ceremony mean to you?" then tell them, "It is the Passover sacrifice to the Lord, who passed over the houses of the Israelites in Egypt and spared our homes when he struck down the Egyptians." ' "

Joshua 4:5-7 says, " 'Go over before the ark of the Lord your God into the middle of the Jordan. Each of you is to take up a stone on his shoulder, according to the number of the tribes of the Israelites, to serve as a sign among you. In the future, when your children ask you, "What do these stones mean?" tell them that the flow of the Jordan was cut off before the ark of the covenant of the Lord.' "

Hebrew parents and children talked. The Lord did not say, "if your children ask you" but "when your children ask you." Fathers were even more involved in the education of their children than the mothers. In a typical ancient Jewish home, communication was virtually constant, and to remove the spiritual significance from their conversation would have almost silenced them.

No segment of Scripture expresses the interweaving of God and family like the Shema, Deuteronomy 6:4-9. Carefully read these verses, trying to absorb the priorities of life God delivered in this directive.

How would you explain to a new Christian the relationship between the things of God and the things of family?

You are probably Gentile by heritage just as I am. Anytime we study the life of someone steeped in an entirely different culture, we have to be very intentional about seeing them in their world rather than ours. We can make countless applications to our world but only after we have viewed historical figures in their own. Not only was ancient Orthodox Judaism an entirely different culture from ours, but God also made sure it compared to none. He did not want His nation to be like any others. Let's hear God talk for Himself in Deuteronomy 14:1-2: " 'You are the children of the Lord your God. … For you are a people holy to the Lord your God. Out of all the peoples on the face of the earth, the Lord has chosen you to be his treasured possession.' "

New Testament Jews were Jews at a time when Judaism had perhaps never been more Jewish. By this expression I mean that although they were under Roman rule, they enjoyed very significant freedom to live out their culture. They were firmly established in their land and had their temple. Every sect of religious life was functioning at full throttle—the Pharisees, Sadducees, and the teachers of the law, to name only a few.

Life in the Galilean villages of Capernaum and Bethsaida must have seemed light-years away from the hub of religious life in Herod's temple in Jerusalem, but one thing varied little from Hebrew to Hebrew. YHWH* was life—Provider, Sustainer, Sovereign Creator of all things. To the Jews, to have little thought of God was to have little thought at all.

If the more sophisticated Jews in the Holy City thought the simple settlers on the Sea of Galilee envied them, they were surely mistaken. Neither had modern conveniences, but who can miss what they never had? Neither was without the inevitable troubles that are part of life. Each had their preferences. Each had points of view. One awakened to

To the Jews, to have little thought of God was to have little thought at all.

*The Jews referred to God in writing with the Tetragrameton (four letters, YHWH), from which we get the name Jehovah or Yahweh. They used the word Adonai (meaning Lord) rather than speak the name of God.

the brilliance of the sun dancing off the gleaming walls of the temple. The other saw the sun strolling on the water. A fisherman would have been hard to convince that God's glory dwelled more powerfully in a building made of stone than in a bright pink and purple sunset over the lake. (I know this for a fact. I am married to a fisherman.)

Two pairs of sons grew up not far from each other on the northern tip of the Sea of Galilee. Four pairs of feet earned their calluses on the pebbles of a familiar shore. From the time their sons were knee high to them, Zebedee and Jonah were responsible not only for making sure their rambunctious offspring didn't drown but also for harnessing their insatiable curiosity. Fathers were walking day-care centers for their sons, and their son's mothers would be expecting them home in one piece.

Peter and Andrew, James and John. They were trees planted by streams of water being raised to bring forth their own fruit in season (see Ps. 1:3). If those fathers had known what would become of their sons, I wonder whether they would have reared them any differently. I doubt it. They were simple men with one simple goal: to teach their sons all they knew.

Our task today is to piece together what our protagonist's life might have been like in childhood and in youth before a Lamb came and turned it upside down. In the following activity, please read only the verse without giving attention to the surrounding verses that will compose tomorrow's text. Here you'll find the first mention of the one destined to become the beloved disciple.

Read Matthew 4:21. How is John identified in his family?

_____

Scholars are almost unanimous in their assumption that John was the younger brother of James. In the earlier reference his name is listed after his brother's, which often indicated birth order. In their world, if any name existed that was more common than James (a Hellenized form of Iakob, or Jacob), it was John.

What is the Old Testament form of John (see 1 Chron. 26:3; Ezra 10:6)?

_____

Because the family used the Hebrew language, this was the name John was actually called. It may sound a little fancier, but the name was as common as could be. I don't feel that James and John were the kinds of boys about whom the neighbors mused, "I can't wait to see what they'll turn out to be. Mark my word. They'll be special!" Those who watched them grow up assumed the sons of Zebedee would be fishermen like their father.

New identities were not common commodities in those days. Look at Matthew 4:21. Not only are James and John referred to as "two other brothers," but John is also simply identified as the brother of James, son of Zebedee. If we're right and James was the older brother, he held the coveted position in the family birth order. Special rights and privileges belonged to him as well as a birthright that assured him a double portion of his father's estate. The firstborn son was a leader in the family, commanding respect for a position he did nothing to earn. John? He was just the younger brother.

Most of us have experienced the ambiguity of being known by little more than our relationship to someone else. I love being Keith Moore's wife, Amanda and Melissa's mother, and Curt's mother-in-law, but that's probably because I've lived enough of life to figure out who I am. I can remember feeling lost in a whole line of siblings growing up.

Peter and Andrew, James and John were raised to bring forth their own fruit in season.

I have fond memories of my mother calling me every name in our big family but mine. I often grinned while she scrambled for the right one, and exasperated, she'd finally say, "If I'm looking at you, I'm talking to you!" I'd giggle, "Yes, Ma'am!" and run off while she was still doing her best to remember my name.

What about you? How are you identified by your relationship to others?

_____

_____

Some things about parenting must be universal. Surely Zebedee looked straight at Jehohanan and accidentally called him Iakob at times. If so, would young John have been the type to let it go unnoticed, or might he have said, "Abba! I am Jehohanan!" These are concepts and thoughts I love to explore imaginatively when studying a character. Either way, John was no doubt accustomed to being Zebedee's other son and James' little brother. However common his name, its meaning was extraordinary: "God has been gracious."[1] Growing up on the shore of Jesus' favorite sea, John had no idea at this point just how gracious God had been. He would soon get a glimpse.

John would soon get a glimpse of just how gracious God had been.

John may have been an ordinary name, and our protagonist may have been an ordinary boy, but based on maternal persuasions through the ages, we can be fairly certain he was extraordinary to his mother. We will discover later in our journey that she considered nothing too good for her sons. Who was this woman anyway, this wife of Zebedee and the mother of James and John? Let's look ahead for just a moment.

Compare Matthew 27:55-56 and Mark 15:40. What might her name have been?

_____

Most scholars I have researched believe that John's mother is positively identified by name in the latter verse. Some scholars go as far as saying that Salome was Jesus' aunt (the sister of His mother, Mary), based on a comparison with John 19:25.

Who is identified in John 19:25? How many relationships are referenced?

_____

_____

As you can see, we have no way of knowing whether John identified three different women or four. Mary the wife of Clopas could have been the one identified as Jesus' maternal aunt, but two daughters in one family with the name Mary seems a little peculiar. On the other hand, to draw a fist-tight conclusion that Salome was Mary's sister from comparing lists like these is probably risky. Although I don't doubt that the families may have known each other and may even have been somehow related, I tend to agree with R. Alan Culpepper, who wrote, "Surely, if John had been Jesus' first cousin, this relationship would have been recognized more prominently in the early Christian traditions about the apostle."[2]

As you and I will learn in the coming weeks, the early church fathers recorded a fair amount of tradition about John, but we find little mention of his being Jesus' maternal

At the cross all who wished to have a relationship with Jesus Christ became blood relatives.

cousin. I am certainly no expert, but from what I have gleaned from those who are, I will write from the basis that familiarity probably existed between the two families, but I'm not convinced of a blood relationship. Thankfully, at the cross all those who wished to have a relationship with Jesus Christ became blood relatives.

As we conclude today's lesson, what do we know about the apostle John so far, based on information we've gathered today? Go ahead and make a brief list of facts. You might also include any fairly solid suppositions.

_____

_____

I have made very few sacrifices to do what God has called me to do. Christ made the significant sacrifices. One occasional sacrifice brings me small waves of heartache from time to time: I don't get many opportunities to cultivate new relationships of great personal depth. I am a people person. I can sit in a shopping mall as happy as a clam to become a student of the people who walk past me! When I drive by a house in the country, I always want to know what the people inside are like. I love people! But my calling prevents my studying and exploring the uniqueness of individuals in depth.

I just realized that in-depth Bible study that focuses primarily on one figure is a creative way God has given me to do the two things I love most. In this hideaway office where I am alone with God to write, I'm about to get to know a "new" person very well. You are, too! What joyful anticipation floods my soul!

Day 3 THEY WERE FISHERMEN

> **TODAY'S TREASURE**
> *"Without delay he called them, and they left their father Zebedee in the boat with the hired men and followed him."—Mark 1:20*

*This time frame is strictly a deduction I have made from comparing time references in John 1:43; 2:1, 12-13. I could certainly be mistaken if time lapses existed that weren't noted in these portions of Scripture.

Passover was just around the corner.* Soon the hillcrest of Eremos in northern Galilee would be covered in red anemones and blue iris. Spring had finally arrived but not a moment too soon for a band of fishermen who spent their days on the water. Winter temperatures ranging from 50 to 65 degrees Fahrenheit during the daytime may not have seemed so cold to landsmen, but fishermen would have told a different story. Sometimes their wet, sandaled feet felt like blocks of ice, and their fingers temporarily lost their dexterity from the cold. During the winter season their few hours at home were spent trying to thaw the chill in their bones. Just about the time they thawed, the boat had to be pushed from the shore back into the water. They were fortunate to get sunshine at all.

What does Luke 5:5 tell you about the hours fishermen sometimes worked?

_____

Obviously, our little band of fishermen worked the graveyard shift at times. I can think of only one thing worse than fishing in the cold: not catching anything. It happens to the best of fishermen. When it happens to Keith, I always ask him the typical sanguine woman question: "But did you have fun with your friends anyway?" My personality is given to the philosophy that the question is not so much whether you succeeded or failed but whether you had fun. I wish I had a picture of Keith's face when I ask him that question. I'd put it in the margin for your amusement. But I don't care what anyone says; company greatly determines how difficult a bad situation can be. From the few facts we're given, I believe the fishermen we're joining today had pretty good company.

Focus for now on the implications Luke 5:8-10 had on the lives of these men before they encountered Christ. What relationship did Peter, James, and John share?
❑ **Competitors**   ❑ **Business partners**   ❑ **Companions**

According to Luke 5:2-3, did these sets of partners share a boat?
❑ **Yes**   ❑ **No**

Read Matthew 4:18-22, focusing on the circumstances rather than Christ's call. Although they were partners, how were the fishermen teamed?

_____

_____

Read John 1:44. Where were Andrew and Peter from?
❑ **Judea**   ❑ **The Jordan**   ❑ **Nazareth**   ❑ **Bethsaida**

Let's discover another fun fact, and then we'll draw a few conclusions from what we've learned. Read Mark 1:20. What detail suggests something about Zebedee's financial status?

_____

Let's tie these bits and pieces together. Take a look at a map and pinpoint the Sea of Galilee. This freshwater lake is called by three additional names in Scripture: the Sea of Chinnereth, which is the Hebrew word for *harp-shaped,* the general outline of the lake; the Lake of Gennesaret, named for a fertile plain nearby; and the Sea of Tiberias because it was associated with the capital of Herod Antipas.[3] At the time Andrew, Peter, James, and John cast nets on those waters, a vigorous fishing industry was booming all over the lake. As you can see, many villages settled on its shores. Not only was it the food basket of the region, but the sight was also breathtaking. It still is. The way the lake is cupped in the center of surrounding hills looks to me like water in the palm of a large hand. With my own eyes I've seen how the early spring sunrise hangs lazily in the clinging mist. Since the first time I saw the Sea of Galilee, I have never wondered why Christ seemed to favor the villages near its shore over the metropolis of Jerusalem.

At the northern tip just where the Jordan River feeds the lake, you'll find Bethsaida. The word *Bethsaida* means "house of fishing,"[4] and it lived up to its name. The Sea of Galilee boasts 18 species of fish,[5] so fishing could be profitable almost anywhere. Bethsaida was located where the warm springs at the foot of Eremos Hill bubbled into the

When Andrew, Peter, James, and John cast nets on those waters, a vigorous fishing industry was booming.

lake, attracting fish looking for a winter blanket. The fish that have since been labeled Peter's fish are tropical and often swarm the warmer temperatures where the springs flow into the lake, giving our fishermen a decided advantage over many of their competitors.

We know for a fact that Andrew and Peter were from Bethsaida, and we can safely assume Zebedee also raised his sons in the village because they were all partners. As we will soon discover, at some point Andrew and Peter moved to nearby Capernaum, where Peter lived with his wife and mother-in-law (see Mark 1:21,29-30). We don't know for certain which of the two villages was the home of James and John at this point in their lives, but we do know they all continued to work together.

Obviously, Zebedee was the one who owned the fishing enterprise. Although I don't want to intimate that he was wealthy (because few villagers were), we'd probably be mistaken to think him poor. The reference to the hired servants tells us that he owned his own business, which was profitable enough to allow him to have servants in addition to two healthy and able sons. He might have easily owned both boats. Peter and Andrew could have fished from one (which was considered "theirs"), while a little farther away (see Mark 1:19) James and John fished from another.

Now that we have an idea what the fishermen's lives were like before they followed Christ, let's read all three Synoptic Gospel versions of their call. God wisely equipped us with four Gospels because we learn far more from hearing several accounts of anything especially noteworthy. The facts one writer included may not have been noted by another because each point of view is tinted by the individual's perspective and priorities. While writing *Jesus, the One and Only,* I learned I could almost always expect Luke to get a little more specific, which made perfect sense to me. He was a doctor, and a good doctor pays attention to details. You'll find this principle to hold true in our reading today.

Read each segment of Scripture below and carefully record any facts unique to each Gospel in the appropriate column. Be sure to look for details!

Matthew 4:18-22	Mark 1:14-20	Luke 5:1-11
_____	_____	_____
_____	_____	_____
_____	_____	_____
_____	_____	_____
_____	_____	_____

I can go no further without musing over Christ's divinely uncanny ability to waltz right into a life and turn it upside down, inside out, and every way but loose. Just think how many times those fishermen had prepared and cast their nets together. We would not be at all off base to imagine that they had caught fish together under Zebedee's instruction since they were young boys, perhaps no older than seven or eight. Picture how many years they had practiced a routine. They weren't fishing for the pure enjoyment of it as my husband does. Fishing was their job. I don't doubt they loved it as most men would, but don't think for a moment it wasn't work. I know you didn't miss Luke's inclusion, " 'Master, we've worked hard all night and haven't caught anything' " (Luke 5:5). They worked hard. Day in. Day out. Then one day Jesus walked up, and everything changed.

We learn far more from hearing several accounts of anything especially noteworthy.

Oh, isn't that exactly like Him? Jesus walks up, catches us in the act of being—again today—exactly who we were yesterday, and offers to turn our routine into adventure. Hallelujah! Have you allowed Christ to do that for you? If you're bored with life and stuck in a rut of routine, you may have believed in Christ, but you may not yet have agreed to follow Him. Christ is a lot of things—but boring? Not on your life! Life with Him is a great adventure. You don't necessarily have to leave behind what you do if He proves your present course to be in His will, but I assure you, He will have you leave its boredom and routine behind. When Jesus Christ takes over our lives, life gets exciting!

As we begin our journey, plot where you feel you are in this season of your life. Keep in mind that even spiritual or religious practices can become routine. Also keep in mind that living in the great adventure doesn't mean you won't have challenges or suffering. It means you can see and take part in Christ's breathtaking work in your life, no matter what your circumstances are.

> When Jesus Christ takes over our lives, life gets exciting!

Where do you see your life right now?

In a routine and a rut   **Living the great adventure**

No matter where we plotted ourselves, I pray that we will need an extension to the right margin at the end of our 10 weeks. May our lives be off the scale with excitement as we live the great adventure!

> **Let's notice another important fact inspired by God for Luke's account.**
> **What name did Simon call Jesus in Luke 5:5?**
> ❏ **Lord**   ❏ **Master**   ❏ **The Christ**   ❏ **Friend**   ❏ **Lamb of God**

That's not the kind of title most people use for a stranger unless they know that the person is worthy of honor. I believe we can assume that these fishermen had familiarity with this man called Jesus. Remember, in day 1 we established that several of those who would become disciples of Jesus had been disciples of John the Baptist. The events occurred in the following sequence.

JOHN 1:35-51	JOHN 2:1-11	MATTHEW 4:18-22; MARK 1:16-20; LUKE 5:1-11
Andrew and John with John the Baptist see Jesus. Andrew and John follow Christ. Andrew introduces Simon (Peter)	Events at wedding feast in Cana (events described John 2:12—4:45)	Call of the four (Simon/ Andrew, James/John)

> **Based on John 1:35-42, who were certainly disciples of John the Baptist?**
> ❏ **Andrew**   ❏ **Peter**   ❏ **James**   ❏ **Matthew**

Many scholars believe that John the apostle was the other of the two disciples mentioned in John 1:35. John as a rule did not identify himself in his writings. We know for certain that Peter met Christ in advance of his encounter on the boat because John 1:42 tells us that Andrew brought him to meet Jesus.

The words "Jesus looked at him and said" sends chills up my spine. According to *Strong's Concordance,* the Greek word for *looked* means "to look on, i.e. ... to observe fixedly, or (absolutely) to discern clearly:—behold, gaze up, look upon."[6] I think Christ looked Peter straight in the eyes with a look that could have drilled a hole through him and said, " 'You are Simon son of John. You will be called Cephas' (which, when translated, is Peter)" (v. 42).

Based on John the Baptist's faithful ministry, Peter, Andrew, James, and John knew Christ at least by reputation. Several of them also knew Him because of the prior encounter described in John 1. When Jesus approached them at their boats, God had them primed and ready to leave everything behind and follow Christ. I'd like to suggest that just as James and John were preparing their nets, they too had been prepared. The word *preparing* (see Mark 1:19) can also mean *repairing*. The exact word is used in Galatians 6:1 for restoring a fallen brother. Oh, how thankful I am that the same God who prepares also repairs and restores.

> **The same God who prepares also repairs and restores.**

At this season of your life, what do you sense that you need most?
❑ **Preparation for a fresh work of God**
❑ **Repairing from a tear**
❑ **Restoration from a kind of fall**

Preparation reminds me of a wonderful verse in Joshua, " 'Consecrate yourselves, for tomorrow the Lord will do amazing things among you' " (3:5). God can perform a miracle in any one of us at any time, but amazing things happen when He prepares us for His mighty work. Included in that mighty work will most assuredly be what we need most—whether a fresh work, a repair from a tear, or a full-scale restoration.

Let's allow God to consecrate us over the next few weeks and lay the groundwork for something spectacular so that by the time we reach the last half of this study, God is amazing and astonishing us. Right this moment let Jesus look you straight in the eyes and tell you that He knows who you are and who He wants to make you. Are you willing to follow Him? That's the only way you and I will ever discover the One who calls us and the one we were born to be. Child, a great adventure awaits you.

Day 4 OLD TIES AND NEW TIES

> **TODAY'S TREASURE**
> *"After this he went down to Capernaum with his mother and brothers and his disciples. There they stayed for a few days."—John 2:12*

One of our primary goals this week is to piece together coinciding facts that help us picture how the ministries of the disciples—and one in particular—began.

Please reread Mark 1:16-20, but this time allow the scene to capture your full imagination. Remember that what we're reading happened to flesh-and-blood people who were busy leading fairly established lives when Christ intervened. Allow me to help you explore the possibilities in the scene by asking you the following questions. Keep in mind that no right or wrong answers exist.

How do you picture Christ's expression and demeanor as He called these four fishermen to follow Him? Briefly explain. This picture will establish our present impressions of Christ and will allow us to measure whether our impressions change over the course of deeper study.

_____

_____

_____

We'll give considerable attention to the group dynamics involved in the circle of disciples, so let's start now. How do you think Peter and Andrew felt about Jesus' stopping by the second boat and calling James and John also? Keep in mind the partnership they shared in business for some time.

_____

_____

_____

Do you think the sight of Peter and Andrew accompanying Christ had any kind of impact on the response of James and John? Whether yes or no, briefly explain your answer.

_____

_____

_____

James and John left their father, Zebedee, in the boat with the hired men (see Mark 1:20). How do you think Zebedee reacted? Keep in mind that Zebedee probably had some familiarity with Jesus. Don't forget that he was a Jewish father with his own plans for his sons. What do you think?

_____

_____

I'm glad God chose to include the name of James and John's father. He wasn't just any man or just any father. He was Zebedee. He had a name, feelings, and plans. He was probably close enough to his sons' births to hear Salome cry out in pain. He probably wept when told he had a son. And then another. No doubt, he praised God for such grace. Daughters were loved, but every man needed a son to carry on the family line, after all. He had two fine sons. He named them himself. They played in his shadow until they were old enough to work, and if I know anything about teenage boys, they still played plenty behind his back even when they were supposed to be working. Just about the time he grew exasperated with them, he'd look in their faces and see himself.

At the time Christ called James and John, I have a feeling they had never had more pleasure or more support. Life is curious. Just about the time you get to reap some of the fruit of your parenting labors, the young, flourishing tree gets transplanted elsewhere. Keith and I are in the season of life I'm describing. Our daughters have never

> Just about the time you get to reap some of the fruit of your parenting labors, the young, flourishing tree gets transplanted elsewhere.

been more delightful, have never been easier to care for, and have never had more to offer in company and stimulating conversation. The summers of their college years have been great fun, and we never secretly wanted to push them back to school or down an aisle. They are simply very little trouble right now. I wonder whether Zebedee felt the same way about his young-adult sons. Just when he was reaping a harvest of parental rewards, they jumped ship. All he had to show for it was a slimy fishing net.

What would happen to the business? What about Zebedee and Sons? No matter how Zebedee felt, God had great compassion for him. After all, He knew how Zebedee felt when John had to be called away from his father's side to fulfill his destiny.

Chances are pretty good that Zebedee thought their sudden departure was a phase they'd get over. Glory to God, they never did. Once we let Jesus Christ really get to us, we never get over Him. " 'Come, follow me,' Jesus said, 'and I will make you fishers of men' " (Mark 1:17). I love the fact that Jesus talks in words and images His listeners can understand. When He said, "I will make you fishers of men," He obviously used terminology Andrew, Peter, James, and John could understand. I am convinced that one part of the sentence applies to every person Jesus Christ calls: "Come, follow me, and I will make you …"

Decades later when God used these fishermen to change the face of religion forever, they still could not boast in themselves. Christ made them the men and the influences they were. I can't express what these thoughts mean to me. I am not falsely modest when I tell you that when Christ called me, He had pitifully little to work with. I was such a broken and scattered mess. So emotionally unhealthy. So insecure and full of fear. I was a wreck and stayed a wreck for longer than I'd like to admit. I have such a long way to go, but this I can say: anything that I am or have of value is completely from Christ. I followed Him, and whatever I am of worth, He made me.

Christ made these fishermen the men and the influences they were.

Do you have a similar testimony? If so, share it on the lines below. Perhaps you are still in the broken, scattered state I described. If so, can you accept by faith what Christ can do if you follow Him? Please comment.

_____

_____

_____

_____

_____

So how does Christ make a man or a woman? We will explore many ways over the weeks to come, but the most immediate way Jesus began building His new followers into the men He wanted them to be was by spending intense time with them and showing them how He worked.

Piecing the Gospels together in a precise chronological order is a task far too challenging for me, and I'm relieved to know that it is also a little too challenging for most Bible commentators. What we know is that Christ and His small and yet incomplete band of followers attended a wedding in Cana together. We are going to wait to explore the wedding until week 5, when we study the uniqueness of John's Gospel, but I'd like for you to view the verse immediately following the celebration.

What does John 2:12 tell you about the relationships involved at this point?

_____

_____

Have you considered that Christ's family and disciples obviously enjoyed at least a brief season of peace and harmony? I didn't give it any thought until researching for this study. The schism in Christ's family didn't develop until a little later (see John 7:3-5). In week 3 we will see the reconciliation brought by the power of the resurrection. For now, however, picture Christ surrounded by both His family and His new disciples.

I am fairly convinced that we don't really know people until we stay with them for a few days. Can I hear an amen? Although I'm grinning, I have almost always been more blessed than less. Not long ago due to a severe flood in Houston, Amanda and I got stranded in Tennessee after a conference. When I learned that the airport was closed, I frantically called Travis, my dear friend and worship leader, and asked whether he had room for two more in his van back to Nashville. Without making a single preparation for us, his young family of four graciously received us into their home for two nights. Although we were already very close friends, we bonded for life. The treasure of having part of my ministry family and part of my natural family in fellowship together was priceless. I am very aware that the experience might not have gone quite so positively!

Because the disciples were new on the scene, they probably weren't quite as comfortable interacting with Christ's family as I was with my worship leader's family. Still, they got to see Christ interact with His own family—a critical opportunity, I think. Soon they would see Him perform all manner of miracles. They had already witnessed His changing water to wine, but the sights they would soon see would nearly take their breath away. You see, people are much harder to change than water. Don't you think?

As they watched Jesus, fellowshipped with Him, and then witnessed His work, what do you think they saw? Consistency? Versatility? Unwavering passion? Did they see a lamb as often as a lion? The center of all attention? Or a teacher who became a student of all those around Him? We know they saw absolute authenticity, but how might you imagine they saw it portrayed?

Record your thoughts below.

_____

_____

Don't think for a minute that exercises like these are a waste of time. The more we grasp the flesh-and-blood reality of these encounters and try to imagine the intimate details the disciples witnessed in Christ, the better! What we're studying isn't religious fiction or simple Christian tradition. Christ walked into and transformed people's lives. You and I want to experience nothing less. We read in Isaiah 53:2 that Jesus

Christ walked into and transformed people's lives.

> had no beauty or majesty to attract [them] to him,
>> nothing in his appearance that [they] should desire him.

Yet Jesus had things about Him that caused grown men to walk away from established lives and to keep following Him to the death.

What do you think some of those things were?

_____

_____

Now that you've had a chance to share your own impressions, let's take a look at several Scriptures that applied to Christ at this time of His ministry.

Read the following Scriptures in your Bible. In what ways would people have been attracted to Him?

Mark 1:40-42 _____

Luke 2:52 _____

Luke 4:14-15 _____

Luke 4:31-32 _____

Christ was everything of value. People knew He was unique even before they knew He was God.

Do you see, Beloved? Christ was everything of value. People knew He was unique even before they knew He was God. He was the rarity. An honest-to-goodness whole person who embodied the fullness of the Godhead (see Col. 2:9). Can you fathom it? I can't, but how I want to!

Jesus had favor. Power. Authority. Compassion. He was the perfect Man. He had hands strong enough to turn over merchants' tables and tender enough to touch the leper's rotting flesh and make him whole. Those who appreciated His uniqueness were drawn to it. Those who were threatened by it either ran or wanted Him destroyed.

As we conclude today's lesson, I sense the Holy Spirit leading me to ask you a question. Are you by any chance threatened by Jesus and His desire for you to follow Him with complete abandon? Don't answer quickly. Meditate on the question for a few minutes and see if the Holy Spirit raises anything to the surface. Are you afraid of anything? Are you jealous over the things He might require? Intimidated? Think about it.

Beloved, if you are willing to cast away all your fears, hindrances, and unanswered questions and follow Him, you're going to see His glory.

Day 5 A HARD ACT TO FOLLOW

TODAY'S TREASURE
"Jesus replied, 'Let us go somewhere else—to the nearby villages—so I can preach there also. That is why I have come.' "—Mark 1:38

The disciples saw Christ perform eye-opening miracles almost from the start. Although we are saving further comments on the wedding at Cana for week 5, we know that it was the location of Christ's first miracle and that John's reference to the time frame of the wedding was "the third day" (John 2:1). The next occurrence in sequence was Christ's trip to Capernaum with His mother, brothers, and disciples (see John 2:12). The three events we will study today probably happened during the same stay in Capernaum, so imagine them falling next in sequence.

Please read Mark 1:21-28. Check your context. How can we know that at least Andrew, Peter, James, and John were with Jesus?

_____

_____

Picture these four fishermen mingling in the crowd gathered that Sabbath in the synagogue. I have an idea that Christ's new disciples didn't just watch Jesus as He preached. I have a feeling that they watched the reactions of others who were listening to Him as well. Mind you, at least Peter and Andrew lived in Capernaum at that time (see Mark 1:29). A town this size had only one Jewish synagogue, so they worshiped with virtually the same people week after week. They knew them personally. Some were relatives, others were neighbors, and others were business associates. What kinds of reactions do you think they saw on these familiar faces as Jesus preached in Capernaum?

Talk about an interesting service! If an amazing message were not enough excitement, just then a man in their synagogue who was possessed by an evil spirit cried out, " 'What do you want with us, Jesus of Nazareth?' " (Mark 1:24). Suddenly their heads turned toward the opponent, almost like spectators in a tennis match. I wonder whether the crowd previously knew that this man had an evil spirit or whether they had been oblivious for years to the nature of his problems. Had they known, I'm not sure they would have allowed him in the synagogue, so my feeling is that the man may have kept it covered to some extent. Goodness knows Satan loves a good disguise. Somehow, however, when the authority of Christ was released in that place, the demons lost their cover. Jesus has a way of bringing the devil right out of some people, doesn't He?

> When the authority of Christ was released, the demons lost their cover.

What happened when Jesus commanded the demons to come out of him (see Mark 1:25-26)?
❏ **They immediately left the man.**　　❏ **They talked back.**

Picture John witnessing these events. Many scholars believe he was the youngest of the disciples. One strong basis for this deduction is his positioning and apparent role at the Passover meal just before Jesus' crucifixion. We'll glance at those events in several weeks, but for now keep in mind that the youngest at the Passover meal usually sat nearest the father or father figure so that he could ask the traditional questions. I will refrain from building any doctrines on this deduction since I could be off base, but I am personally convinced enough that John was the youngest that I'll adopt this position. If he was, can you imagine his face while Jesus encountered—then cast out—these demons?

Write down what you think may have been some of the statements or questions going through John's mind as this event unfolded.

_____

_____

I think John probably experienced a combination of emotions. Young men dearly love competitions, so he had to savor seeing his new team win, even if only one Player was involved in the match. I have to think the encounter also scared him half to death. One thing that might have offset his fear was that he had to be indescribably impressed with his new mentor. John wasn't the only one. Mark 1:22 tells us the crowds were amazed by Christ's teachings, but Mark 1:27 intensifies the adjectives by saying they were "so amazed" by His demonstration of authority over the demons. We do love a show, don't we? When I think how patient Christ has been with our human preference for divine fireworks, I am more amazed than ever. Christ knows us intimately. He knows how to get our attention, but He also desires that we grow up and seek His presence and glory even more than the display of His might. John and the other disciples would see many miracles before they were irresistibly challenged to mature.

I have a feeling that by the time the fishermen reached Capernaum with Jesus, so did the news of their leaving Zebedee holding the net. I don't doubt for a minute that these young men reveled in the grand reaction people had to their new leader. What could be more exciting than being the *khavura,* or "circle of friends"[7] of the most powerful and popular new man on the scene? But the day was far from over.

> **Read what happened next in Mark 1:29-34. What were the obvious living arrangements at the house in this scene?**

_____

Think of events such as Jesus' birth, baptism, crucifixion, and resurrection as primary events that can indeed be placed in time sequence. Think of the events like the ones we're studying today as secondary events. We won't often be able to put the secondary events of the four Gospels into an unquestionable chronological order. Based on identical time sequencing in Mark and Luke and on the fact that nothing in Matthew or John refutes it, however, I believe we can rightly assume that the first healing of the sick ever witnessed by the disciples was in Simon Peter's home.

Surely an early turning point came in the hearts and minds of the disciples when healing hit home. I know it did for me. Seeing Him work in a church service is one thing. Witnessing His healing in the life of your own family is another. That's when a person begins to get it through her head that Jesus doesn't just love church. He loves people.

> **Compare Mark 1:21,29. When did this healing occur?**
> ❑ **On the Sabbath** ❑ **On Passover** ❑ **On the Lord's Day**

Christ raised the Pharisees' ire on several occasions by picking this particular day for healings—as if He were making a point. In a future session we're going to see that in many ways this was the perfect day of the week for healing. I didn't realize until researching for today's lesson that even Jesus' first healing was on the Sabbath. Obviously, Christ saw the purpose of the day far differently than many of His contemporaries. Apparently, Simon Peter's mother was healed just in time to rise from the bed and get ready for company.

> **What happened literally at her front door after sunset (see Mark 1:32-34)?**

_____

_____

Christ desires that we seek His presence and glory even more than the display of His might.

Have you ever seen an instantaneous physical healing like those described in this text? I've known people God healed physically, but I haven't had many chances to watch an instant healing take place before my very eyes. Can you imagine what these sights were like for the disciples? Matthew's Gospel records a graphic scene that occurred very close to the same time. Meditate on Matthew 4:24, pausing to picture every description.

What kinds of feelings did you have the last time you encountered someone who was suffering terribly?

_____

_____

Few of us choose to confront suffering because we feel so helpless. Imagine the contrast between the agony of seeing human suffering and the ecstasy of seeing someone healed. What would such an experience have been like for Mother Teresa, for instance, as she daily died to her own desire for personal comfort and confronted the unimaginable suffering in Calcutta? Somehow my mind can hardly even fathom the range of emotions. Picture being one of Christ's disciples. After all, John was a human being just like you.

How do you suppose these kinds of sights affected John?

_____

_____

Rewind to the scene in Mark 1:33-34. John had observed hundreds of Sabbaths. Imagine that he awakened that morning with a fresh wave of, _I can hardly believe what I've done! I wonder what my mom and dad are thinking right now._ John is excited and unsure, and his soul is filled with the realization that something new is looming on the horizon. Perhaps Scriptures swirl through his mind as he recites morning prayers of thanksgiving for God's provisions: "It is of the Lord's mercies that we are not consumed, because his compassions fail not. They are new every morning: great is thy faithfulness" (Lam. 3:22-23, KJV).

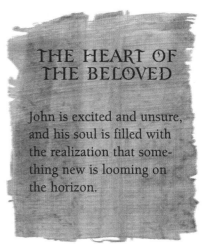

THE HEART OF THE BELOVED

John is excited and unsure, and his soul is filled with the realization that something new is looming on the horizon.

John prepares to go to the synagogue for services just as he has done all his life, only this time he gets a bit more than he bargained for. The scroll is unrolled, and the Scripture for the day's service is read. Then Jesus takes the role of rabbi, sits down, and nearly preaches the locks off their heads.

Just then a man possessed by demons starts shouting, and John sees Jesus get stern—perhaps for the first time. In an astounding show of power Jesus casts out the demons, causing the man to shake violently. John feels that he will never forget the sound of those demons shrieking as long as he lives. He and the other disciples walk together to Simon Peter's house, whispering all the way about what they've seen. Simon Peter's mother-in-law is sick with a fever, so Jesus takes her by the hand and helps her up. The fever leaves her so instantaneously that she begins to serve them.

Then they begin to hear sounds at the door. Murmurings. Shrieking. Crying. Sounds of moaning. Sounds of hope. And hope says, _What He did for her, He might do for me._ That He did. When John awakened that morning, his mind could not have conceived just how many mercies were new that particular sunrise. Imagine being John. Imagine all he had seen during the course of the day.

If you were John, when you pulled a blanket over yourself that night, what part of the day or piece of a scene would you have thought about the most?

_____

_____

I can only imagine the things that went through the mind of the young disciple. He probably tossed and turned most of the night. Perhaps he and James whispered to each other from their pallets until they were overtaken by exhaustion.

As I imagine all that had happened that Saturday and all they had seen, I know one of the thoughts that would have crowded my head: _Is there anything the man can't do?_ John watched Jesus practically bring the house down with His teaching. He watched Him confront and cast out a hoard of demons from a man who came to synagogue. He watched Him not only heal Simon's mother-in-law but also instantly restore her strength. Then every manner of distress landed on their doorstep.

I love Matthew Henry's words of commentary on the scene at the door: "How powerful the Physician was; he healed all that were brought to him, though ever so many. Nor was it some one particular disease, that Christ set up for the cure of, but he healed those that were sick of divers [various, diverse] diseases, for his word was a panpharmacon—a salve for every sore."[8] Jesus' Word was a panpharmacon—a salve for every sore. Ah, yes. I have yet to have an ailment that God had no salve to soothe. But what may be even more peculiar is that I have yet to have an ailment of soul that God's Word was not the first to point out, diagnose, then heal. His Word is far more glorious, powerful, and fully applicable than we have any idea of.

You very likely did not pick up this particular Bible study because you sought healing. You would surely have picked other titles. But based on my own experience and many references in Scripture, you will undoubtedly receive some fresh diagnoses and, if you cooperate, a new measure of healing. As will I. I'm counting on it.

That's the nature of His Word. As Psalm 107:20 says, "He sent forth his word and healed them." How often God had to send forth His Word and begin the healing to get me healthy enough even to face the diagnosis! I want you to revel in something wonderful. Every time God has prepared us with His Word and gotten us to a point that we can receive a hard pill to swallow from Him, healing has already begun. Once He confronts us, we never need to be overwhelmed by how far we have to go. If we've heard Him through His Word, healing has already begun. Take heart. He is the Panpharmacon.

If we've heard God through His Word, healing has already begun.

---

[1]R. Alan Culpepper, _John, the Son of Zebedee: The Life of a Legend_ (Minneapolis: First Fortress Press, 2000), 7.
[2]Ibid., 9.
[3]Ronald F. Youngblood, ed., _Nelson's New Illustrated Bible Dictionary_ (Nashville: Thomas Nelson, 1995), s.v. "Galilee, Sea of."
[4]Ibid., s.v. "Bethsaida."
[5]Culpepper, _John,_ 11.
[6]James Strong, _New Strong's Exhaustive Concordance_ (Nashville: Thomas Nelson, 1995), 1689.
[7]Christo Botha and Dom David Foster, trans., _With Jesus Through Galilee According to the Fifth Gospel_ (Rosh Pina, Israel: Corazin Publishing, 1992), 32.
[8]Matthew Henry, _Matthew Henry's Commentary on the Whole Bible,_ vol. 5, _Matthew to John_ (n.p.: Fleming H. Revell Company, n.d.), 456.

VIDEO RESPONSE SHEET

Group Session 1

Sometimes we also may have the desire to take our _____ and

_____ _____ ___ _____ in our worlds: in our _____

_____, in our _____, in our _____, etc. We've got to

be so careful what we rationalize by Scripture. Before we proceed, we are wise to remember a few

important things. We'll make six points today based on the calling of John.

Read Mark 3:13-19 and John 2:12-17.

1. Christ could not _____ in His _____ or _____. **See Ephesians 4:26-27.**

   Anger and rage are highly motivational, but they are extremely destructive.

2. Godly _____ is measured by the _____ of "_____."

3. God looks upon the _____ beneath the action. We can even have a

   _____ _____ about a _____ _____ and

   find ourselves disciplined by God.

4. Paradoxically, we receive our calling as _____ _____ ____ _____

   but can only fulfill it _____ _____. **See Matthew 18:2-3.** " 'Unless you change and

   become _____, you will never _____

   _____.' "

5. Though _____ is important, Christ seems to have an affinity for

   _____ _____.

6. The kind of change God desires comes one primary way. **See Mark 3:14:** "that they might

   be with him and that he might send them out."

SIGHTS AND INSIGHTS

Day 1
A Solitary Place

Day 2
Three and One

Day 3
Right-Handed Disciples

Day 4
Reclining Next to Him

Day 5
From the Edge of a Garden

Can you imagine walking beside Christ? Knowing His sandal size? Recognizing His accent and favorite figures of speech? Over the next two weeks we will look at snapshot scenes in the Gospels in which John accompanied Jesus. Think of yourself as the 13th disciple—one who was invited into each scene we'll study. Remember not to spiritualize John. He was as flesh and blood as we are, but what he witnessed reached far beyond the natural realm. Let's stand by this young disciple's side and gaze on scenes that marked him forever. May we be marked as well.

Principal Questions

Day 1: According to John 11:41-42, what confidence did Christ have in His praying?

Day 2: Based on Mark 5:35, what was the reasoning of those who discouraged Jairus from bothering the teacher anymore?

Day 3: What is the obvious risk of great revelation, and how are we told in 2 Corinthians 12:7 that God safeguarded the apostle Paul against it?

Day 4: Based on Luke 19:41-44, why was Jesus apparently so grief-stricken?

Day 5: What happened as soon as Judas took the bread at the Passover?

Day 1 A SOLITARY PLACE

TODAY'S TREASURE

"Very early in the morning, while it was still dark, Jesus got up, left the house and went off to a solitary place, where he prayed. Simon and his companions went to look for him."—Mark 1:35-36

Today we get to walk in a scene with a few of Christ's first disciples and find Him praying all by Himself or with invisible company that we can't grasp. I love Christ's alone moments in Scripture. As I continue to learn of Him, my concept of the public Jesus develops more, but I am still deeply drawn to the mystery of the private Jesus.

I suppose I've always been a bit drawn to the mysterious in a person. My husband, Keith, is a man very few people know intimately. Somehow, knowing him makes me feel special. I am also indescribably drawn to the mysterious side of Christ. What I know about Him gives me a desire to know what I don't and can't know for now.

We all have our concepts of heaven, and our images don't change the reality a bit. Still, I long for heaven to be not only a place of magnificent corporate worship but also a place of quiet, private encounters with Jesus Christ. I can't wait to be with all my siblings in Christ and sit around the table with Moses, Paul, and the apostle John. As selfish as this may seem, though, I've got to be honest with you. I want Jesus alone. At least for a few minutes each millennium! My dearest times with Him on this planet have been in the secret places. That's heaven to me.

Like the disciples we'll study today, I want to walk up on a scene and suddenly find Jesus there. Unlike them, however, I don't want to drag Him back to the masses. I want to keep Him to myself a moment. I like to picture that He might turn around, see that it is I, and reach out His hand for mine. Then He might gently draw me to sit beside Him and allow me to share what has momentarily captured His attention. Maybe a mountain view of the crystal sea. Or the sight of children playing in a flowery meadow with furry lion cubs (see Isa. 11:6).

Do I have too much imagination for you? Maybe so, but I believe heaven will be far more creative than most believers picture it. Surely a God who created this world with all its magnificence, diversity, and experiences has not designed an eternal home that is like a one-scene, one-act play. Nor do I imagine that we'll always be in one huge corporate gathering. How in the world could private encounters happen with millions of the redeemed in heaven? The way I see it, that's one reason we have eternity. Plenty of time for each of us to have Jesus all to ourselves. I think we have lots of surprises ahead.

> Heaven will be far more creative than most believers picture it.

Please read Mark 1:29-39. You'll notice that your reading overlaps our previous study so that we can recapture the context and time sequence. Briefly recap what Christ's previous 24 hours entailed (see vv. 21-35).

_____

_____

After that kind of day I might have considered sleeping in. Not Jesus. While the others may have whispered from their makeshift beds about all they had seen, the One with whom He longed to speak wasn't crawling into the next pallet. While it was still dark, Jesus got up, left the house, and went off to a solitary place where He prayed.

Don't you imagine that Jesus had trouble feeling at home anywhere? Perhaps that's why He said, " 'The Son of Man has no place to lay his head' " (Luke 9:58). He slept in plenty of places, but none of them was His true home. He slipped out of the house that morning after the Sabbath; He had a Sunday-morning service to attend. If it had been my childhood church, the placard that hung on the wall would have read, Today's Attendance: 2.

Christ calls Himself " 'the bright Morning Star' " (Rev. 22:16). The Morning Star is the planet Venus, seen in the eastern sky before or at sunrise. I've seen it many mornings. When I get up to have my morning prayer time, I love the comfort of knowing that the sun will rise during that precious time with God. I often step out on the porch, look at the sky, and behold one star that shines far brighter than the rest. That morning not far from the lapping waters of Galilee's shore, the bright Morning Star rose while it was still dark and lit the desolation with the lamp of glory. Only God saw. "Oh, Child," our Heavenly Father says to us today, "would you rise for only Me to see?"

How was the place Jesus went described?_____

The original word for *solitary* (*erhmos*) means "being in a state of isolation, … of an area isolated, unfrequented, abandoned, empty, desolate."[1] A place locals through the centuries have called Eremos (solitary) Heights is located just outside Capernaum. Bargil Pixner, an author who has lived at Tabgha by the Sea of Galilee for 12 years, describes the area traditionally believed to be the Eremos where Christ went as having rugged rocks of red granite and naked, windswept cliffs. A friendlier part of it is called the Eremos Hill. With its array of blossoms, birdsongs, and splendid view of lake, the area residents call it God's Eye. It became the mountain of the new covenant, the mount of the Beatitudes.[2]

Christ taught, " 'When you pray, go into your room, close the door and pray to your Father, who is unseen' " (Matt. 6:6). He had no home of His own, but when the One who spoke the earth into existence prayed, the entire Eremos Heights could be His closet if He wanted it to be!

Where is your favorite place to pray? Why does this place work for you?

_____

_____

Christ's prayers had a freedom and familiarity others could not comprehend.

Jesus went to Eremos for one reason: to be alone with His Father. Oh, how I would love to know how He prayed! What He said! How long He talked! And then I wonder how He heard His Father respond, either with His ears or His heart. Christ's prayers were unique. He had a freedom and familiarity that others cloaked in human flesh could not comprehend. Surely that's one reason the disciples pled with Him at a different time, " 'Lord, teach us to pray' " (Luke 11:1). Hebrew men were taught to pray from the time they could speak. They recited benedictions and petitions off and on all day long. They knew how to pray as men taught, but when they beheld Christ captivated by the presence of His Father for hours at a time, they must have meant, "Teach us to pray like that!"

I think John indicates one wonderful reason Christ was so drawn to prayer and could pray for hours. Read John 11:41-42. What confidence did Christ have in His praying?

_____

_____

Let's really give this some thought for a minute. How differently would we pray if we were convinced of two critical factors: that our Father is the omnipotent Creator and Sustainer of the universe and that He always hears us?

_____

_____

Do we not find our minds wandering and ourselves even a tad bored in prayer at times because we wonder whether our words are bouncing off the ceiling? How differently would we pray if Christ appeared bodily and sat in a chair across from each of us, leaning forward to concentrate on what we're saying? Beloved, if only we would realize that although He is invisible to us, that is in essence what He does! He intercedes for us at the right hand of the Father. When we pray, He is so close to us that He may as well be leaning over the edge of heaven and bending down to hear. His presence through His Holy Spirit literally surrounds you as you pray. His eyes are fixed on your face, on every word you say, and on every expression you make. Can you imagine how the angels marvel over our boredom when we pray as they behold our Heavenly Father listening intently to our every word?

> **I want to give you a personal prayer assignment to practice in your own "prayer closet" and then discuss in your small group. Every time you pray for the next week, begin your prayer with Christ's words straight from John 11:42: " 'I knew that you always hear me.' " Then conclude it with Christ's words in John 11:41: " 'Father, I thank you that you have heard me.' " Practice God's presence! Pray as if He's really listening—because He is!**

The disciples were far too immature to consider the enormity of the scene they walked in on in Mark 1:35-37. When they blurted out, " 'Everyone is looking for you!' " they gave us an insight into their state of mind. Forget what Jesus does in private! They wanted to be seen in public with the popular Jesus!

We're not going to be too hard on them, because they were demonstrating a normal part of adolescent Christianity. We are the same way in our spiritual immaturity. At first we are far more excited about corporate worship than private worship.

Frankly, we don't know Jesus well enough to have as much to say one-on-One. We love the excitement of being in the masses of those enthralled by Christ, and we always will. However, as we mature and Jesus becomes an increasingly greater personal reality to us, I think we come to treasure time in the solitary places with Him more than anything.

> As we mature, we come to treasure time in the solitary places with Jesus more than anything.

Mark 1:36 tells us that Simon and his companions went to look for Jesus. Check the context in previous verses. Who were they?

_____

I think we can be almost certain that our John was among them. The only companions we've met so far in Mark's Gospel are Andrew, Peter, James, and John; so very likely the small group consisted of all or some of these four. Notice they weren't called disciples. I'm not sure they qualified as learners and pupils yet! Whoever the companions were, the original language suggests that they were tracking Jesus down, almost like a manhunt. The Greek word is often used in a hostile sense.[3] I'm not suggesting that they were hostile toward Jesus but rather that they were quite anxious and maybe even a little put out with Him for not being where all the people were. We see no indication that they hesitated for a moment of respect or awe when they found Jesus praying. They barreled on the scene with, " 'Everyone is looking for you!' "

I suspect that the companions tracking down Jesus may have been Peter, James, and John. Later in His ministry Jesus chose these three men to watch Him on several occasions in the "inner places." Something caused Jesus to single them out. Scripture proves that it wasn't their spiritual maturity. I think two primary motivations compelled Christ to draw the three into intimate places: the fact that they just didn't get it at times and the fact that Jesus knew once they did get it, they'd really get it! I can just imagine Christ thinking, *So you're not the boundaries types, are you? OK, I'll take you behind some ordinary boundaries, but I'll hold you responsible for what you learn while you're there.*

I have a friend whose little boy thought he was the teacher's pet because she seated him right in front of her desk. He didn't realize for years that this action was motivated by his discipline problems. Why didn't she just send him to the principal instead of expending so much energy on him? Because she knew the child had a student in him, and she was determined to find it. And she did.

Over the next two weeks we're going to see Peter, James, and John get their desks moved to the front of the class. Just like children, at times they might be tempted to think the Rabbi moved them there because they were the Teacher's pets.

> Something caused Jesus to single them out. Scripture proves that it wasn't their spiritual maturity.

Day 2 THREE AND ONE

TODAY'S TREASURE
"After six days Jesus took Peter, James and John with him and led them up a high mountain, where they were all alone."—Mark 9:2

Unless we remember our objective, some of us may be frustrated over the leapfrogging we're about to begin! Although I wish we could go through every step the disciples took with Christ, the purpose of this journey is to draw riches from the life and letters of John. We've had the privilege of taking the first steps of his encounters with Jesus slowly because he was among the first disciples chosen. Now we will pick up the pace rather dramatically as we hop from scene to scene. As we focus on the Synoptic Gospels in weeks 1–3, we will concentrate on scenes where John is named or known to be present.

Keep in mind that Jesus had many followers but that He chose twelve to walk nearest to Him and appointed them apostles. Tomorrow's lesson will center on events close to the last Passover Jesus and His disciples observed together. Every moment the twelve spent with Jesus was significant, but today we're going to look at two scenes with some common denominators that no doubt had a profound effect on John. Try your best to view each occurrence from John's point of view. Keep in mind that he was probably the youngest of the disciples and the younger brother of one. Think of him as flesh and blood, and imagine what each experience might have been like for him.

Scene 1: Read Mark 5:35-43. Why do you think Jesus singled out Peter, James, and John to go with Him? (Just your opinion.)

_____

_____

Now pretend you are John and you keep a journal or a diary. In one paragraph, what entry would you have made that evening before you fell asleep?

_____

_____

_____

_____

_____

_____

How does Scripture intimate that others wanted to go with Jesus to the ruler's house?

_____

I have no idea what was in the minds of the three men who were allowed to follow Jesus to a place the others weren't invited, but I know what would have gone through mine. Women tend to be so relational that I hardly would have been able to enjoy the privilege without fretting over others being left out. Then, of course, I would have worried about whether they would be angry at me when we got back. I would imagine for days that they were acting a little weird. Knowing I would have fretted myself half to death, Jesus wouldn't have bothered letting me come. No telling how many things I've missed because I make a knot out of the simplest string.

I would have hated to miss the eyeful the three got that particular day. Raising the stone-cold dead is nothing less than divine. This scene was not business as usual, no matter how many miracles the three had seen and even performed.

I have been with people near their times of death and was utterly amazed each time how quickly the body grew cold. In spiritual terms the soul keeps a body warm. Physical death occurs when the soul, the immaterial part of us, departs the body. At its exodus the warmth of life departs as well. We can be comforted by the fresh realization that life is in the soul and the soul continues living. Death has relatively little finality to a believer, and I don't mean in only eternal terms.

Death has relatively little finality to a believer.

35

Why did some men discourage Jairus from bothering the teacher (see Mark 5:35)?

_____

A loved one's death is not a time to quit bothering Jesus. He may not raise our loved one from the dead, but He does countless things to get us through our losses. Comfort is our most obvious need. I often talk to people who are virtually paralyzed by unresolved grief. Sometimes the deceased is not a loved one but an unforgiven or unforgiving one with whom they needed to make peace. Hopelessness may ensue. Depression can result. Sometimes we think all parties have to be alive for us to gain peace.

Needless to say, the ideal time to make peace with others is while everyone's still breathing, but if it's too late, bother the Teacher! He doesn't have our limitations or rationalizations. Has a death left you with unfinished business? Finish it with Jesus.

Describe the scene in Mark 9:2-10 in two-word statements. I'll get you started: "Jesus led; three followed."

_____

_____

Much time elapsed between the two scenes we're studying today. Significant events occurred, such as Jesus' feeding the five thousand and walking on the water. What makes these two scenes priorities for our study is the inclusion of only three disciples. Christ does nothing haphazardly. He undoubtedly had reasons for taking these observers.

In Mark 5:37 the three are listed as Peter; James; and John, the brother of James. John is no longer named like a tagalong. In Scripture we see his identity undoubtedly emerging. Also note that Jesus didn't just let Peter, James, and John come along. He took them.

God's will is His divine intention. Just as Jesus was intentional toward experiences and exposures of the three, He is intentional toward us. Christ never bosses us or appoints us to something only to presume authority. His will always has purpose. Sometimes we go our own ways, and God has mercy on us and shows us something there. Other times we beg Him to allow us to go a certain place, and He consents. Still other times God takes us places we never intended to go and reveals Himself to us in ways we didn't even know He existed.

All three Gospels record this scene. Each supplies unique bits and pieces of information.

Compare each Scripture passage and note each unique piece of information in the proper column below—no matter how insignificant it may seem.

Matthew 17:1-9	Mark 9:2-10	Luke 9:18-36
_____	_____	_____
_____	_____	_____
_____	_____	_____
_____	_____	_____
_____	_____	_____

Jesus is intentional toward us.

Don't be alarmed by the difference in the time segments. "After six days" and "about eight days" can easily be figured into the same period of time because the Jews often counted any portion of a day as an additional day. Luke's word, "about," relieves us of any concern about contradiction. Can you even imagine what the three disciples beheld? This scene is another of those I hope God has recorded on divine videotape.

Matthew's Gospel supplies the unique fact that the three disciples fell face down on the ground. I am convinced that the people of God miss many appropriate opportunities to fall facedown, not in an emotional frenzy but in complete awe of God. We don't have a clue whom we're dealing with. I believe one of Jesus' chief reasons for transfiguring Himself before the three was to say, "I am not like you. This is just a glimpse of who I am." Remember, He had equipped them with supernatural power to perform some of the same miracles He performed. What would keep them from thinking that just maybe in time they might be His peers? God forbid the thought!

Jesus is not a superhuman. He is God—the beloved, divine Son of Him who occupies the throne of all creation. In Psalm 50:21 God said, "You thought I was altogether like you." One primary reason Jesus takes us places we've never been is to show us that He's not like anyone else.

> One primary reason Jesus takes us places we've never been is to show us that He's not like anyone else.

Where has God taken you personally to transfigure your perception of Him?

_____

_____

_____

Glory came down on the mountain that night. When the cloudy pillar enveloped them and the voice of the Almighty became audible, the observers clung to the dirt of earth in terror. Rightly so.

Mark shares at least two additional facts. First, he tells us Christ's clothes dazzled with a whiteness whiter than anyone in the world could bleach them. You and I can't fathom whiter-than-white. Our finite minds can embrace only earth's rendition of white—like fresh-falling snow. The divine goes much further than the whiteness of snow.

What is one thing that is whiter than snow, according to Psalm 51:7?

_____

Anything we are and anything we have that is whiter than snow comes from Christ alone. I have lived long enough to sin against many people. I have sought forgiveness from those God brought to my mind and have been forgiven many times, but no one could make me clean. Only Jesus, whose dazzling glories are whiter than anyone in the world, could bleach them.

Mark also tells us that Peter made the daft suggestion of building three tabernacles because he did not know what to say. He was too frightened.

Have you ever noticed how often we say something completely ridiculous when we don't know what to say? Oh, that God would have put our brains in our tongues! In His wisdom He gave us twice as many ears as mouths, but we seem to have missed the point.

God responded from the heavens, " 'This is my Son, whom I love. ... Listen to him!' " (Matt. 17:5). My translation: "Shut thee up!"

One of Luke's primary inclusions is the fact that Moses and Elijah were there discussing Christ's departure. A more literal translation would be *exodus*. That puts chills all over me. If any two former mortals knew anything about distinctive departures, Moses and Elijah did. One died alone with God and was buried by Him; the other was taken up in a whirlwind with chariots of fire. Jesus' assignment was far more radical, and the effects would be completely revolutionary. They had much to discuss.

We've studied two scenes today. Both involved Christ's power over the dead. Jairus' daughter was raised from the dead. Neither Moses nor Elijah was returned to his mortal body on earth; yet they were both very much alive.

Read Mark 9:9-10. What did they discuss as they came down the mountain?

_____

_____

Why you think Jesus let the three disciples follow Him to Jairus' house and to the transfiguration? What points do you think He was trying to make to Peter, James, and John?

_____

_____

_____

What do Jesus' actions say to you today?

_____

_____

_____

Jesus is Lord over the living … and the dead.

Beloved, Jesus is Lord over the living … and the dead.

Day 3 RIGHT-HANDED DISCIPLES

TODAY'S TREASURE
"They replied, 'Let one of us sit at your right hand and the other at your left in your glory.' "—Mark 10:37

In our previous lesson our protagonist; his brother; and his buddy, Peter, saw sights the others could hardly have imagined. Christ showed them His glory through two miracles. You might say you'd have to be dead to be unaffected by such sights, but obviously, both cases highly affected the dead! No one remained unchanged. But how were they changing?

That's the question. Before we look at how the three assimilated their private invitations, let's make sure we're prepared to apply some of these truths to ourselves. The Book of Ephesians was not written to the twelve disciples. It was inspired and intended for all of us through the ages who would place our faith in Jesus.

What does Ephesians 1:3 tell you about yourself?

_____

_____

Under the Holy Spirit's inspiration, what did Paul pray for us (see Eph. 1:17)?

_____

_____

Scripture clearly teaches that we who have trusted Christ are also chosen (see Eph. 1:4) and called (see Eph.1:18). He leaves us on earth to have an influence for God's kingdom. He primarily equips us for our tasks by revealing Himself to us. If you want to serve Christ, get to know Him intimately and be ready to meet your calling head-on! God wants to give us a spirit of wisdom and revelation so that we'll know what to do with what He reveals.

On day 2 we talked about the highly intentional will of God. We also know that we've been chosen and called to various kinds of ministries, whether vocational or not. These concepts are wrapped up in the difficult package we could call election. At the risk of more simplicity than my biblically intellectual friends can stand, my personal belief is that God will call anyone who will come. He looks on the heart.

God has been so merciful to me that I cannot imagine His withholding grace from anyone who seeks Him. I believe He chooses those who have the heart to choose Him. Can I answer all the questions this stand invariably raises? Not on your life! Neither could Paul. Check out Romans 11:33-34. I defer to A. W. Tozer, who wrote, "God will not hold us responsible to understand the mysteries of election, predestination and the divine sovereignty. The best and safest way to deal with these truths is to raise our eyes to God and in deepest reverence say, 'O Lord, Thou knowest.' Those things belong to the deep and mysterious Profound of God's omniscience. Prying into them may make theologians, but it will never make saints."[5]

God reveals Himself to us so that He can reveal Himself to the world. How we react to God's revelation through His Word, through nature, and through circumstances says much about our maturity. The enemy entices and puffs up even the most mature believers because God chooses them.

What is the obvious risk of great revelation, and how did God safeguard Paul (see 2 Cor. 12:7)?

_____

_____

> God wants to give us a spirit of wisdom and revelation so that we'll know what to do with what He reveals.

Somebody might have needed to stick a thorn in Peter, James, and John as well and burst their balloon egos. Did you notice in our previous lesson that the three didn't fall facedown on the ground until God spoke from the cloud (see Matt. 17:5-6)? Can you imagine still being able to stand on your feet and talk while Christ dazzled with glory and Elijah and Moses popped onto the scene? Nope, the three weren't thinking very clearly. Sometimes we don't when our heads are too heady.

The voice of God interrupted the scene, saying, "You three don't get it, do you? You can't 'see' what you're seeing, so shut up and listen!" Clearly, they didn't exactly assimilate the revelation with maturity. Luke recorded three additional scenes with the transfiguration.

How did the disciples misread election and revelation in each passage? Be sure to look for John. He's about to rise to the top like a bug in a bowl of cream.

Luke 9:46-48 _____

_____

Luke 9:49-50 _____

_____

Luke 9:51-55 _____

_____

I'm sitting here shaking my head. Oh, not just at them. At myself. At the whole lot of us. Sometimes I wonder why God doesn't give up on us when we show attitudes like these. Only His mercy keeps us from being consumed (see Lam. 3:22-23). I constantly thank Him for hanging in there with me. I would have given up on myself a long time ago. I am so grateful that God is both near-sighted and far-sighted. He sees us as we really are, and (praise Him!) He sees us as we'll really be.

Perhaps John's age didn't help. Life simply hadn't had time to beat him over the head with humility. In contrast, 40 years on the far side of the desert being followed by a flock of aggravating people were enough to humble the exclusivity right out of Moses.

Read a wonderfully peculiar account in Numbers 11:24-30 and record any contrasts or comparisons to the scenes we're studying today.

_____

_____

I'll never forget standing in the resource room of my office with a friend who asked, "What does it feel like to look at all these books with your name on them?" My face screwed up into a knot, and I said, "All they represent to me is one holy beatin' after another!" I am sad to say that much of what I've learned has come with the rod of God, and if I start feeling cocky about our progress, I fully expect His discipline again (see Rev. 3:19).

After the three strikes recorded in Luke 9, Christ's enduring love and patience are obvious in His unwillingness to throw back His thumb and yell, "Out!" Particularly since He knew what was coming next.

God sees us as we really are, and He sees us as we'll really be.

40

Take a good look at Mark 10:35-45. Didn't James and John sum up the approach of spiritual toddlerhood? " 'We want you to do for us whatever we ask.' " In what ways do we ascribe to the same philosophy?

_____

_____

We relate too closely to judge James and John harshly, don't we? Let's face it. All of us have to go through spiritual toddlerhood and adolescence to get to a place of maturity. We don't ordinarily leap up; we grow up. The danger is when we refuse to grow. To get stuck in this stage is about as appealing as an adult who still acts like a two-year-old.

For a few moments James and John did nothing but descend deeper in the quicksand of self-absorption. (Never doubt that it's quicksand.) James and John made only three statements: (1) " 'Teacher, … we want you to do for us whatever we ask.' " (2) " 'Let one of us sit at your right and the other at your left in your glory.' " (3) " 'We can.' "

Meditate on each statement and try to capture their emotions and attitudes. Do you detect a growing audacity with each statement? If so, how?

_____

_____

They would have dug themselves deeper if they'd been given the opportunity. Had Christ told them He might consider one on His right and one on His left, how long would it have taken them to rumble over who would sit where? Oh, brother! Their famous last two words really get me. Christ asked, " 'Can you drink the cup I drink or be baptized with the baptism I am baptized with?' " and they answered without hesitation, " 'We can.' " They didn't have any idea what they were talking about, because they didn't have any idea what Christ was talking about. Soon they would. One day they would sip from the cup and know the baptism of His suffering, but now they needed a baby bottle, not a cup.

Our problem is often the same. We let Christ's human image mislead us into downsizing Him: _If He stooped a little, and we stood on our tiptoes, we'd be just about side-by-side. One at His left. One at His right._ On the contrary. When the Word became flesh to dwell among us, human flesh wrapped its way around the fullness of the Godhead bodily (see Col. 2:9).

> We let Christ's human image mislead us into downsizing Him.

How did Isaiah react to His election, call, and revelation in Isaiah 6:5?
❏ **Asked how God would compensate his faithfulness**
❏ **Proclaimed his adequacy for the task**
❏ **Declared himself ruined and undone before God's holiness**

I am convinced that if we really got the concept of being chosen and called by Jesus Christ, we'd be too humbled to get up and go! The Spirit of God would have to set us on our feet, like Ezekiel, to get us off our faces (see Ezek. 2:1-2). Yes, we've been chosen, and yes, we've been called. We'll know we're grasping the concept when humility cloaks our humanity.

So what's it going to be? "Teacher, we want You to do for us whatever we ask"? or "Teach us to do for You whatever You ask"?

Day 4 RECLINING NEXT TO HIM

TODAY'S TREASURE

"One of them, the disciple whom Jesus loved, was reclining next to him."—John 13:23

The final week of Christ's life as the God-man started exactly as the disciples preferred: the fanfare of a triumphal entry. A great deal of excitement had surrounded them since the voice of Jesus awakened a man who had been dead for four days. The longer the chief priests "let" Christ get away, the more complicated their schemes became. John 12: 10-11 tells us they planned to kill Lazarus, too, because many of the Jews were going over to Jesus and putting their faith in him.

The week of the great feast arrived, and so many Jews were in Jerusalem that a donkey couldn't even hear himself bray. Surely the disciples had joined their families in many pilgrimages to the holy city to observe the Passover, but this year they attended with One who appeared to be the Master of ceremonies. Their impatient, ambitious feet seemed finally about to walk on pay dirt. They were about to be important. Or at least that's what they thought. My most recent memory work has been from James 3. I keep thinking about verses 13-16. Concentrate on the portion that speaks of "humility that comes from wisdom."

 Read James 3:13-16. Why do you think humility is so wise?

_____

_____

> Wisdom might have warned the disciples differently had they been listening.

I have learned one thing about the wisdom of humility. Expressed in the words of my country heritage, if you're riding high on the horse one day, you'd be wisest not to feel too uppity, lest you be rolling in the manure the next day. Circumstantially, the disciples didn't have the least hint that trouble was coming. Wisdom might have warned them differently had they been listening. Christ told them on several occasions what awaited Him, but they, like us, cut and pasted the parts of His sermons they liked and deleted the rest.

Word traveled quickly that Jesus was on His way to the city, so a crowd gathered to meet Him, waving palm branches and shouting, " 'Hosanna! Blessed is he who comes in the name of the Lord! Blessed is the King of Israel!' " (John 12:13).

The disciples should have been tipped off that this week was going to be unlike anything they had ever experienced with Jesus. Right in the middle of the parade approaching Jerusalem, Jesus took a good look at the landscape of the city and had a crying fit. Luke 19:41 simply tells us that Jesus wept over it, but the Greek uses the strongest word for *grief* in the New Testament text. The wording suggests that His grief was not only deep but also demonstrative.

Take a look at Luke 19:41-44. Why was Jesus apparently so grief-stricken?

_____

_____

Imagine Peter, James, and John glancing at one another. Perhaps they even shrugged their shoulders. Just about the time they thought Jesus had pulled Himself together, however, what did He do next (see Luke 19:45-47)?

_____

_____

Imagine you are one of the three. Based on what we've learned so far about them, what do you think might have been going through their minds while Jesus was driving out the salesmen who were packed in the temple courts?
❑ He's lost His mind!
❑ God's temple needs cleaning.
❑ He's going to get us all killed.
❑ What a man!
❑ What will people think?

Obviously, the week of Christ's passion began almost as passionately as it ended. In between, only Jesus could still have had the presence of mind to perform some of the duties that meant the most to Him.

What did Jesus do between the Sunday of the triumphal entry and the actual observance of the Passover meal, according to Luke 19:47?
❑ He continually taught His disciples.
❑ He privately prepared Himself for the events awaiting Him.
❑ He taught every day at the temple.

As Jesus taught, all the people hung on His words. Soon they would yell, "Crucify Him!" and He would hang on theirs (see Luke 23:21). Unlike the disciples, Jesus knew what was coming and became the embodiment of the humility that comes from wisdom. Because the disciples brought knapsacks full of selfish ambition to town, they no doubt felt the disorder James 3:16 says the ambitious are bound to experience. Life can be so confusing when it's all about us.

Between Luke 19:47 and Luke 21:38, you'll find a sampling of the teachings Christ offered in the temple on Monday, Tuesday, and Wednesday. Luke 22:1-6 follows with Satan's possession of Judas and the subsequent deal he made with the chief priests and officers of the temple. "Then," according to Luke 22:7, "came the day of Unleavened Bread on which the Passover lamb had to be sacrificed."

What did Jesus send Peter and John to do (see Luke 22:7-34)?

_____

_____

_____

Christ's appointments are never haphazard. He can accomplish anything He desires by merely thinking it into existence. He assigns us to certain tasks because the experience is often as important as the accomplishment. Sometimes more so. For example, God

Christ's appointments are never haphazard.

didn't shine a light on the Damascus road to show off. He did it so that a man named Saul would be changed forever. Perhaps the most profound example is that the point of our salvation was not a cross but that the Son of God hung on that cross.

God can do anything He wants. He sovereignly chooses to employ mortals to flesh out an invisible work in the visible realm—even Jesus the perfect Word made flesh. I believe not only that Peter and John were chosen for the job of preparing the Passover but also that the job was chosen for them. When I considered this scene in *Jesus, the One and Only,* I shared what I believe is far more than a coincidence: Peter and John's repetitive references in their letters to Christ as the Lamb. They seemed to have gotten the concept of the Paschal Lamb like none of the other writers of the New Testament. I believe a tremendous part of their understanding came in retrospect after their preparation for the last Passover with Christ.

God added an insight in our present study as I became more deeply aware of the early influence John the Baptist had on Peter and John. We know that each was either directly discipled by the Baptizer or indirectly influenced through his brother. The former is the more probable option.

By what name did John the Baptist first introduce them to Christ (see John 1:29)?

Jesus would not rest until He taught Peter and John exactly what that title meant. The pair didn't run by the Old City market and grab a plastic-wrapped package of trimmed lamb for a buck fifty a pound. They picked out a live lamb and had the sweet thing slaughtered. Very likely, they held it still for the knife.

You and I can hardly imagine all that was involved in preparing for a Passover, but you can be sure that none of it was wasted. That's one of the things I love about Christ. He's not into waste management. If Jesus gives us a task or assigns us to a difficult season, every ounce of our experience is meant for our instruction and completion if only we'll let Him finish the work.

> If Jesus gives us a task or assigns us to a difficult season, He means it for our instruction and completion.

The other day I came across a verse that causes me to stop, meditate, and ask big things from God every time I see it. Psalm 25:14 says, "The Lord confides in those who fear him." I desperately want God to be able to confide in me, don't you? The *King James Version* puts it this way: "The secret of the Lord is with them that fear him." I want God to tell me His secrets! I believe these hidden treasures are not secret because He tells them only to a chosen few but because not many of us seek to know Him and tarry with Him long enough to find out.

I believe as Peter and John prepared the Passover meal that day, they were privy to many secrets that became clearer to them over time. Ecclesiastes 3:11 says that God makes everything beautiful in its time. I truly believe that if we're willing to see, God uses every difficulty and assignment to confide deep things to us and that the lessons are not complete until their beauty has been revealed. I fear, however, that we are so often attention-deficit that we settle for bearable when beauty is just around the corner.

Surely many years and Passover celebrations passed before Peter and John fully assimilated the profound significance of the one in which Jesus became the Lamb. John could never get over it. From the pen of an elderly, shaking hand we find more than 20 references to the Lamb in the Book of Revelation. And it was Peter, his sidekick, who wrote, "You know that it was not with perishable things such as silver or gold that you were redeemed from the empty way of life handed down to you from your forefathers, but with the precious blood of Christ, a lamb without blemish or defect" (1 Pet. 1:18-19).

"From the empty way of life handed down to you from your forefathers." When I think of Jewish heritage, I don't imagine empty! We Americans are such a hodgepodge that many of us lack the rich traditions of less alloyed cultures. Who could have enjoyed richer ways of life and more traditions than those passed down by Jewish forefathers? Yet Peter called them empty. Why? I think once he saw their fulfillment in Jesus Christ, he knew they were empty without Him. Once he knew the true Passover Lamb, an Old Testament Passover meant nothing without its fulfillment. Jesus became everything; all former things were empty without Him. Thank goodness for Christ's patience to make all things beautiful over time.

> Thank goodness for Christ's patience to make all things beautiful over time.

How does Luke 22:24 show that they didn't grasp the significance of their Passover experience that evening?

_____

_____

Hmm. Sounds like a good time for a pitcher and a towel. But we'll push the hold button on washing the disciple's feet until we consider the uniqueness of John's Gospel. I wonder how often the disciples looked back with humiliation on their argument. I can relate. If you can tolerate another colloquialism, I have had some humdingers—moments when I said something so entirely ludicrous that I can't even think about it without my whole face screwing up in a knot. You too? I have a feeling we're going to have to take some good-natured ribbing about some of those things in heaven. I hope they're funny by then.

Let's conclude with a snapshot moment that precipitated the dispute over who was the greatest. Jesus told His disciples that one among them would betray Him. At this exact moment John's Gospel adds a very important tidbit of information.

Read John 13:22-26. Assuming "the disciple whom Jesus loved" is our John, what was his place at the table?

_____

You have just found one of the chief clues that many scholars use to pinpoint John as the youngest disciple. At the traditional Jewish Passover, the youngest child who can talk often sits nearest the father or father figure at the table and asks the traditional questions. The room was small enough for Peter to ask Jesus a question even if he were seated at the opposite end of the table. The fact that he prompted John to ask the question suggests that John may have assumed the role as the official petitioner that evening.

I also love imagining that the youngest might have had the least protocol. He acted the way he felt and not just the way he felt was proper. So he leaned against Jesus. Glory! There's nothing doctrinal about John's leaning on Jesus! It wasn't law and wasn't prescribed in the Passover book of rules. John didn't have to lean on Jesus to talk to Him. Christ could hear him just fine. John leaned on Him because he wanted to. Because he loved Him. Because Jesus was … leanable. Approachable. Lovable. Be still, my heart. I cannot wait.

Both of my daughters are very affectionate, but my older is without a doubt more proper. My younger wouldn't know the word _protocol_ if it were tattooed on her forehead. (I hope I don't give her any ideas.) I have often said if she is with me, she is somehow on me. As my mother would say, attached to my person. From the clues we gather, I like to think that John was somehow the same way with Jesus. His affection for Jesus wasn't encumbered by silly things like protocol. I love that about him.

THE HEART OF THE BELOVED

John didn't have to lean on Jesus to talk to Him. Christ could hear him just fine. John leaned on Him because he wanted to. Because he loved Him. Because Jesus was … leanable. Approachable.

One of our primary tasks is to explore the deep affection that flowed like a teeming brook between Jesus and John. I'll be honest with you. I want what they had. I want what God and David had. I want what Christ and Paul had. If a mortal can experience it with the Immortal Invisible, I want it. I want "to know this love that surpasses knowledge—that [I] may be filled to the measure of all the fullness of God" (Eph. 3:19). All else is just an empty way of life handed down by bored and unmotivated forefathers. No thanks. Give me Jesus.

Day 5 FROM THE EDGE OF A GARDEN

TODAY'S TREASURE
"He took Peter and the two sons of Zebedee along with him, and he began to be sorrowful and troubled."—Matthew 26:37

When Peter and John prepared the Passover, they could never have imagined the events to follow. They prepared a table for 13. They had no idea they were preparing a table before their enemy. At that point they didn't know that an enemy sat among them. Few things shake us from the core like the sudden revelation of a Judas. Maybe because we can't believe we didn't see it. Maybe because we're terrified that if one of us could be Judas, couldn't we all? Aren't we all self-centered, vain, and ambitious? Did he seem altogether different? Didn't he say, "Surely not I" like the rest of us? We are terrified by our similarities! And we should be. But one thing sets us apart. He sold his soul to the devil.

John's Gospel tells us something none of the Synoptics include. Read John 13:21-30. What happened as soon as Judas took the bread?

Jesus often teaches us lessons He knows we won't fully assimilate until later.

John 13:28 tells us that no one at the meal understood. Over the course of years and countless replays of the scene in the apostle John's mind, he knew that the devil entered Judas at that table right before their very eyes. How did he know? Christ taught in John 14:26 that the Holy Spirit is also the Holy Reminder. He can reveal the truth even in something past; He reminds us of what He was teaching us at the time when we were unable to grasp. Jesus often teaches us lessons He knows we won't fully assimilate until later.

Grasp that Judas was not inhabited by any old demon. Satan is not omnipresent. He can be in only one place at a time. The prince of the power of the air flew like a fiery dart into the willing vessel of Judas, one of the twelve. Oh, we can follow. Closely. And still not belong to Jesus. We can talk the talk. We can blend right in. We can seem so sincere.

I believe in retrospect John saw the devil in Judas' eyes. I think he saw him in Judas' hands reaching for the dipped bread. For the briefest moment two hands held the same bread. One soiled by silver and the other a thin glove of flesh cloaking the hand of God. John saw the devil in Judas' feet as they walked away, for if we are ever truly with Christ, we cannot leave Him—a concept John taught later (see 1 John 2:19). He knew all too well.

Later, the same hands that betrayed Christ tied a knot in a rope and looped it around his own neck. Those same feet spasmed, jerked, and then dangled lifelessly. I think perhaps Judas took his own life because the same devil he betrayed Christ to please then betrayed him. The devil used him and left him just as surely as Judas used Christ and left Him. Judas was not even a warrior of hell. He was discarded like a soiled rag. Less than nothing. That's Satan's way. He is friend to no one. He only pretends. He is the real Judas, the betrayer. I wonder, has the devil ever betrayed you? Has he ever talked you into something, used you, then left you dangling? He has certainly betrayed me.

Your answer may need to stay general, but briefly share how Satan has betrayed you.

_____

_____

Soon after Christ confronted Judas and he departed, Christ and His disciples observed the ordinance of the new covenant, sang a hymn, and went out to the Mount of Olives (see Matt. 26:30). Again, what they could not assimilate in the teaching of the bread and the wine, the Holy Reminder would later explain to them. The Mount of Olives stands east and directly across from the old city, overlooking the temple. So pointed was the view that several decades later the Roman commander Titus headquartered on its northern ridge, successfully planning the city's destruction, and named it Mount Scopus, or "Lookout Hill."[5]

"The whole mount must have been heavily wooded. As its name implies, it was covered with dense olive groves. It was from this woodland that the people, under Nehemiah's command, gathered their branches of olive, … myrtle, and palm to make booths when the Feast of Tabernacles was restored after their years of captivity in Babylon (see Neh. 8:15)."[6]

According to Luke 22:39 (choose the correct answer)—
❑ **Jesus had obviously been often to the Mount of Olives;**
❑ **Jesus had never been to the Mount of Olives;**
❑ **Jesus had never taken the disciples to the Mount of Olives.**

Unlike the disciples who climbed the hill beside Him, Jesus knew its significance—both past and future. No wonder He had been there so many times. On the previous Sunday He stood on Lookout Hill over His beloved city and baptized the Mount of Olives with His tears: " 'If you, even you, had only known on this day what would bring you peace!' " (Luke 19:42). This most profound of all Passover nights, Jesus would anoint the Mount of Olives with sweat like drops of blood falling to the ground.

Jesus would anoint the Mount of Olives with sweat like drops of blood.

Read Matthew 26:36-46. Allow the diagram below to represent Gethsemane. Label Christ and the 11 remaining disciples as they are described in the most intense part of Christ's anguish.

Peter, James, and John were once again drawn out from the others. Gethsemane is the third time they are documented as eyewitness to a scene the others did not observe. We have mentioned all three this week. I want to give you an exercise that will cause you to really think. No right or wrong answer exists. Nothing was haphazard about the three scenes Peter, James, and John were invited to observe. In the margin I have drawn a circle representing all twelve of the disciples, then a triangle around it representing the three scenes in which Peter, James, and John left the circle and went to further extremes with Christ. We don't know exactly why Jesus chose these three experiences for this small band of disciples, but we can surmise what we think may have been their points.

Draw a triangle in the space below and label the three points with the three extreme experiences Peter, James, and John shared with Jesus. Which one will you put at the top or bottom and why? Do you see any relationship among the three experiences? If so, please describe it in the space around or below the diagram you've drawn.

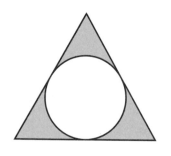

○ Experiences of the 12
▲ Experiences of the 3

I think we can rest assured that the disciples had never seen Jesus as the three saw Him in Gethsemane. I have studied this scene many times before but never from the disciples' point of view. I want you to imagine that you are one of the three.

What has Jesus represented to the disciples for the past three years? Name as many things as you can.

_____

_____

I said that Jesus at least represented security and strength to His disciples. I hope you mentioned plenty of others things also. Grown men don't follow someone for three years with virtually no income unless they are completely taken with Him. I believe Jesus was their whole lives. In Jesus their pasts made sense; their present was totally immersed in Him; all their hopes for the future rested in His faithfulness to do what He promised. Never in a million years would they have expected Him to fulfill them this way: " 'My soul is overwhelmed with sorrow to the point of death. Stay here and keep watch with me' " (Matt. 26:38).

Wait a second! This was their Rock! Their strong Tower! What in the world is wrong with Him? Why is He on the ground like that? Why is He writhing in anguish? Why is His hair drenched in sweat? It's freezing out here! Why does His sweat look like blood drops falling to the ground? Why does He keep asking for a cup to be taken from Him? What cup? He's crying " 'Abba!' " (Mark 14:36). What's He so upset about? Is it because one of us betrayed Him? Why won't He stop? I hate seeing someone cry like that. I thought nothing could get to Him. Why won't He stop?

In Jesus the disciples' pasts made sense; their present was immersed in Him; their future rested in His faithfulness.

When was the last time you saw someone you consider to be a rock in unabashed anguish, virtually inconsolable, and overwhelmed with sorrow? Describe how you felt.

_____

_____

I believe the disciples experienced many emotions as they watched their strong Tower fall to His knees with His face to the ground. Luke 22:45 tells us that the three disciples finally fell asleep from the exhaustion of their own sorrow. They had no idea what was coming, so why do you think they sorrowed so deeply?

_____

_____

The disciples may not have realized that Jesus was no less God that moment than He was on the mount of transfiguration or when He raised the dead. Their Rock and their strong Tower was not falling apart. He was falling on His knees. That takes strength. I always wonder how the mountain kept from splitting in two when the weight of the Word made flesh fell to His knees on it. Oh, how creation must have groaned!

There in the garden the Son of God bore His private cross. Very soon He would bear it publicly, but when He rose from knees bruised with anguish, His face, dusted with earth, was set like flint. I want to leave you with one last point that I find critical to our understanding about the heart of God. Christ knew what He was going to have to do when He came to planet Earth. Remember? He is the Lamb slain from the foundation of the world. He was as good as dead from the beginning. Jesus lived for one purpose alone: to do the will of His Father. Yet He still felt.

Jesus is the precise image of His Father, who also feels. God is holy and righteous. Our salvation necessitates a cross; our poor decisions necessitate chastisement. The refusal of the lost to believe necessitates judgment. But God still feels. Beloved, God still feels.

And so will we. Sometimes obeying God in a matter will be the hardest thing we've ever done in our lives. We are not wrong to feel. We are wrong to disobey. Hash it out with God. Ask for the cup to be removed, but resolve to do His will no matter what. Glory is at stake. That's why He drew the three close enough to see—to teach them to pray, not sleep, in their anguish. This time they slept. They had little power to do otherwise. But a time would come when each would rise from his own Gethsemane and bear his own cross.

> Ask for the cup to be removed, but resolve to do His will no matter what.

[1] Frederick W. Danker, ed., _A Greek-English Lexicon of the New Testament and Other Early Christian Literature_, 3rd ed. (Chicago: University of Chicago Press, 2000), 391.

[2] Christo Botha and Dom David Foster, trans., _With Jesus Through Galilee According to the Fifth Gospel_ (Rosh Pina, Israel: Corazin Publishing, 1992), 39.

[3] Frank E. Gaebelein and James D. Douglas, _The Expositor's Bible Commentary_, vol. 8 (Grand Rapids: Zondervan Corporation, 1984), 629.

[4] A.W. Tozer, _The Pursuit of God_ (Camp Hill, PA: Christian Publications, 1993), 61–62.

[5] Ronald F. Youngblood, ed., _Nelson's New Illustrated Bible Dictionary_ (Nashville: Thomas Nelson, 1995), s.v. "Mount of Olives."

[6] Ibid.

VIDEO RESPONSE SHEET
Group Session 2

Reflect on John 18:15-18,25-27.

1. Few experiences lend more opportunity to be _____ by someone we've

_____ _____ than a traumatic event.

2. Each of us is wise to ask the following question: Who have I given enough _____

to _____ ___ ____ _____ by his or her _____ actions toward Christ?

3. Sudden uncharacteristic actions do not by themselves render the person or ministry _____.

See 2 Corinthians 11:2-3.

4. Wise is the man or woman who realizes he or she, too, could momentarily _____ Christ. May we

never _____ from _____ something that—in due time—we may _____ ___.

Read John 18:28-31,38-40; 19:12-16.

1. Chaotic events don't place us suddenly out of control nearly as much as they remind us how

_____ _____ we had _____ _____. **See 2 Thessalonians 2:3.**

2. When we feel tremendously _____ ___ _____ in one area, without God's help

we will ordinarily _____ a _____ _____ on another area.

3. We will never develop _____ _____ in God's sovereign control

until we let Him _____ ___ _____ _____ when life seems out of control.

4. Keep in mind that Satan's first goal in a believer's life in trauma is to encourage

_____ of _____ with God.

5. God may not always answer _____ _____, but He will always _____ ___.

Psalm 65:5: "You answer us with awesome _____ of _____, O God our Savior."

Jeremiah 33:3: " ' "Call to me and I will answer you and tell you _____ and

_____ _____ _____ _____ _____ _____." ' "

Psalm 69:13: "O God, answer me with your _____ _____."

DEFINING MOMENTS

Day 1
Standing Nearby

Day 2
A Race to the Tomb

Day 3
What About Him?

Day 4
If and When

Day 5
Just a Handful

Are you keeping up with our pace? Catching up with the youngest disciple is rather like catching up with any adolescent boy. He practically has us out of breath. At least we're not likely to get bored! The Word of God is alive, and God wants to ignite a fresh passion in us this week through perhaps the most familiar accounts in the life of Christ. In the latter half of our study we'll consider many truths that are far less familiar to us, but we can get there only by way of the cross. Before this study I had never looked at the events surrounding the cross and glorious resurrection over the shoulder of one of the disciples. The experience profoundly affected me. I hope you gain an entirely new perspective, as well. Ask God to free you from any bondage that familiarity can breed. Then completely immerse yourself in every scene.

Principal Questions

Day 1: Based on what you studied in day 1, how would you describe John?

Day 2: According to Ephesians 1:19-20, what does God promise us if we keep believing?

Day 3: Based on Acts 1:3, what length of time did Christ use to reveal Himself after He rose from the dead?

Day 4: In Acts 1:8 what did Jesus tell His followers they would receive?

Day 5: What does Galatians 3:29 say about you?

Day 1 STANDING NEARBY

TODAY'S TREASURE
"When Jesus saw his mother there, and the disciple whom he loved standing nearby, he said to his mother, 'Dear woman, here is your son,' and to the disciple, 'Here is your mother.' "—John 19:26-27

No Broadway play can capture the raw, gaping emotions of real-life drama.

Have you ever been in circumstances you could never have imagined and thought, *How did we get here?* I remember feeling that way when we sat in the ICU waiting room while Keith's beautiful 23-year-old sister lay dying with an aneurysm. Just a few nights earlier we had all laughed until our sides split. Just that morning Keith, Amanda (a toddler at the time), and I went to church and then shared a pizza for lunch. Through a rapid string of events, our entire lives changed radically. No Broadway play can capture the raw, gaping emotions of real-life drama when you want to scream, "No! This can't be happening!" Days that you desperately wish would drop off the calendar so that you can go back to life as it had been.

Describe the last time you felt this way. _____

_____

_____

You and I have some concept of the way John must have felt in the scene depicted in John 19:17-27. Read these verses. Can you imagine how John's head must have been spinning? Don't you know he wished someone would wake him from his nightmare? This scene encases a profoundly tender and emotional interchange among Jesus, John, and Mary, but take care not to tag it a warm and fuzzy moment and try to snuggle up to it. The events John observed were horrible. We can appreciate the depth of the tenderness only against the backdrop of the horror. Most of us have studied the cross of Christ many times, but today we will try and capture it from where John's sandals flattened the dirt.

Let's rewind the events to place John accurately in the scenes. We know without a doubt that he was an eyewitness to the occurrences described in John 18:1-11.

Read these verses and record the dramatic things John saw.

_____

_____

Mentally recapture our previous lesson as John, James, and Peter most closely witnessed Christ's agony in the garden of Gethsemane. Their witness dissolved into sorrow and then sleep. They were awakened by their leader's voice: " 'Are you still sleeping and resting? Look, the hour is near, and the Son of Man is betrayed into the hands of sinners. Rise, let us go! Here comes my betrayer!' " (Matt. 26:45).

Like me, you've probably slept when you should have been awake and alert. Imagine John trying to shake off the weariness and guilt he felt for falling asleep. Picture his young face as he saw a detachment of soldiers climbing the hill carrying torches, lanterns, and weapons.

To me one of the most amazing moments in the final hours of Christ's life happened when He faced the mob. He answered their demand for Jesus of Nazareth by saying, " 'I am he,' " and the crowd drew back and fell to the ground (John 18:5,8). Our English versions add *He,* but the word doesn't appear in the Greek. Jesus literally said, " 'I am.' " When the Son of God announced the name by which God said He'd be remembered through all generations (see Ex. 3:14-15), God buckled the knee on every leg in the mob. John himself recorded the scene. Imagine how many times he had replayed those images in his head by the time he wrote it down. John also saw a sword take the ear off the high priest's servant and was the only Gospel writer who divulged that Peter was the swordsman.

John 18:15 tells us another important detail. Many scholars believe the description "another disciple" refers to John. If so, what did he alone do?

_____

While several of the disciples followed from a distance, John appears to have been the closest eyewitness of the twelve as the final hours unfolded. Whether or not he saw the events described in John 19:1-16, he very likely stood close enough to hear them. Try to resist overfamiliarity and read this account with a fresh breath of the Spirit.

Camp on verse 16: "Finally Pilate handed him over to them to be crucified." Finally? Hadn't these events happened so quickly that John's mind could hardly fathom what he had seen? Hadn't they just accompanied Christ down the Mount of Olives a few days earlier as the masses waved palm branches and proclaimed Jesus Messiah? Obviously, it means Pilate finally handed Christ over after He had been tossed from court to court like a tennis ball. I'd like to interject, however, an additional kind of *finally.*

Meditate on the following Scriptures. Write *finally* after each passage.

" 'I will put enmity between you and the woman, and between your off-spring and hers; he will crush your head, and you will strike his heel' " (Gen. 3:15). _____

" 'I will make you into a great nation and I will bless you; I will make your name great and you will be a blessing … and all peoples on earth will be blessed through you' " (Gen. 12:2-3). _____

" 'Go down and bring Aaron up with you. But the priests and the people must not force their way through to come up to the Lord, or he will break out against them' " (Ex. 19:24). _____

"King Solomon and the entire assembly of Israel that had gathered about him were before the ark, sacrificing so many sheep and cattle that they could not be recorded or counted" (2 Chron. 5:6). _____

"Then came the day of Unleavened Bread on which the Passover lamb had to be sacrificed" (Luke 22:7). _____

Finally, a public road was about to be paved from the holy of holies, through the holy place, out into the court of the Israelite men, right on to the court of women, and out into the court of the Gentiles—right to your heart and mine. Finally, a perfect, unblemished Lamb would be sacrificed to fulfill the righteous requirements of the temple's blazing altar. Finally, something would happen to reconcile believing humanity to God once and for all. After thousands of years of humanity's folly, someone in a cloak of flesh would do it right. Finally! Glory, glory to God!

Something would happen to reconcile believing humanity to God once and for all.

Retrospect and the recorded Word give us more insight than the disciples had. In the immediacy of the moment reflected in John 19:16, *finally* simply meant that Pilate made a decision after a long, excruciating night, but to us it represents the best of good news. We don't know how distant John was forced to remain, but can you imagine the verdict filtering through the ranks? Jesus is going to be crucified. The verdict is in: crucifixion!

Mind you, the verdict was illegal, but it was certainly lethal. They all knew too well what crucifixion entailed. It was the worst possible nightmare. John could not have assimilated the information calmly. Imagine the hot knife of shock searing his stomach.

 What thoughts might have gone through John's mind as he heard the verdict?

_____

_____

After beating Jesus within inches of His life, soldiers held His hands and feet against the crude wood and fastened Him there with a hammer and three long nails. Whether or not John saw the pounding of the hammer, heaven could hear the pounding of his heart. At a time when any thinking man would want to run for his life, John, probably the youngest of all the disciples, stayed near the cross.

Above young John hung his world, his hero, his attachment, his future, his leader, the love of his life. Three years earlier he was trying to gain his daddy's approval with a boat and net. He hadn't asked for Jesus. Jesus asked for him. And here he stood. Isaiah tells us that by the time the foes of Jesus finished with Him, "his appearance was so disfigured beyond that of any man and his form marred beyond human likeness" (Isa. 52:14).

"When Jesus saw his mother there, and the disciple whom he loved standing nearby, he said to his mother, 'Dear woman, here is your son' " (John 19:26). Don't take it lightly. Hear it. Not the way the passion plays do it. Hear the real thing. Hear a voice erupting from labored outburst as Jesus tried to lift Himself up and draw breath to speak.

Because Jesus' condition made speech harder than dying, every word spoken from the cross is critical. Chronic pain is jealous like few other things. It doesn't like to share. A man in pain can hardly think of anything else; yet Jesus did. Perhaps His heart's pain exceeded the pain of His shredded frame. The look on His mother's face. Her horror. Her suffering.

Then He gazed straight into the young face of the one standing nearby. Less than 24 hours earlier John's face had nestled against His chest in innocent affection. John was the baby of the family, as we call Melissa, and he knew it. He no doubt reveled in its privilege. If anyone had an excuse to run from the cross, perhaps it was John. But he didn't.

Jesus saw the disciple whom He loved standing nearby. I believe love and compassion hemorrhaged from His heart. "To the disciple, [He said,] 'Here is your mother.' From that time on, this disciple took her into his home" (John 19:27).

> If anyone had an excuse to run from the cross, perhaps it was John. But he didn't.

Why do you suppose Jesus gave this responsibility to John rather than to His own brothers? No right or wrong answer exists.

_____

_____

If the cross is about anything, it is about reconciliation: "He himself is our peace, who has made the two one and has destroyed the barrier, the dividing wall of hostility"

(Eph. 2:14). I think the unbelief of Christ's brothers had raised a wall of hostility between them and His disciples. As Christ gazed on His beloved mother and His beloved disciple, He saw His own two worlds desperately in need of reconciliation and a woman who no doubt was torn between the two.

Simeon's prophecy to Mary was fulfilled before Jesus' very eyes: " 'A sword will pierce your own soul too' " (Luke 2:35). How like Jesus to start stitching a heart back together even as the knife was tearing it apart. One day soon His family and His disciples would be united, but the firstfruit of that harvest waved beneath the cross of Christ: "From that time on, this disciple took her into his home" (John 19:27).

How perfectly appropriate! Right at the foot of the cross we discover the element that set John apart from the rest. I am a huge fan of Peter and can relate to him far more readily than John, but the inspired words the Holy Spirit later entrusted to the Son of Thunder (see Mark 3:17) suggest a profound uniqueness. I am reminded of a saint about whom God said, " 'My servant Caleb has a different spirit and follows me wholeheartedly' " (see Num. 14:24). God didn't mean a different Holy Spirit. God referred to something wonderful about Caleb's human spirit that made him unique. I believe John had something similar. These were fallible men prone to the dictates of their own flesh just like the rest of us, but they had something that was almost incomparable when overtaken by the Holy Spirit. They were simply different.

You and I have arrived at a red-letter moment on which much of the remainder of our journey hinges. I am convinced we've stumbled on the very thing that set John apart and made him the fertile soil into which God could sow the seeds of such a Gospel, such epistles, and such a revelation. John remained nearby Jesus, whether his leader was on the mount of transfiguration or in the depths of Gethsemane's suffering. John affectionately leaned on Him during the feast but also followed Him into the courts for the trials. John clung to Jesus when He raised the dead, and he clung to Jesus when He became the dead.

John stood nearby when human reason implied that his faithful leader's mission had failed. He could not have comprehended that the plan of the ages was going perfectly. Yet he remained. He who looked on a face that "shone like the sun" (Matt. 17:2) was willing to look on a face that was bloody and spit upon. He stayed nearby during Christ's brightest hour and His darkest hour. The young disciple knew Jesus in the extreme. John was willing to look when others covered their eyes. And he beheld Him. How can we behold what we are unwilling to see?

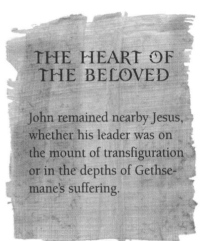

THE HEART OF THE BELOVED

John remained nearby Jesus, whether his leader was on the mount of transfiguration or in the depths of Gethsemane's suffering.

**Wouldn't it be a good time to ask God for a spirit like John's—
a spirit to follow Jesus anywhere? Take time to pray.**

We cannot claim to know anyone intimately whom we've not known in the intensity of both agony and elation. Anyone with eyes willing to truly behold Jesus will at times be confused and shocked by what she sees. You see, if we're willing to be taken to the extreme of His glory where we gain intimate knowledge, we will undoubtedly see Him in situations that we cannot explain and that sometimes disturb. Then comes the question: Will we walk away from Jesus when our human understanding sees Him look weak and defeated? Do you know what I mean by that question?

What will we do when we can't explain what Jesus is doing? Will we remain nearby when He doesn't stop a tragedy? Based on earthly evidence, human reasoning concludes that He is either mean or weak. Think, Beloved, about what I'm saying. Will we cling when our human reasoning implies that evil has defeated Him? Or that evil seems to be found in Him? Will we stand by faith when human logic says to run?

That's what will make us different.

Day 2 A RACE TO THE TOMB

TODAY'S TREASURE

"Peter and the other disciple started for the tomb. Both were running, but the other disciple outran Peter and reached the tomb first."—John 20:3-4

Sometimes violent circumstances shake the earth beneath our feet. We feel as if a canyon suddenly appeared and we've been hurled into it. Our emotions swing wildly and we think we'll be torn in two. Imagine how those who most loved Jesus felt at His death.

 Read John 19:28-30. Reflect on the events of the previous 3 years for John and 33 years for Mary. What kinds of feelings do you think they might have experienced?

_____

_____

When someone suffers extreme pain, we feel relief when it ends, even if by death. Then true to our self-destructive, self-condemning natures, guilt often follows. To add to the heap, the finality of the death ushers in feelings of hopelessness. Why? Because humanity has bone-deep indoctrination in the statement, Where there is life, there is hope.

Not in God's strange economy. That day of all days, where there was death, there was hope. Who could have fathomed it? And strangely, even now for those of us in Christ, our greatest hope is in what lies beyond our deaths. We stand on the edge of our clifflike emotions looking into the deep cavern of our grief, and we're sure that the jump will kill us. For those of us who entrust our feeble selves to our faithful Creator, in ways I can neither explain nor describe, it doesn't. Life is filled with large and small "deaths." In Jesus, when one of these deaths comes, we have a unique opportunity to take it to the cross. We can remain nearby and suffer its grief. Then we also experience the resurrection.

We say, "But part of me has died." And indeed it has. Hear the words of Christ echo from the grave, " 'I tell you the truth, unless a kernel of wheat falls to the ground and dies, it remains only a single seed. But if it dies, it produces many seeds' " (John 12:24). As a child who bears the name of Christ, if a part of you has died, it is meant to produce many seeds in time. Has it? Have we lived long enough and cooperated enough to see tender shoots come forth from the barren ground? Oh, Beloved. Don't give up!

What does God promise us if we keep believing (see Eph. 1:19-20)?
❏ **To wipe away all tears and sorrows**
❏ **His resurrection power to us who believe**
❏ **That whatever we pray, believing, we shall have**

Grief's final stage has not come until we allow God to bring forth resurrection life.

We hear about the phases of grief: shock, anger, depression, and acceptance. Many believe that the acceptance of death is grief's final stage, but if we're in Christ, the final stage has not come until we allow God to bring forth resurrection life. Yes, we have to come to acceptance but not just acceptance of death. Acceptance of resurrection life. Don't stop until you experience it. Though it tarry, it shall come!

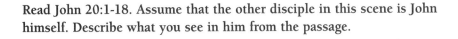

Read John 20:1-18. Assume that the other disciple in this scene is John himself. Describe what you see in him from the passage.

_____

_____

We have no idea where Mary found Peter and John, but she found them together—as usual. They were dear friends, weren't they? They most likely knew each other all their lives. They walked away from their nets on the same day and followed this magnetic man from Nazareth. A miracle man. But more than that. The Messiah. Or that's what they thought. Was He? How could He be?

They wanted to believe they lived the great adventure together for the past three years. They had seen things people would not even believe. And now they had seen something they themselves could not believe. Their fearless leader beaten to a bloody pulp and nailed to a criminal's cross. Jesus was dead. And to top it off, missing.

" 'They have taken the Lord out of the tomb, and we don't know where they have put him!' " (John 20:2). Their feet began moving before their minds could think. They were running. Harder. Faster. Hearts pounding. Adrenaline pumping. Fear surging. *Where is He? What is He? WHO is He?* So many questions. So many doubts. Flickers of hope. But why? It was hopeless, after all. Wasn't it?

They had walked side by side for years. Now they ran side by side. I realize I'm introducing something into the picture that wasn't intended by the author, but at this emotionally heightened moment in Scripture, I am amused that the man John incidentally tells us that he outran Peter. Ever competitive, aren't they? Then the same youth that outran Peter appeared to chicken out of going into the tomb. Both instances seem to imply his younger age. We're told in John 20:8, "Finally the other disciple, who had reached the tomb first, also went inside." You can just imagine Peter saying, "Come on, John! It's OK. Mary was right. No one's here. But look at this!" Strips of linen were lying there, and the one that had been wrapped around Jesus' head was folded all by itself. Now who in the world do you think folded that cloth?

Jesus probably rose right out of those grave clothes. I wonder if an angel God summoned to guard the tomb and to tell the news picked it up and folded the cloth.

Read 1 Peter 1:10-12. What did Peter write about angels?

_____

_____

As glorious as celestial beings are, I don't think they can comprehend the greatness and grace of so radical a salvation. They were created to praise the very One whom humanity, His prize creation, rejected and killed. Surely they were horrified that the Father didn't summon them to stop the madness. If the archangel Michael and the devil disputed over the body of Moses (see Jude 9), can you imagine the confrontation over this body? The whole plan must have seemed preposterous. Two angels were assigned to watch over the body of the Beloved One. One at His head. One at His feet. Total silence. Not a twitch. Weeping endured for a long winter's night. Would joy ever come in the morning?

The Father had waited long enough. He didn't even let the sun come up. He created the day. He'd say when it was morning. After all, the darkness is light to Him

> " 'They have taken the Lord, … and we don't know where they have put him!' " Their feet began moving before their minds could think.

(see Ps. 139:12). Suddenly, the Lord God omnipotent raised His mighty arm and unleashed strength beyond comprehension. Somehow I don't think the cold, lifeless body of Christ gradually grew warm. I'm convinced the blood instantaneously flashed hot through His veins, and He stood to His feet so fast that the grave clothes couldn't stick to Him. Clothed in resurrection raiment, Christ Jesus, the Savior of the world, stepped out of the tomb before the stone had a chance to get out of the way.

What happened next, according to Matthew 28:2-4? _____

_____

_____

I've been called the drama queen more than a few times. May I have the honor of presenting to you His Truly, God Almighty, the King of drama? Compared to Him, I'm nothing but a knot on a log. Yep, He's got the drama thing going, and I for one don't want to be caught sitting when a standing ovation is in order.

Let's go back to our John 20 text again. Recall that Mary tarried long enough to see the resurrected Lord Jesus face-to-face. Read verses 17-18 again. How I thank God that He appointed His Son to bring dignity to women. In a very tender way, she was the very first one Christ sent forth to bring the best news of all. Jesus is alive! May we be moved every single time the news hits us afresh.

Read John 20:19-23. Picture the scene. Mary took the news as Christ instructed. Time passed slowly as the disciples tried to assimilate Mary's report. Somewhere in this time frame Jesus appeared to Peter in an encounter that I believe was so private that we are intentionally left without a single detail (see 1 Cor. 15:5). We have no reason to believe that John had yet seen Jesus. Sit back and imagine the room. Feel the oppression of fear in the air. Picture bars across the doors and the captives inside who only a short time before wielded power to cast out demons and heal the sick. Had they been stripped of their authority? Of their abilities? No indeed. The enemy always sends fear to render victims powerless.

Suddenly Jesus walked through their barriers, into their hiding places, and appeared among them. We've been there. As a father has compassion on his children, Jesus has compassion on us (see Ps. 103:13). He knew that their finite minds needed Him to show them His hands and side. Don't we constantly expect people to heal from life's beatings and lose their scars? I'm somehow comforted to know that Christ still has His.

Stop to pray. Pour out your heart to Jesus about your scars and His.

Someone as young as John might have been thinking or saying, "We won!"

Picture their expressions. Feel the oppression lift. Now look in your imagination and find our friend John. Wait for a few seconds and picture Jesus' eyes fastened on John alone. Somehow I imagine young John's eyebrows pinned to his hairline, eyes as big as saucers. I think he probably froze until the love of Christ melted him like butter. I wonder if he broke out in such a toothy grin that Jesus wanted to laugh. Someone as young as John was probably thinking the same things as the others; he might have been thinking or saying, "We won!" And indeed they had. They had won Christ.

Day 3 WHAT ABOUT HIM?

TODAY'S TREASURE

"When Peter saw him, he asked, 'Lord, what about him?' "—John 21:21

One of the postresurrection images of Christ I love most is when He has to tell Mary Magdalene to peel herself from Him so that each of them can be released to do what God had called them to do (see John 20:17). The moment she recognized Jesus, she obviously latched on to Him for dear life as if to say, "Now that I've found you, I will never let you go!" Although you and I have never seen Christ face-to-face, we're not altogether different. We sometimes receive a fresh revelation of Christ in a moment of crisis. Then we may not want to budge from it for the rest of our days.

> We sometimes receive a fresh revelation of Christ in a crisis. We may not want to budge from it.

Christ seems to say to us, "Yes, this revelation is a gift to you, but be careful not to get stuck here. Don't cling to your sightings of Me. Let those moments be fuel for your future. Walk by faith and not by sight. There's work to be done! Rest assured I'll always be with you because now that I've found you, I will never let you go."

I don't doubt that once they saw their resurrected Savior, the disciples wanted to hang on to Him just as tightly as Mary Magdalene did. And they were just as unable to do so.

According to Acts 1:3, what length of time did Christ use to reveal Himself after He rose from the dead? ❏ **40 days**   ❏ **10 days**   ❏ **50 days**

Today we're going to sit on the shore of the Sea of Galilee, also called the Sea of Tiberias, and watch one of the last encounters Christ had with the disciples before He returned with them to the Mount of Olives. Our eyes will be on the events recorded in John 21. Although the disciple-oriented spotlight seems to be on Peter, I also want you to focus on John's role.

First read John 21:1-14. Who was in the boat? _____

_____

My husband would tell you that seven men in your average boat is at least five too many, but Peter and the others had obviously returned to the commercial vessel where Peter earned his living for years. He seems to have ascribed to the philosophy "When you don't know what to do, do what you used to do." Even though the disciples must have been ecstatic to have Christ in their midst, I believe He purposely let those days become an identity challenge for them. Notice Jesus didn't hang around with them every minute.

How many times had the disciples seen Christ by now (see John 21:14)? ____

The fact that Jesus didn't bind Himself to the disciples during His postresurrection tenure must have been confusing to them. I'm not sure they knew how they fit into Christ's work from this side of the grave. Surely the thought occurred to them, *What need does anyone powerful enough to walk out of a tomb have for us?* They didn't understand that Christ's primary purpose during those 40 days was for people to understand that He is God. Keep in mind, Jesus had more on His agenda than appearing to His disciples.

To whom did Christ reveal Himself, according to 1 Corinthians 15:5-7?

_____

_____

What are we supposed to do when God is busy letting people know who He is and we're not sure where we fit into the present revelation (see Ps. 46:10)?

_____

Yep. Be still and know it ourselves. Don't default into our past. Don't jump the gun for our future. Just behold and know. Instructions will come when the time is right. In the meantime, being is so much harder than doing, isn't it? Thankfully, Jesus knew where to find His disciples anyway, and He interrupted their doing with His own being. John seemed to better grasp what Christ had come to be than the others at this point.

Being is so much harder than doing, isn't it?

John is attributed only four words in this scene. What are they? _____

_____

Oh, that we would come to recognize what is the Lord and what is not. The second John announced Jesus, Peter jumped from the boat and swam to Him with all his might. I can't let this moment pass without putting the flashlight on one of Peter's sterling moments. In our Christian circles we often surround ourselves with people of similar practice of faith. We have unspoken codes. Spiritual practices that we consider acceptable. We also agree on things that are not. Things that are weird. Behaviors that are just, well—overboard. Then someone among us jumps ship and decides he or she doesn't care what the rest of us think. Nothing is going to get between Peter and Jesus. Glory! As much as I love John, in this scene I want to be Peter!

Actually, I remember well when I began to break the unspoken code of just how far my church compadres and I would go with this "spiritual thing." Years ago those closest to me charged me with going overboard—you can believe they disapproved, too. Do you know what, Beloved? I wouldn't climb back in that boat for anything.

Have you jumped out of the boat of the comfortable and acceptable? Do you want Jesus even if you have to make a fool of yourself to get to Him? If so, elaborate. If not, what's holding you back?

_____

_____

Intimacy with Christ doesn't always feel warm and fuzzy. Just ask Peter. That water was cold! This scene took place during the latter part of our month of May. Days are very warm in that part of Galilee, but the temperature drops dramatically during the night. This fishing trip took place before breakfast (see John 21:12). No wonder the other disciples followed in the boat! I believe Jesus esteemed Peter's impetuous determination to get to Him. I am also convinced that this act was an important part of Peter's restoration. Notice he didn't ask to walk on water. This time he was willing to dog-paddle in ice water to get to Jesus.

I am convinced Peter's solo pursuit wrote the perfect invitation in the sand for Christ to single him out in the redemptive scene that followed. His leap from the boat may have suggested that at this point Peter truly loved Christ " 'more than these' " (John 21:15).

Read John 21:15-23, looking for John in the snapshot. What did Christ say to Peter (see v. 19)?

_____

Three years earlier Peter had heard the same words, and to his credit, he had done it. But he had done it in his own strength and with his own agenda, his own ambition.

What happened the previous time we saw Peter warming himself by a fire (see Luke 22:55-57)?

_____

_____

What was the obvious motivation Christ wanted for Peter to follow Him (see John 21)? ❑ **Lordship** ❑ **Love** ❑ **Leadership**

Oh, Beloved, can you see the significance? No other motivation will last! We might feed the sheep or serve the flock based on other motivations for a while, but only one thing will compel us to follow the Lord Jesus Christ faithfully to the death: love! No one had more spiritual tenacity than the apostle Paul, and he made no bones about what kept him on the path amid unparalleled pain and persecution.

> Only love will compel us to follow the Lord Jesus Christ faithfully to the death!

In 2 Corinthians 5:14 Paul wrote, "_____ compels us!"

Carefully read James 1:12. What is the evidence of love's tenacity?

_____

_____

Our callings may differ, but if we're going to follow Jesus Christ in the power of the crucified life, our compellings will be the same. Only love compels to the death. Life is hard. Opposition is huge. Circumstances will happen in all our lives that will defy all discipline, determination, and conviction. Love keeps burning when everything else disintegrates in an ashen heap. Pray for this one thing more than you pray for your next breath.

I am convinced that love is everything, but I wasn't the first one convinced. I simply follow in a long line of believers who failed their way into the discovery that love is the highest priority and motivating force in the entire life of faith. Generations before any of us wised up, a young disciple named John was so drawn to Christ's discourse on love that he couldn't help but listen as Jesus and Peter walked away from the others to talk. I believe the conversation in John 21:15-23 began in the group of eight. Perhaps in the course of the question and answer, Jesus quite naturally stood up, brushed Himself off, and took a few steps away from the small circle of men. Peter, unnerved by his own interpretation of the repetitive question, probably jumped to his feet and followed.

Peter was grieved because Jesus questioned his love a third time. " 'Lord, you know all things; you know that I love you' " (John 21:17). Mind you, he was still drenched from his zeal. Jesus then prophesied why Peter's love for Him would be so critical. Peter would be asked to glorify God by giving his own life. Only love could make him willing.

As if to say, "Knowing all this and with your eyes wide open," Christ reissued the call " 'Follow me!' " Don't downplay it for an instant. The cost of the call was huge. We don't know why Peter looked behind him to see John following. Perhaps John stepped on a branch. Perhaps he groaned when he heard Christ foretell his friend's future.

I don't believe John trailed them from selfish curiosity. I think he sensed the enormity of what the risen Teacher was teaching. This was no tiptoed eavesdropping. I think he was drawn like a magnet. I believe Scripture will prove that John, perhaps like no other disciple in that circle, assimilated the profound implications of what his beloved Savior was saying: "You are My called ones. You have tough futures ahead of you, but the glory God will gain will be immeasurable. Love is the only motivation that can afford this kind of cost."

"When Peter saw him, he asked, _____?" (v. 21).

Oh, for the Bible on videotape! We would be far better equipped to interpret a scene accurately if we could see the speaker's expressions and hear his tone of voice. Because we have no such help, words like Peter's have almost as many interpretations as I have commentaries. They each say something different about Peter's motivation for asking this question. Here's the good news: that means we can speculate without getting too far off base.

What do you think was in Peter's voice?
❑ **Deep concern for John**   ❑ **Jealousy**   ❑ **Other:** _____

No matter what your interpretation is, I think we can all admit that the question sometimes plagues us, as well. Perhaps you have served near someone else, and God has called you to suffer some difficult circumstances while he or she seems to flourish in relative ease. Or perhaps your heart has broken for someone who works hard and serves diligently but has difficulty for a constant companion. Maybe one of your children seems blessed and gifted by God, and you keep looking at the other and asking, "Lord, what about him?"

Which scenario has been most common to you? Elaborate.

_____

How does Christ's response speak to the scenario you described (see John 21:22)?

_____

_____

Over and over Jesus tells us, "You can trust Me!"

Over and over Jesus tells us, "You can trust Me!" In this scene He says to His present-day disciples, "You can trust Me with you and with them. I am the same God to all of you, but I have a different plan for each of you. You won't miss it if you keep following. Remember, I've been a carpenter. Custom blueprints are My specialty. God's glory is My goal. You're not ready until you'd swim or walk it all by yourself. Now fill your canteen to the brim with love and follow Me."

Day 4 IF AND WHEN

TODAY'S TREASURE
" 'You will receive power when the Holy Spirit comes on you.' "—Acts 1:8

Let's not work up to something profound today. Let's jump right in! Try to grasp this: They saw Him. They touched Him. The disciples came face-to-face and hand-to-wounded-hand with the resurrected Lord of hosts. Yes, we walk by faith, but do you realize that our faith is based on Rock-solid fact? Today we are going to stand on the sidelines and watch the disciples experience some pretty wild things that happened just as Scripture says. Our reading begins with Acts 1:1-12. You may be very familiar with the scene described in these verses, but sometimes overfamiliarity can be the biggest treasure thief of all. Rewind the verses, and let's replay them in slow motion.

Where had Christ and His disciples gathered (see v. 12)?
❑ Sea of Tiberias ❑ Mount of Olives ❑ Jerusalem

Read verse 11 and take the angels' words literally. To what location does Zechariah 14:4 say the Lord will return?

_____

Think of several reasons God may have for not telling His followers (both past and present) the times and dates of the kingdom.

_____

_____

Fill in the blanks: " 'You _____ receive _____ when the Holy Spirit comes on you' " (Acts 1:8).

We can apply this portion of the verse as readily as Christ's original disciples. The Holy Spirit comes no other way but in power; His omnipotence is part of His essence. Before our lesson concludes, we'll also see that when we receive what the Holy Spirit is fully equipped to apply to us, the effects show. In fact, that's the point.

> The Holy Spirit comes only in power; His omnipotence is part of His essence.

Read 2 Corinthians 4:7, in which Paul speaks of the "treasure" of the Holy Spirit. Besides the multifaceted ministries of the Holy Spirit to each believer, what is God's goal in giving us this treasure?

_____

_____

Beloved, God wants to hang out all over you! Don't you see? That's why circumstances and challenges are often beyond us! If life were completely manageable, we'd manage in our own

If we only knew what we have, our lives could be so different!

strength, and no one would see the living proof of God's existence in us. We are here to become witnesses to an injured world in desperate need of a Savior. Do you belong to Jesus Christ? If so, the Holy Spirit dwells in you (see Rom. 8:9) and brings glory to Christ through you. As He does, your whole life becomes a living witness. Our assignments may differ, but we have the same Holy Spirit that Christ promised to His first disciples. If we only knew what we have, our lives could be so different!

After Christ gave His chosen apostles the assurance of the coming power of the Holy Spirit, He was taken up before their very eyes, and a cloud hid him from their sight (see Acts 1:9). Try to imagine being on the Mount of Olives that day. Verse 11 implies that they were all standing, so they were basically eye to eye with Jesus, not letting a single word from His mouth fall to the ground. He promised them the power of the Holy Spirit; then, without warning, the disciples realized that they were glancing somewhat upward as He seemed a tad taller. As He rose a head above them, surely some of them looked down and saw that His feet were no longer on the ground.

What was Christ doing as He lifted off the ground (see Luke 24:50-51)?

Perhaps by now your imagination has drawn a rough sketch of the apostle John on the your mind's canvas. Picture him and the others bug-eyed, with their mouths gaping open. Had my grandmother been one of the disciples (a frighteningly funny thought), she would have stood there saying, "Now don't that just beat all?" I feel sure they said something comparable in Hebrew.

Just about the time they might have tried to rub the supernatural sight out of their eyes, God threw a cloudy cloak of shekinah glory over His beloved Son and swept Him home. Oh, don't you know that the Father had been watching earth's clock for that precious moment to finally arrive? Although Christ was no prodigal, He was most assuredly a son who journeyed to a foreign land. I can almost hear the Father say to His servants, " 'Quick! Bring the best robe and put it on him. Put a ring on his finger and sandals on his feet. Bring the fattened calf and kill it. Let's have a feast and celebrate. For this son of mine was dead and is alive again' " (Luke 15:22-24).

Had the angels not broken their stare, the remains of 11 stiff carcasses might still be on the Mount of Olives today. I wonder whether their words to the disciples about Christ's return stirred up memories of a very recent conversation between Jesus and Peter, overheard by John. Turn to John 21:21-23 and recapture the conversation. By the time this dialogue took place, Peter knew that he must believe anything Christ said. Just as surely as the prophecy of Peter's three-strike denial was fulfilled, the foretelling of his death would be fulfilled. How sobering this news must have been! Not only to him but also to his best friend, John.

Meanwhile, the implication of Christ's words may have led both Peter and John to wonder whether the younger son of Zebedee would live to see Christ's return. We know for a fact that such a rumor spread. Whether or not Peter and John temporarily mistook Christ's *if* for a *when,* plenty of others did. (Remember, the Gospel was written years later when retrospect made statements like these much clearer.) Beloved, few words in Scripture are bigger than *if.* Watch for it and be careful not to make it a *when.* The Word of God is full of unconditional promises, but plenty of others hinge on an *if.*

Today we've discussed a priority promise Christ gave in Acts 1:8.
Is it an "if" or a "when" statement?   ❑ If   ❑ When

Those of us in Christ may keep wondering *if* we have the power to be victorious in the challenge before us, but God's wondering *when* we're going to believe Him!

We'll look only briefly at our second reading passage in Acts 1:12-26. As you read, remember that most of the disciples were from the villages around the Sea of Galilee.

Why did the disciples return to Jerusalem (see Acts 1:4-5)?
❑ **Jerusalem was home.** ❑ **Fishing** ❑ **Jesus was sending the Holy Spirit.**

Scripture tells us their return to the city was a "Sabbath day's walk," which would have been about ¾ mile. I have walked that brief trek a number of times, and it is straight downhill until you ascend the temple mount to the city gates. One can hardly keep from walking fast due to the incline, but somehow I'm imagining their mouths were traveling faster than their feet. (You're imagining that mine was, too!) We are told the disciples went upstairs to the room where they were staying. The Greek words and sentence structure indicate that the location was well known and was highly significant to the disciples.[1]

Who joined the disciples in this room? _____

_____

List several reasons this mix of people has significance, based on your own opinion or understanding.

_____

_____

_____

How large was that first New Testament cell group, according to Acts 1:15?
❑ 25   ❑ 50   ❑ 120   ❑ 500

You may attend a church about this size and wonder with frustration what God could do with such a small group of people. Dear One, when the Holy Spirit falls on a place, it doesn't matter how small the group—things start happening! Remember, the Holy Spirit comes in order to get results! Let's find out what can happen when the Holy Spirit interrupts a prayer meeting. You and I are about to behold the disciples' *when!*

When the Holy Spirit falls, things happen!

Carefully read Acts 2:1-21. Then glance over the various headings in Leviticus 23, focusing your attention especially on verses 15-16 and 22.

This awesome chapter records the annual feasts God appointed to Israel. I am convinced every one of them is ultimately fulfilled in Jesus Christ. In context with today's lesson we'll emphasize three. The most important was (and is) Passover (see Lev. 23:4-8).

What does 1 Corinthians 5:7 tell us? _____

_____

_____

The feast that immediately followed Passover was Firstfruits, when a sheaf of the first grain of the harvest was waved before the Lord for His acceptance (see Lev. 23:11). This was the day after the Passover Sabbath, obviously falling on a Sunday.

> **Now read 1 Corinthians 15:20-23. What significance does *firstfruits* have in Christ?**

Fifty (*pente*) days after Passover came the Feast of Weeks, later called Pentecost. It was the celebration of seven weeks of harvest. The one sheaf waved on Firstfruits turned into an entire harvest celebrated seven weeks and one day later. The Feast of Weeks was the presentation of an offering of new grain to the Lord (see Lev. 23:16). In other words, it was the celebration of harvest reaped. Now do you see the significance of what happened on Pentecost? Fifty days earlier Christ, the Passover Lamb, was crucified. On the day of Firstfruits, that very Sunday morning, His life was waved acceptable before God as the firstfruit from the dead. Fifty days after Passover, the Holy Spirit came just as Christ promised. And He came to bring glory to Christ! The Holy Spirit reveals Himself many ways in Scripture.

> **How did the Holy Spirit reveal His all-surpassing power in simple jars of clay that day (see Acts 2:1-21)?**

The Holy Spirit comes to bring glory to Christ and to bring results.

> **What were the results that first Pentecost after Christ, our Passover Lamb, was offered (see Acts 2:46-47)?**

Christ tarries only so that the harvest can reach its peak.

I present the first harvest reaped by the life, death, and resurrection of Jesus—Pentecost! I believe we also live in a form of Pentecost. Christ tarries only so that the harvest can reach its peak and be reaped to God's glory. He does not will for any to perish but for all to come to repentance (see 2 Pet. 3:9). He desires everyone and forces no one, but He will not wait forever. One day the ultimate Feast of Trumpets (see Lev. 23:23; 1 Thess. 4:16) will come, and we will meet Jesus in the air. The books will be opened and closed for the last time, and the final judgment will take place (see Rev. 20:11-15). The Day of Atonement will be past (see Lev. 23:26; Rom. 3:23-25). Those who were covered by the blood of the Passover Lamb will tabernacle (see Lev. 23:33) with God forever. And so shall we ever be with the Lord (see 1 Thess. 4:17).

" 'The father said to his servants, "Quick! Bring the best robe and put it on him. Put a ring on his finger and sandals on his feet. Bring the fattened calf and kill it. Let's have a feast and celebrate. For this son of mine was dead and is alive again." So they began to celebrate' " (Luke 15:22-24).

I feel like starting early. I'm going to put on some praise music and maybe even my dancing shoes!

Day 5 JUST A HANDFUL

We have an appointment with Peter and John in just a few minutes at Solomon's temple, but first I need to run ahead and "sacrifice thank offerings to God, fulfill your vows to the Most High" (Ps. 50:14). The rocks will cry out if I don't stop and make a thank offering. My heart overflows with inexpressible gratitude to God for the treasure of His Word. He has single-handedly used His Word to heal, free, thrill, and lead me. I love it so much that sometimes when I finish reading a passage that has opened a fresh spring in the deep well of my soul, I cannot help but gently, reverently kiss the page.

The Word is the only truly divine substance that is touchable and tangible in this earthly realm. I do not worship a book. I worship the One who breathed life onto the page in human vocabulary so that mortal creatures could hear the very voice of God. I could weep at the thought. Often a dear sister who has been touched by one of the Bible studies will thank me for writing it. A lump wells in my throat as I try to articulate to you what I want to say to her: "Beloved, I thank you. Do you realize that your desire for these studies is the very thing God uses to keep this woman who was once so broken and self-destructive in a perpetual state of healing and filling? Life in the Word has released me from life in the pit, Dear One, and caused my soul to dance in meadows of wildflowers and swim in coral reefs! I trek to exotic places on the other side of the globe and step back in time to an ancient civilization—all without leaving my office! I am awash with gratitude to God and to this small slice of the body of Christ that gives me such an invitation."

At the end of our previous lesson, we celebrated the Pentecost of 3,000 souls. Added to the strong cell group of 120, Solomon's temple would have paled in comparison to the gleaming harvest. Before we get to the heart of today's lesson, read the description of the early church in Acts 2:42-47. Pretend you are looking for a local church and you're reading reviews of those in your area written by the newspaper's religious editor.

In just a few sentences what would he have to say about this church?

_____

_____

Now that's a church I want to attend! Let's get to our appointment with Peter and John. Read all of Acts 3, but let's center our attention on the first 13 verses. What is the most remarkable part of the account?

_____

Can you believe the change in Peter already? Primarily, the difference is the anointing of the Holy Spirit, but I believe his former failure was a huge part of his present victory. We wonder why God allows some of us, yours truly included, to be sifted like wheat; yet when we assess the difference in Peter, the reason is clear. God allows only servants to

God allows only servants to be sifted who have something that needs sifting!

be sifted who have something that needs sifting! If we feel that we're being sifted because God has allowed the enemy to play havoc in our lives, we are wise to cut to the chase and find out what God wants sifted. God saw the same thing in my earlier ministry that I believe He saw in Peter's. It is spelled p-r-i-d-e. Let me assure you, God's methods of separating the chaff from the grain are very effective.

What you have in this chapter of Scripture is a pair of mighty fine servants. Allow me to highlight a few things I love about Peter and John in this scene. First, they cherished their heritage. Please don't miss the fact that the Jerusalem church was Jewish!

Where did the believers meet daily (see Acts 2:46)? _____

Acts 3 opens with Peter and John on their way to the three o'clock prayer time at the temple, which coincided with the evening sacrifice. The thought never occurred to them to cast off their Judaism for their new faith in Christ. Nothing could have been more absurd. Jesus was Jewish! Their Messiah fulfilled their Jewish heritage. No longer obligated to the letter of the law, Christ had met its righteous requirements. They were free to enjoy its precepts and practices as expressions of their faith in Jesus.

Can you imagine how their belief in Christ and their newfound knowledge of Jesus as the answer to every symbolic practice spiced up their participation? Suddenly the black and white of their ritual prayer services turned technicolor with the life of the Holy Spirit. I snicker when I think that the Pentecost observers thought the disciples had been drinking. Don't you suspect the critics secretly wanted a sip of whatever they were having?

Last year I stumbled onto a definition of a Hebrew word that I want to share with you. Take a look at the well-loved Scripture, Jeremiah 29:11. The Hebrew word for *future* includes the following explanation: its general meaning is "after, later, behind, following. The Hebrew way of thinking has been compared to a man rowing a boat; he backs into the future while looking toward where he has been. Therefore, what is 'behind' and what is 'future' come from the same root, `ahar."[2]

Try to grasp this: God cherishes your heritage, too. You may balk, "What are you talking about? My past is horrible!" Listen carefully, Beloved. We are no longer under the law and authority of our pasts, but like Peter and John, we are free to use them as they lend expression to our faith in Jesus. You can't become the servant God is calling you to be without the threads of your past being knit into the technicolor fabric of your future. If your heritage had nothing to do with your future, God is far too practical to have allowed it. I am convinced this is true in my life. I don't believe Satan would have gained permission from God to defile my young life had my faithful Heavenly Father not known without a doubt how He could use it. The earlier definition told us the Hebrew words for *past* and *future* come from the same root. God is never more glorified than when He brings an oak of righteousness (see Isa. 61:3) out of a once damaged root.

I love the image of the rowboat. Don't read more into the word picture than you should—it's simply food for thought. Certainly, we want to keep our eyes on Jesus. Some of us so focus on our pasts that we don't row to our futures. Others try to turn their backs on their pasts with such denial that they can't make any progress.

> You can't become the servant God is calling you to be without the threads of your past being knit into the technicolor fabric of your future.

If we're going to become the effective servants God desires us to be, how do you think we should balance past and future?

_____

_____

Not convinced? Perhaps you're thinking, *I'd take Peter and John's Jewish heritage over mine any day!* Wonderful! Because in addition to your own, you have their heritage, too!

What does Galatians 3:29 say about you? _____

_____

Second, Peter and John were not so busy getting to the prayer meeting that they missed the beggar at the gate. Don't miss the significance of the location at the gate called Beautiful. Leave it to God to appoint a bitter reality in our beautiful scene. Try as we may to avoid the misery, misfortune, and injustice around us, they will find us. My city is filled with gated and extravagant planned communities with walls around them to keep the niceties in and the unpleasantries out. I don't have a single problem with great wealth as long as folks still have a clue about the rest of the world. God is too faithful to let us hide forever. We have to come out from behind those protective walls sooner or later, and when we do, one of these days we're going to have a head-on collision with reality. The kind of reality that begs the question, *What are you going to do about this?*

Peter and John could have glanced at the nearest sundial and said, "Oops! We're almost late for a prayer meeting. Beg on, Brother!"

Instead, "Peter looked _____, as did John" (Acts 3:4).

Refreshing, isn't it? I'm not much for looking suffering and poverty straight in the face. I'll face it, all right. But slightly to one side or the other. Not Peter and John. They looked straight at him and likewise demanded that he look straight at them.

Why do you think Peter required such a thing? _____

_____

Peter may have had many reasons for telling the beggar to look at them, but several things occur to me. The man was crippled from birth. Actually, "from the womb" is a more literal translation of the Greek. He was taken to the temple daily. Verse 3 says he saw Peter and John, but the inference is that he didn't really look at them. I think he had begged so long that he saw himself as nothing more than a beggar. He had ceased to look people in the eye. He didn't want to look in the face of anything that made him feel any more inferior. I'm convinced that his begging had become tragically rote. Completely mechanical. Dear One, I want to say something that may seem harsh. Sometimes we decide God is mean because He won't give us what we're begging for. We don't realize that He has a higher mercy for our crippled estate. We want a Holy Enabler. God wants to be our Healer.

We want a Holy Enabler. God wants to be our Healer.

Have you ever begged for something that you realize would have done nothing but help keep you in your crippled estate? I sure have! Share below.

_____

_____

Third, Peter and John gave what they had. I love the words " 'Silver or gold I do not have, but what I have I give you. In the name of Jesus Christ of Nazareth, walk' " (v. 6).

God never asks us to give
what we don't have.

God never asks us to give what we don't have. Somehow I'm relieved by that assurance. This verse recently came alive for me. Soon after the terrorist attack on the Twin Towers, clergy and church leaders in New York City were overwhelmed by the task of ministering to their flocks after such unprecedented disaster. The American Association of Christian Counselors was asked to lead a training conference dealing with grief specifically caused by trauma. The AACC quickly pulled together their most experienced Christian counselors and also asked a handful of Christian speakers to join them. I'm still mystified to have been among them.

On my way to New York I poured out my heart to God and told Him I did not begin to know how to tell people to deal with such tragedy. I kept saying, "Lord, I'm over my head here. I'm out of my league. I don't know what I'm talking about, and I have nothing in my catalog of experience to draw from!" The Holy Spirit reminded me of this Scripture. God seemed to say, "Beth, I'm not sending you to New York City as a Christian counselor. Don't try to be what you're not. Go and do what I've taught you to do. Teach My Word." Although I was still very intimidated by the task, God's reminder was profound. I began my message with Acts 3:6. I confessed my tremendous lack of experience and credentials but pledged that such as I have, I would give.

I was so relieved not to have to try to be something I'm not or to do something I don't. Can you relate in any way? If so, how?

Fourth, Peter took the beggar by the hand and helped him up. I love this part of the account. Peter and John knew better than anyone that the power to heal the man came solely from the Holy Spirit. The man wasn't healed because Peter took him by the hand and helped him up. To me, the tender representation here is that Peter offered the man a handful of faith to help him get to his feet. After all, this man had been crippled all his life. What reason did he have to believe he could be healed? He thought all he wanted was a little money. When the beggar grabbed Peter's hand, he felt the strength in his grip. The confidence of his faith. In one clasp Peter offered a handful of faith, and that was all the man needed to get to his feet.

Can you see him? Close your eyes and watch! Watch the beggar jump to his feet, see his cup tumble down the temple steps and the few coins spin in the afternoon sunshine. Look at his face! Watch him dance on legs thin from atrophy. Look! Look straight at him! That's him jumping and praising God through the temple courts. Laugh over the horrified expressions on pious faces. Look for others in the crowd who are ecstatic with joy and decide to grab a handful of faith for themselves. They recognize him as the man who used to sit begging at the temple gate called Beautiful. They are filled with wonder and amazement at what happened to him. Yep, his past made his present so miraculous. And we wonder why ...

Fifth, Peter and John took no credit for the miracle. After all, if man can do it, it really isn't a miracle, now is it? Miracles are from God—for the likes of crippled man. Someone reading today has been begging God for trivial things like silver and gold when God wants to raise her to her feet to jump, dance, and praise Him. Why do we want God to help us stay the way we are? Grab a handful of faith and be changed!

[1]Frank E. Gaebelein and J. D. Douglas, *The Expositor's Bible Commentary,* vol. 9 (Grand Rapids: Zondervan Publishing, 1981), 260.
[2]Spiros Zodhiates, "Lexical Aids to the Old Testament," 344, in Spiros Zodhiates, Warren Baker, and David Kemp, *The Hebrew-Greek Key Study Bible* (Chattanooga, TN: AMG Publishers, 1996), 503.

VIDEO RESPONSE SHEET

Group Session 3

Read Acts 4:23-32.
The Greek word *deesis* refers to a _____ _____ for which one prays.

How did God respond to their prayers?

- The place where they were meeting was _____. The Greek word means "to move

    to and fro, shake … to put into a state of waving, _____, vibratory motion."

- They _____ filled with the Holy Spirit.

- They _____ spoke the Word of God boldly.

1. They neither _____ nor _____ the seriousness of the problem (v. 23).

2. The believers _____ for prayer in a way God highly honors. (The Greek word is *homothumadon.*)

    - *Homos* means _____ and the _____.

    - *Thumos* means _____, _____. Also, "With one mind, with _____

        _____, in one accord, all together." *Thumos* can also mean _____

    as well as mind or thought.

    If God honors His people coming together with ONE MIND and passion, whose mind is right?

    Philippians 2:5 (KJV) says, "Let _____ _____ be in you, which was also

    in _____ _____." What kind of mind did He have?

    - He made Himself of _____ _____.

    - He took on the _____ _____ _____ _____.

    - He _____ Himself. Proverbs 13:10 says, "Pride only breeds quarrels."

3. They corporately _____ God. In doing so, they _____ Him and reminded

    themselves to whom _____ _____ (Acts 4:24).

4. They cited _____ _____ to their challenge (vv. 25-26).

5. They reminded themselves that anything God allows to _____ _____ _____,
    He will use to bring about great glory.

6. Then they asked _____ _____.

BEYOND THE LIMITS

Day 1

A New Fire

Day 2

Devastation

Day 3

The Right Hand of Fellowship

Day 4

Lessons from Obscurity

Day 5

The One Jesus Loved

The Word of God never gets old to me. No matter how often I've studied a scene, I can always gain fresh insight from a new perspective. The Bible is like a priceless gem held up to a light. If you tilt it and look from a different angle, you see all sorts of new colors. Before I first walked the journey you are taking through God's Word, I hadn't given significant thought to John's place in the early church. Neither had I considered the tremendous impact the benchmark events had on him individually. May God grant each of us a new depth of understanding into the Spirit of God as it pierces the souls of humans.

Principal Questions

Day 1: According to John 4:9, what was the situation at the time of the disciples' ministry?

Day 2: Why might John have been with Christ's biological family?

Day 3: How do we know from Paul's testimony that John held a primary role in the Christian church in Jerusalem (see Gal. 2:9)?

Day 4: According to Hebrews 2:14-15, what kind of freedom did Christ give us?

Day 5: How do you imagine John felt as the solitary remaining apostle?

Day 1 A NEW FIRE

Next we behold the dramatic unfolding of a new chapter in the lives of Christ's first followers. We witnessed in week 3 that the New Testament church often gathered for prayer in the temple courts. They savored their Jewish heritage and viewed their faith in Christ as its fulfillment. With the coming of persecution, however, the disciples faced a virtual end to their freedom to practice their faith unafraid on temple grounds.

What caused the rift (see Acts 4:13-20)? _____

_____

Over the next several chapters in the Book of Acts persecution increased like stones hurled by a mob. The reality of the Jewish establishment's intentions rose to the surface as Stephen fell to his knees. I am convinced he was bloodied and bruised by a gnawing and growing paranoia in their souls: What if they were wrong about Jesus of Nazareth? What if they crucified the Son of glory? They would do everything they could to silence those who made them question their own actions, but the Sanhedrin underestimated the tenacity of Christ's followers, who inverted their muzzles and made them megaphones.

Read Acts 8:1-4. How could verse 4 change the way you pray about the persecution of Christians today?

_____

_____

I can't wait for you to read a fitting quotation from a book more than a century old. In *The Two St. Johns of the New Testament* James Stalker described how the early believers were themselves astonished as "the fences within which their religious life had been confined broke down, and they were carried into one new territory after another as preachers of Christ; the oddest circumstances sometimes giving the providential impulse to fresh developments. Not infrequently it was by persecution that the new faith was driven out of one place into another, where, but for this reason, it might never have been heard of; so that the opposition which threatened to extinguish the fire of the Gospel only scattered its embers far and wide; and wherever they fell a new fire was kindled."[1]

What amazing providence! When Christ told His disciples that they would receive power and become witnesses not only in Jerusalem but also to the uttermost parts of the earth, they never expected His means! No, His ways are not our ways. Our ways would always be comfortable. Convenient. Certainly without hurt or harm. We would always ask that God use the favor of the masses to increase our harvests, not the fervor of opposition. If you've walked with God very long, I have little doubt that He has used what you perceived as very negative means to achieve a positive result.

His ways are not our ways. Our ways would always be comfortable.

How has God allowed something to push down your fence so that He could expand your horizon?

_____

_____

God is faithful, isn't He? Even when He turns the ignition on a holy bulldozer to plow down a confining fence.

Now read Acts 8:4-25, giving attention to the role John played. Where did the apostles in Jerusalem send Peter and John and why?

_____

_____

If we were studying the Book of Acts, I would explore the disciples' encounter with Simon the Sorcerer with you; but because our goal is to study the life, heart, and spirit of John, something else seizes my attention. Does the location of Samaria and its relationship to John ring a bell to you? The first bell this reference probably rings is the word Christ spoke over the 11 disciples before His ascension (see Acts 1:8).

When Christ commanded His disciples to be witnesses in Samaria, He probably raised a few eyebrows. Jerusalem? No problem. Judea? Absolutely. Ends of the earth? We're Your men, Jesus. But Samaria? Jews despised the Samaritans! If Gentiles were the target of the Jews' prejudices, then the Samaritans were the bulls-eye. And the feelings were mutual. Jews considered Samaritans to be a mongrel breed, border people who lived in the strip of land between the Jews and the Gentiles.

> When Christ commanded His disciples to be witnesses in Samaria, He probably raised a few eyebrows.

What was the situation at the time of the disciples' ministry (see John 4:9)?

_____

The idealists among us might be thinking, _But surely since they followed Christ, the disciples didn't have those kinds of prejudices toward people. After all, they were Christians._ Hmm. I hear another bell ringing. Take a good look at Luke 9:51-56. You can see the ill feelings on both sides. However, get a load of our friends James and John.

What did they suggest? _____

_____

Don't assume they were being overdramatic and didn't really mean what they said. Jesus clearly took great offense, turned on His heel, and gave them a swift rebuke. The gospel had not reached the Samaritans yet. All those people of age would have perished in their sins. Believers often charge the lost with not taking hell seriously enough, but I'm not sure we take it very seriously ourselves. To hope someone burns in hell is profoundly offensive to God and proves we lack His heart (see Ezek. 33:11; 2 Pet. 2:9). James and John didn't volunteer to call fire down from heaven to save Jesus the trouble. They wanted to wield that kind of power. They wanted to be the hosts of a fireworks spectacular.

Scripture tells us Jesus looks on the heart. I wonder if Jesus saw something in young John's heart even more lethal than his big brother's. Instead of threatening His childish followers with a dose of their own medicine, Jesus chose a far more effective route. He assigned John to be an ambassador of life to the very people he volunteered to destroy. Don't think for an instant this was coincidental. Even as the words fell from Jesus' lips, He may very likely have looked straight at John when He said, " 'and Samaria' " (Acts 1:8).

Earlier I mentioned our naïveté to think that followers of Christ are automatically void of prejudices. Whether our preferred prejudices are toward other denominations, world religions, colors, or economics, they are usually so deeply engrained that we refuse to see them as sin. We just consider our prejudices to be the way we are, but prejudice is sin. It is the prejudgment and stereotyping of a whole group of people.

Read Luke 9:54 to discover a key word: " 'Lord, do you want us to call fire

down from heaven to _____ them?' "

Prejudice destroys. Entire world wars have been fought and multiplied millions slain over nothing more than what many would term harmless prejudice.

Among God's most redemptive tools for dealing with prejudice is appointing His guilty children to get to know a person from the group they have judged. I was reared in one denomination and had few relationships with anyone outside it. Much prejudice comes from pure ignorance. I grew up judging some groups of people I simply didn't understand. God wasn't about to let me stay in my bubble—He intended to develop a heart in me for the entire body of Christ. His redemptive way of accomplishing His goal was to place me in the position of getting to know others who practice their Christian faith differently.

The most obvious work God did in my life involved a woman from one of those churches that my old church would have considered maniacal and unsound. They did not make that judgment from firsthand knowledge, of course. They simply dumped the church into one huge category. I was in my 20s and developed a friendship with her before I knew where she went to church. I fell in love with her heart for God. She had such a love for His Word. We often boasted in Him and developed a deep friendship. When I found out where she went to church, I was stunned. She wasn't crazy. She wasn't a maniac. She wasn't unsound. When my other friends made fun of people from that church, I couldn't bring myself to join in anymore. The jokes weren't funny. I learned a very important lesson I hope never to forget. Do we even know the people we stereotype and judge? Perhaps the better question is, Would we be willing to get to know someone and take the chance that God will change our prejudiced minds?

> Would we take the chance that God will change our prejudiced minds?

I don't think for a second that John missed the point when the apostles sent him to the Samaritans. He came face-to-face with them. They too were created in the image of God. They too loved their children and worried over their welfare. They too bruised when they were hit and wept when they were sad. They seemed so different from a distance. Somehow up close they didn't seem nearly so weird. Mind you, these were the same people on whom John had been so anxious to call down destruction.

Why is it so much easier to hate from a distance?

_____

Acts 8:15 tells us that Peter and John prayed for the Samaritans. Persistent prayer is a prejudice-buster every time if we'll let it be. Then something really amazing happened.

Take another look at Acts 8:17. Then Peter and John _____,

and they _____.

Well, well, well. They got their wish after all. They called down fire on them, all right. The kind of fire that destroys things like hatred, meanness, and prejudice for those who let this Holy Fire consume them. The kind of fire that destroys the old and births the new. Our God is a consuming Fire, and that day He lit the hearts of Samaritans at the hands of Jews.

I want to say something simple but very profound to me: how I praise God that we sinful, selfish, ignorant mortals can change. John wasn't stuck with his old prejudices. God neither gave up on Him nor overlooked the transgression. God was gracious enough to push the envelope until change happened. Acts 8:25 concludes the segment with the words "Peter and John returned to Jerusalem, preaching the gospel in many Samaritan villages." How like Jesus. He turned John's prejudice into a fiery passion.

When we continually walk with Christ, we can't stay the same.

When we continually walk with Christ, we can't stay the same. We can cease cooperating, but we'll have to cease walking close to Jesus to do it. We can fake the walk only so long. If we truly pursue intimacy with Christ, change will happen. Praise God, it will happen. Beloved, I want to ask you a question as I ask myself the same.

How has God dramatically changed your attitude toward some target of your personal prejudice?

_____

_____

I'd like to conclude with a look at a fascinating account in Mark 8:22-26. What peculiar details do you notice about this event?

_____

This account is one of the times in Scripture we see an incomplete healing that necessitated a second work of Christ. Because Jesus knew just what He was doing, He obviously had a point to make to the blind man or perhaps to His observers. (The next verse intimates that His disciples were with Him.) I like the *King James Version* of Mark 8:24. When asked if he saw anything, the man looked up and answered, "I see men as trees, walking." I am convinced that no matter how many Bible studies we attend and no matter how we serve our churches, until the way we view others dramatically changes, we will not know the deep healing of Christ and the restoration of our souls. We need to see people clearly (see v. 25), just as Christ sees them. The blind man wasn't healed until he saw men the way Christ saw them.

How does 2 Corinthians 5:16-17 support this concept? _____

_____

Beloved, do we still see men as trees, walking? Do we see them as distortions of who they really are? Would we be willing to allow God to change our minds and adjust our sight? We're only half-healed until we do.

Day 2 DEVASTATION

TODAY'S TREASURE

"He had James, the brother of John, put to death with the sword."—Acts 12:2

I had no idea when I began this Bible study how differently we could view the scenes by seeing them through John's eyes. The series I wrote prior to our present journey was *Jesus, the One and Only.* I have researched some of the same scenes, but the perspective has dramatically changed as I've attempted to look over John's shoulder rather than Jesus'. Had God not specifically appointed us to walk beside John, I may never have viewed today's dramatic scriptural account from his point of view. May the Holy Spirit help us grasp the significance of these events.

Read Acts 12:1-25. Why might the events recorded in verses 1-17 have affected John more than any of the other believers in the infant church?

_____

_____

Don't let the reference to John in verse 12 confuse you. John Mark was the cousin of Barnabas and the writer of the second Gospel. We have no way of knowing for certain whether John the apostle was among those gathered and praying at Mary's house. He may have been among those referenced in Acts 12:17.

Whom did Peter want informed about the events he had experienced?

_____

The James referenced in this passage is the younger sibling of Jesus, and I believe the brothers in this passage were Christ's other biological half-brothers. Remember that they became believers after the resurrection and were participants in the prayer meetings recorded in Acts 1:14. Keep in mind that John very likely may have been with the group at John Mark's, but another possibility exists.

Why might John have been with Christ's biological family? John 19:27 is your hint.

_____

_____

Focus on Acts 12:25. What dramatic conversion has taken place between our Scripture reading in Acts 8 and the events we're studying today? (Glance at Acts 9.)

_____

Now return to Acts 12:2 and read it out loud. Let its weight fall on you. How is James identified in this passage?

Inseparable as boys. John, the younger, always tagging along. His entire early identity was wrapped up in his brother's: "James son of Zebedee and his brother John" (Mark 1:19). The other day I sat on an airplane next to a mom with two little boys. The older couldn't have been more than 3 years and the younger about 18 months. Being a mother, I know how hard keeping a hat or cap on a toddler can be; yet the little guy kept a baseball cap firmly on his head the entire flight. Would you like to know why? Because big brother wore a baseball cap just like it. Don't you know James and John were exactly the same way? Almost every little brother wants to be just like the big one.

My daughters love each other dearly, but they were raised differently than my older sister and I. Amanda and Melissa had their own rooms and could use the word *mine* and mean it. Raised on a shoestring, from our early adolescence Gay and I shared the same small room and the same double bed. Beyond our underwear I am hard-pressed to think of a single thing either of us could have called "mine." We whispered late into the night and laughed until the bed frame shook. We'd hear Major Dad stomping down the hall to warn us, and we'd immediately fake a dual snore—which brought on uncontrollable laughter and a good (but useless) scolding. We were inseparable.

I remember the call that came to our home informing us that Gay had flipped our old Volkswagen bus on the highway as she pulled out of a local burger joint. She was practically unscathed, but I remember having one of my first realizations that we were indeed two separate people and that one of us could live and the other die. I wept almost as if it had happened.

I have studied and even taught Acts 12 many times. I love the story of Peter's deliverance from prison, but until today I never saw the events from John's point of view. How devastated he must have been! By this time the disciples knew the Jewish leaders could make good on their threats. They crucified Christ and stoned Stephen. They told Peter and John to stop speaking in the name of Jesus or else. They chose "or else." Glance back at an important Scripture from day 1.

> The disciples knew the Jewish leaders could make good on their threats.

Who scattered because of the persecution, and who remained in Jerusalem, according to Acts 8:1?

Yes, John and Peter trekked to Samaria, but the apostles' ministries remained intact in Jerusalem. We assume they simply did not yet feel released by the Holy Spirit to center their ministries elsewhere. In a terrible wave of persecution, James was arrested.

I wonder if John saw them seize his brother. If not, who broke the news to him? Can you imagine the terror that tore through his heart? Remember, John was the apostle who had connections when Jesus was arrested and was able to get into the priest's courtyard. Don't you know he tried to pull every favor and call on every connection he had?

John probably couldn't sleep or eat. He no doubt fell facedown on the floor and begged God to spare his brother's life. Beloved, don't hurry past this scene. James was John's flesh and blood. All the disciples were terrified, but none of them could relate to John's horror. Surely prayer meetings took place. Don't forget, these men had the power and authority of the Holy Spirit to heal diseases and cast out demons. No doubt, they named and claimed James' release and demanded his life in prayer. After all, the disciples were promised power and were told they would be Christ's witnesses all over Jerusalem, Judea, Samaria, and the uttermost parts of the earth. His ministry had just begun! No, this couldn't be the end. He would surely be delivered!

Then they killed him. I pity the person who came to John with the news. In 2 Samuel 1 David was so horrified by the report of Saul's and Jonathan's deaths that he had the one who claimed to have killed them slain. Although John had no such inclination, don't you imagine that he wanted to shake the bad news out of the bearer's mouth and demand a different ending? Don't you imagine that he tried his hardest to shake the reality out of his own head? James was the first disciple martyred. Reality must have hit like an unexpected tidal wave, crashing on the shores of servant lives.

More than any of the other 10, John must have replayed the events a thousand times, wondering whether his big brother had been terrified or calm. Did he think of their parents? Hadn't Zebedee been through enough? How was he going to tell his mother? Did James feel any pain? Was it quick? Was he to be taken next? Then before he had time to steady from reeling, he learned that he was not next. Peter was. Have you ever felt as if a percussionist slammed king-size cymbals on each side of your head? *Not Peter! This was too much! Not James and Peter! Not both of them, Lord! Please, please, no, Lord!*

- "When he arrived at the house of Jairus, he did not let anyone go in with him except Peter, John, and James" (Luke 8:51).
- "About eight days after Jesus said this, he took Peter, John and James with him and went up onto a mountain to pray" (Luke 9:28).
- "Jesus sent Peter and John, saying, 'Go and make preparations for us to eat the Passover' " (Luke 22:8).
- "He took Peter and the two sons of Zebedee along with him, and he began to be sorrowful and troubled" (Matt. 26:37).
- "She came running to Simon Peter and the other disciple, the one Jesus loved, and said, 'They have taken the Lord out of the tomb, and we don't know where they have put Him!' " (John 20:2).
- "Peter turned and saw that the disciple whom Jesus loved was following them. … When Peter saw him, he asked, 'Lord, what about him?' " (John 21:20-21).

Yeah, Lord! What about me? How will I go on without James and Peter? What are You doing? What aren't You doing? Will You let them kill all of us? John had good reason to believe Peter might never make it out of that prison, but he did. God granted a miracle scarcely before the blood of John's big brother was off the floor.

What kind of conflicting emotions do you think John might have experienced about Peter's miraculous release?

_____

I believe something huge happened for young John in this traumatic turn of events. I think he came to the startling realization that we are each on our own before God. Every life is separate and distinct. We may think we have partnerships in life or ministry without which we cannot exist or operate. We may think that everything in the Christian experience is about body life, but it's not. Yes, we're all parts of the body of Christ, and we function in each generation as parts of a whole; but until we each stand before God with a shocking awareness of our solitary standing, I'm not sure we have a clue about our part.

We are each on our own before God.

I don't believe that one of us who is serious about God will forego this test. It's no 30-minute quiz; it's a lifelong essay test written in blood. Will we loose our hold on anything and anyone else as a prerequisite to following Christ in the intensity of aloneness? If you can answer quickly, I'm not sure you grasp the question's seriousness.

 Would you be willing to live—and die—alone with Christ? _____

_____

I have a wonderful staff of coworkers at Living Proof Ministries. I would not trade them for anything! I'm crazy about my husband and get a bigger kick out of my two young-adult daughters than anyone else in the world. I am very involved in my church and am often surrounded by scores of people. Yet moments come when the awareness of my solitary estate before God so radically overwhelms me that I fall to my knees and weep. Bitterly. Frighteningly. The feeling is so intense that at times I can hardly bear it. I heard an internationally known speaker say something the other day that I, in my much smaller world of ministry, could totally understand. She said, "I'm so far out on a limb with God now, if I even think of walking by sight instead of faith, I'm dead." Amen.

That goes for all of us who have truly chosen to follow Jesus Christ. Size of ministry makes no difference. How much of your life you've invested in Jesus is the issue. Have we held some back for ourselves—just in case He's not as real, as powerful, as active as we thought? Just in case He doesn't come through? Just in case He really can't be taken at His Word? Or have we banked everything we have and everything we are on the reality that Jesus Christ is Lord of all the earth? We will never fulfill our destinies until our hope is built on nothing less.

How about you? Do you have a just-in-case plan, or are you totally out on a limb with God? Comment below.

_____

We can lock arms with fellow servants just as the disciples did. We will experience a measure of God's anointing and perform some significant works. For the parts of the whole to work as God intended them, however, each part must stand on its own before a highly personal God. If we insist on a boat full of company, we'll miss the waves where we ride only one at a time. When a wave of loneliness suddenly erupts, ride it. Let your stomach rise and fall with fear and peculiar excitement. Don't fight the feeling. Don't just busy yourself. Ride the wave straight into the presence of God and experience the adventure of feeling you're the only one there.

The intensity of your solitary estate is often most obvious when you fight to reconcile the facts of life with the words of faith. Do you grapple with questions like, Why did God let my brother die but perform a miracle for my best friend? I'm not sure John ever figured this one out. He was thankful his friend's life was spared, but why was James' life seemingly less significant? Why was he the first to go? Why, Lord? And what about me?

Solitude is not so much the place we find answers as the place we decide if we're going on, possibly alone—without them. Many of us will. Why? Because the privilege of wrestling with such a holy and mysterious God still beats the numbness and pitiful mediocrity of life otherwise. Sometimes we don't realize how real He is until we've experienced the awesomeness of His answerless presence. He knows that what we crave far more than explanations is the unshakable conviction that He is utterly, supremely God.

We crave the unshakable conviction that He is utterly, supremely God.

Day 3 THE RIGHT HAND OF FELLOWSHIP

TODAY'S TREASURE
"James, Peter and John, those reputed to be pillars, gave me and Barnabas the right hand of fellowship when they recognized the grace given to me."—Galatians 2:9

A previous slight mention of Saul's dramatic conversion planted a seed for today's study. What did the persecutor-turned-preacher have to do with John? Actually, Paul's testimony offers us several important insights into John and will supply us a valuable time line.

Carefully read Galatians 1:11—2:10. Label the following time line, including each event and the length of time Paul mentioned in these verses. Begin with his conversion and end with the reference to John in Galatians 2:9.

Paul's conversion   *Galatians 2:9*

The fact that Luke made no mention in the Book of Acts of the three years Paul spent in the desert and Damascus is not unusual. It simply wasn't vital to the information he desired to relay. Take a good look at Acts 9:19. This verse obviously picks up at the time of Paul's return to Damascus. The three years encompassed his original stay in Damascus, his flight to the desert, his return to Damascus, and his travel time to Jerusalem.

Read Acts 9:19-31. How did John and the other disciples in Jerusalem react to Paul's attempt to join them and why (see v. 26)?

What insight into their attitudes can you draw from Acts 8:1-3; 9:1-2?

Don't miss these words in Acts 9:1: "murderous threats against the Lord's disciples." Peter, John, and the others had plenty of reasons to take Saul's actions personally. Furthermore, they hadn't received the same vision God gave to Ananias in Damascus about the validity of Saul's conversion. Saul was a brilliant man. For all they knew, he could have faked his professed conversion as a means of getting close to them and exposing their continuing evangelism after they had been warned to cease.

Acts 9 and Galatians 1 may seem contradictory in reference to Paul's time with the apostles. Galatians 1:19 tells us he saw only Peter, but I believe the reference's intent is the time he spent getting acquainted. The other apostles may have heard Barnabas stand up for Paul, but Peter was the only one who really got to know the new convert. John did not get to know Paul at this time and may have purposely remained somewhat distant.

Now fast-forward your thoughts on the time line to the death of James, John's beloved brother. We have no reason to believe that much time passed between Paul's conversion and the martyrdom of James. We know that Stephen was martyred before Paul's conversion and that Paul, in fact, gave approval to Stephen's death.

Only Peter really got to know the new convert.

81

Don't you imagine that John had some pretty strong feelings about Paul?

Even though several years had passed, according to the time line in Galatians 1—2, don't you imagine that John had some pretty strong feelings about Paul? He made murderous threats against the lives of the disciples prior to his encounter with Christ. Paul was among the most radical activists among the haters of the Way.

Even though Paul dramatically gave his life to Christ before James was seized and killed, had I been John, I would have had difficulty embracing him. I'm afraid I might have had thoughts like, *If not for people exactly like you, my brother might still be alive.*

Maybe John felt none of what I'm describing, but I believe Christ's first ragtag band of followers wasn't unlike us at all. Yes, the Holy Spirit had come to them, and yes, they had matured somewhat, but grief and loss don't always engender extremely rational feelings. None of the other apostles had lost a sibling at this point. I just have to wonder how John felt about Paul those first several years.

Let's pick up the time line where the apostle John appears: "Fourteen years later I went up again to Jerusalem" (Gal. 2). Acts 15 describes this trip in greater detail. The meetings are often called the Jerusalem Conference or Council. We can draw few specifics about John during the years falling between Acts' previous mention of him and the events in chapter 15. We'll consider the lack of facts in day 4, but for now we know that he continued to serve faithfully and that he and Peter obviously retained Jerusalem as their home base.

How do we know from Paul's testimony that John held a primary role in the Christian church in Jerusalem (see Gal. 2:9)?

_____

This James is Christ's younger half-brother, who became part of the backbone of the infant church after the resurrection. The Holy Spirit also inspired him to pen the Book of James. John's brother James was slain about a decade earlier. Now Jesus' brother James partnered with Peter and John to form what Paul called pillars of the church.

According to Galatians 2:2, how did Paul approach the leaders (including James, Peter, and John)?
❏ Boldly ❏ Privately ❏ Openly ❏ One by one

What reason did Paul give for approaching them this way?

_____

Mark the following true or false, according to Acts 15:1-5.
_____ Men from Judea began to teach the principle of salvation through faith alone.
_____ Paul and Barnabas went to Jerusalem to defend the conversion of the Gentiles.
_____ The party of the Pharisees believed that Gentiles must become Jewish to be saved.
_____ Paul met privately with the church leaders because he was uncertain of his message.

Paul didn't meet with them privately because he was unsure of the revelation God gave him but rather because he did not know whether they would accept it. The answers to the exercise are false, true, true, false.

Now read Acts 15:6-19 and describe the outcome of the meeting.

_____

_____

Paul used far fewer words to describe the outcome in Galatians 2:9. He simply said, "James, Peter, and John, those reputed to be pillars, gave me and Barnabas the right hand of fellowship." Picture the five men mentioned in Galatians 2:9 conferring together and giving approval to one another:

- James, the unbelieving mocker turned preacher
- Peter, the one sifted like wheat, denying Christ three times and then having enough faith to return and strengthen his brothers
- John, the Son of Thunder, who asked whether he could sit at Christ's side in the kingdom and destroy the Samaritans with fire from heaven
- Paul, a former religious madman who approved the murder of Stephen and helped fuel a persecution that resulted in the murder of James
- Barnabas, the Son of Encouragement, who risked getting hammered by the early church by building a bridge between unlikely brothers

That's just it. We're all unlikely brothers. In Christ's church the pillars were never designed to match. Each one is distinct. What need would cookie-cutter disciples meet? Not only does Christ choose variegated pillars, but everything else within His church is marked by His creative distinctiveness, as well. None of us were meant to match. We were meant to fit together. Two identical puzzle pieces don't fit. Oh, that we would celebrate that difference!

> None of us were meant to match. We were meant to fit together.

What did Paul say James, Peter, and John recognized in him that caused them to extend the right hand of fellowship (see Gal. 2:9)?

_____

_____

What do you think that means?

_____

_____

How does 1 Peter 4:10 echo this concept? _____

_____

Beloved, we don't have to agree on every point of doctrine. We don't even have to always get along. Galatians 2 continues with the record of a fairly heated argument between Peter and Paul. However, God expects us to respect one another and acknowledge the grace God extends to all who are in Christ. Paul came to the leaders in private, but the inference of the right hand of fellowship tells us that they gave him a very public stamp of approval. He needed that approval, and I believe God would have held the pillars of the church responsible for not extending it.

After all, what is the bottom line, according to 1 Corinthians 3:5-9?

_____

_____

To fulfill our kingdom purposes on earth, we could all use a hand of fellowship from another in ministry, couldn't we? When I think back on those God so graciously appointed to extend such a hand to me, I am deeply humbled and awed.

 Answer one of the following questions: Who has extended you a hand of fellowship and how? Or to whom have you graciously extended one and how?

_____

_____

Before we close, I want to share one more personal example with you. When LifeWay approached me with a contract to tape the first series, *A Woman's Heart: God's Dwelling Place,* I was pitifully wet behind the ears. I don't know much about what I'm doing now, but I assure you I knew nothing then. I was petrified. The enemy came against me with such conflict and fear, I think I would have backed out had I not signed a contract. I felt that I desperately needed advice; I needed someone to tell me whether my feelings were normal. I still feel like an idiot over what I did next, but I was desperate. I called Kay Arthur's office and asked to speak to her. I had no idea what I was doing. I had never seen her in person or had the privilege of taking one of her courses. Don't get the idea that I in any way saw a comparison. I just wanted to talk to a woman who had taught the Word on videotape, no matter what gulf of knowledge and experience separated us.

God wasn't about to let me get in touch with Kay Arthur. First of all, He wanted me to rely on Him alone. Furthermore, He knew He had already extended the right hand of fellowship to me through sufficient people. God knew how impressionable I was and that I had not yet allowed Him to fully develop my style. I have so much respect for Kay that if I could have, I would have wanted God to make me just like her. What need whatsoever would God have had for such a person? Kay does an excellent job of being Kay. Why would God have wanted me to approach Bible study in exactly the same way? He already had her!

Today I could pick up the phone, call Kay, and laugh and talk for an hour if we had the time. I will never see myself worthy to help her with her heels, but I call her a friend. We met privately five or six years ago, but through the years, both of us felt the call of God to do something far more public. We both have gone out of our way to demonstrate publicly that we are united in Christ Jesus and we serve the same God, albeit with different styles. I have taught some of her books. Kay has invited me to several of her conferences to lead prayer and to speak. She has extended to me something more precious than gold: the hand of fellowship. She knows I have a lot to learn. We wouldn't agree on every interpretation. She is simply a woman who recognizes grace when she sees it. I am so grateful.

Fourteen years lapsed between the time Paul first tried to fit in with the apostles and when he finally received the right hand of fellowship. I'd like to suggest that the hand didn't come a moment behind schedule. What use would God have had for Paul if he simply turned out to be another James? Another Peter? Another John? His mission was distinct. And so, Beloved, is yours. By any chance were you frustrated by the earlier question about whether or not you've received someone's hand of fellowship? If so, would you consider that the time may not be quite right? Has something come to you privately that you long for publicly? God knows what He's doing! He knows when you're ready! Trust God. He is busy making you someone no one else has ever been.

Trust God. He is busy making you someone no one else has ever been.

Day 4 LESSONS FROM OBSCURITY

TODAY'S TREASURE
"From that time on, this disciple took her into his home."—John 19:27

Today we arrive at a very intriguing place characterized not by John's appearance but by his conspicuous absence. On day 5 we will begin turning our attention to John's writings, but let's not hurry. Today let's glance at the great apostle's role in the Book of Acts and then tarry over his disappearance from the pages. I am convinced that what John didn't do may have nearly as much to say as what he did.

Acts 12:2, when Luke refers to James' death, is the last mention of John. I am very intrigued by the fact that John appears only a handful of times in Luke's annals of the early church, and he is never quoted. Our John seems to appear only as an aside to Peter. Although the Book of Acts traces almost every move Paul made, after James' death John's ministry continues with very little notice.

I wonder what the apostles thought about Paul's gaining so much of the spotlight. I think we'd be pretty naïve to think they didn't notice. John was in the audience of twelve when Christ told Peter He would build His church on the foundation of Peter's confession. After the resurrection John also heard Christ tell Peter what his future held. John may have felt that Peter at least had an important future—even if it ultimately required his life. John, on the other hand, knew nothing about his own future. All he may have known was that Peter's ministry was skyrocketing.

John? Christ simply asked him to take care of His mother. Goodness knows John loved Mary. He took her into his home just as he promised, but somehow in the midst of the responsibility, neither Scripture nor tradition gives us any indication that he ever had a family of his own. Of course, to have known Mary so well was to gain priceless insight into Christ. After all, who knew Him better? Surely she recounted many stories as the evening oil in the lamp grew low. Scripture paints John as curious, so he must have asked Mary a thousand questions through the years: "What did Gabriel look like when he brought the news? Did you instantly know he was an angel? What was his voice like? Did you almost lose hope that James and your other sons would ever believe?"

What does Luke 2:19 share that might suggest Mary had much to say?

_____

If Mary was like most aging mothers, I imagine she told the stories more often as her life hastened toward its end. I don't think I've ever meditated on Mary's death before. The New Testament records very little about the deaths of the members of the infant church. The Old Testament, on the other hand, records many deaths of the saints. I can't help but wonder whether, from God's standpoint, the glory of heaven eclipsed the pain and suffering involved in the deaths of some of His servants.

Still, I wonder what Mary's homegoing was like. If John and Christ's half-brothers had any notion that she was dying, they were no doubt by her side. A natural death must have seemed so different to the eyewitnesses of the resurrected Lord Jesus. They knew firsthand the reality of life beyond the grave. Though they surely felt pain, they probably experienced little fear.

A natural death must have seemed so different to the eyewitnesses of the resurrected Lord Jesus.

According to Hebrews 2:14-15, what kind of freedom did Christ give us?

Can you imagine how anxious Mary was to be reunited with her firstborn son? I have little doubt that those nearby reassured her through her final hours with words of their imminent encounter. As He does with all of us, God counted her steps and kept her tears in a bottle (see Ps. 56:8, KJV). Both were full, and it was time. As He narrowed that solitary life to an earthbound close, He could easily see beyond the weathered face lined by time. Surely God smiled as He remembered the astonishment on her adolescent face when she realized that she had been chosen over every other woman. A girl of most humble means would bear the Messiah. Then perhaps He laughed out loud as she broke into the praises recorded in Luke 1:46-55. The Greek translation of her words " 'my spirit rejoices in God my Savior' " (v. 47) intimates that she was exulting with her whole inner being. The years that followed were tumultuous but exquisite. Mary had the unspeakable privilege of being a player in the plan of the ages.

I like to think Mary was surrounded by loved ones as she inhaled her last ounce of earthly air. I imagine her sons gathered around her. All of them. The one she adopted at the cross. And the One she surrendered to the grave. I wonder whether they knew that their Brother was right there among them—more present in His invisibility than they could ever be. Mary bade farewell to mortality and was ushered to immortality on the arm of a handsome Prince. Her Son. Her God.

John's cross-drawn job was done. What now? Perhaps he did what we sometimes do. When I am confounded by what I don't know, I rehearse in my mind what I do know. John knew that the last thing Christ told the apostles is that they would be witnesses in Jerusalem, Judea, Samaria, and the uttermost parts of the earth. Of course, I am offering supposition, but I wonder whether he thought, *I've served here in Jerusalem for years. I've preached to Samaritans, and I know Judea like the back of my hand. I'm no longer a young man. Who knows how much longer I have? I'm heading to the uttermost.*

Christ's early followers were adventurers! They were pioneers! If they listened to us sit around and decide whether we could work a Bible study to prison inmates around our nail appointments, they'd be mortified. In our postmodern era we associate church life with buildings and programs. Church life to them was moving in the adrenaline and excitement of the Holy Spirit at the risk of life and limb. They were willing to do things we'd think couldn't possibly be God's will (risking our necks, for example) for the sheer joy of what lay before them. They ran the race. They didn't window-shop.

I don't mean to be harsh, but I fear they might look at us and think virtually none of us look like disciple material. But you know what I'd want to say to that first motley crew? "None of you looked like disciple material either when Christ dragged you from your safe little lives." My point? We can still become disciple material! I desperately want to! I want to live the great adventure, don't you? Even if that great adventure leads me into obscurity. Stay tuned to see what I mean.

Most historians and scholars believe John moved to Ephesus and also traveled to Rome at some point. Some believe his trip to Rome came soon after his departure from Jerusalem, but I am inclined to believe the opposite carries more circumstantial support. I think John settled in Ephesus first and his venture to Rome happened before his exile in Patmos and probably led to it. R. Alan Culpepper, considered by many a modern-day expert on the life of John, wrote, "While the New Testament never mentions the activities of the apostle John in his later years, early Christian writers, though not unanimous, furnish strong evidence that he spent several decades in residence in Ephesus."[2]

We can still become disciple material!

Those familiar with Paul's life may recall that he spent several crucial years ministering in Ephesus. Most scholars agree that John's time in Ephesus followed Paul's by a matter of years, but Luke's record of Paul's encounters adds important insights as we imagine John ministering there.

Record the most noteworthy elements about Paul's stay in Ephesus, based on Acts 19:8-20,23-41.

_____

_____

I hope you included the highly unusual supernatural works God performed through the apostle Paul. When I researched the study *To Live Is Christ,* the reason God chose to do such astonishing works in Ephesus became clearer to me. Ancient Ephesus was one of the most pronounced centers of black magic in the entire world, so God made sure to perform works that wouldn't simply impress. They would baffle. Through Paul God showed Himself mighty in Ephesus. Later John followed and built on that heritage.

To the best of our understanding, after maintaining a home base in Jerusalem and serving as one of the pillars of the church, John moved to Ephesus. He faithfully served in Jerusalem. Scripture says nothing about his specific ministry after James' death. It records nothing about his tenure in Ephesus. Though we have much information about Paul's ministry there, we know virtually nothing about John's. As far as we are concerned, John served in biblical obscurity for much longer than the other apostles served, period. Beloved, that is precisely the most important point of today's lesson.

How do we know that John didn't start doubting his identity and his significance somewhere along the way? Peter was no doubt the front-runner in Jerusalem and the early church. Next to him the Book of Acts implies that James, Christ's half-brother, was most prominent. Furthermore, John went to Ephesus and built on the foundation laid by none other than Paul, the former persecutor and latecomer on the scene. You may be thinking, *But what difference does that make?* In an ideal world, none. But this is no ideal world.

In the dead of the night when insecurities crawl on us like fleas, all of us have terrifying bouts of insecurity and panics of insignificance. Our human natures pitifully fall to the temptation to pull out the tape measure and gauge ourselves against people who seem more gifted and anointed by God.

> We are tempted to measure ourselves against people who seem more gifted and anointed.

John went on to outlive every other apostle, while all of them were counted worthy to give their lives for Christ. Did John ever wonder whether he was too little of a threat to kill? We may want to think he was surely too mature and filled with the Spirit to have such thoughts, but keep in mind that this is the same disciple who asked to sit at Jesus' side in the kingdom. Yes, John was a new creature, but if Satan worked on him the way he works on me, he targeted his weak times and hit him with the same brand of temptations that worked in the old days. John's old fleshly desires for significance had been huge. I can't imagine Satan not targeting them again.

How about you? When you're weak, down, or tired, doesn't Satan occasionally try to awaken old temptations in you? If so, how?

_____

What response helps you overcome? _____

_____

The answers God gives us in our tomorrows often flow from our faithful todays.

One way we can respond is by choosing to believe what we *know* rather than what we *feel*. If John struggled with his identity in the era of the early church, that's exactly what he must have done. We know he chose to believe because of the incomparable fruit he produced after years of relative obscurity. In spite of others seeming more powerfully used by God and in the midst of decades hidden in the shadows, John remained faithful to his task. Beloved, there is no obscurity to Christ Jesus. The eyes of *El Roi* ("the God who sees," Gen. 16:13) gaze approvingly on every effort you make and every ounce of faith you exercise in Jesus' name. You have not been forgotten! You have no idea what may lie ahead! God spent this time testing and proving John's character so that he could be trusted with the greatest revelation. The answers God gives us in our tomorrows often flow from our faithful todays.

Day 5 THE ONE JESUS LOVED

TODAY'S TREASURE
"His disciples stared at one another, at a loss to know which of them he meant. One of them, the disciple whom Jesus loved, was reclining next to him."—John 13:22-23

I stumbled onto a quote in Culpepper's book on John that I can't shake out of my head. "Saints … die to the world only to rise to a more intense life."[3] I've turned the quote over in my mind a hundred times, and I'm convinced it's true. John may be the perfect example. I believe God had something so divinely unique to entrust to this chosen apostle that He had to slay the call of the world in him. Mind you, not the call *to* the world but the call *of* the world.

What is the difference? _____

_____

I don't think John was unlike Abraham or Moses. God chose these men and refined them through the crucible of time to prepare them for their tasks. The obvious difference is that God mightily used John soon after his calling, but I'd like to suggest that his latter works undoubtedly fall into the category "greater works than these" (John 5:20, KJV). Critical years of further preparation separated John's earlier and latter works.

As God sought to kill the world in His chosen vessels and crucify them to their own plans and agendas, their terms in waiting were not empty and lifeless. Rather, their lives greatly intensified. Our callings are not so different.

What do Galatians 2:20; 6:14 have to say to us on this matter?
❏ **We find our purpose in unselfish servanthood.**
❏ **We find our purpose through crucifixion with Christ.**
❏ **We must wait through years of preparation.**

We likewise will never be of great use to God if we do not allow Him to crucify us to our-selves and the world's call. Our consolations, however, are exceedingly great! We trade in the pitifully small and potentially disastrous for the wildest ride mortal creatures can ever know. We don't die to self just to accept nothingness. We lay down our lives and the world's call to receive something far more intense—God's call! God intends for the time we spend awaiting further enlightenment and fuller harvest to bulge with relationship.

Months, then years, then even decades may have blown off the calendar of John's life in obscurity, but don't consider for an instant that they were spent in inactivity or emptiness. No way! Please do not miss the following point, because it is critical to the study of John's life and our own application: *During John's interim years of obscurity, one of the most intense relationships in the entire Word of God developed.* Please turn up the volume on this entry and read the italicized words again. The point is so critical that I'm typing standing up!

Yes, Christ used John to cast out demons, heal the sick, and spread the good news through word of mouth, but somewhere along the way God built a man to whom He could entrust some of the most profound words ever recorded on parchment. What kind of person writes, "In the beginning was the Word, and the Word was with God, and the Word was God" (John 1:1)? What kind of human is entrusted with the love letters of 1, 2, and 3 John? And who could ever be chosen to pen the incomparable Revelation? Yet all were entrusted to a person once simply known as the brother of James.

THE HEART OF THE BELOVED

Somewhere along the way God built a man to whom He could entrust some of the most profound words ever recorded on parchment.

Something happened, Beloved. Something big. Something intense. No one knows for certain the exact order of John's writings, but I am most comfortable with the theory of many scholars who believe that the order was given to John in the order they appear in Scripture. Most scholars believe that the weightiest evidences suggest that they were all written within a matter of years, anyway. This time frame would fall in the A.D. 80s and 90s. If so, decades passed while John the apostle served in places like Jerusalem and Ephesus and the other disciples were martyred one by one.

Can you imagine being John as news landed like a newspaper with a thud on his doorstep? One obituary followed another. "Firm tradition places Peter in Rome in the A.D. 60s, where he and Paul were martyred under the reign of Nero."[4] One was cruci-fied, the other beheaded. How John must have grieved! But they were neither the first nor the last. One by one each apostle stepped through the crimson door of violent death to everlasting life until only one remained.

> **What kinds of things do you imagine John felt as the solitary remaining apostle? In your response keep in mind that his awareness of that fact most likely preceded a single word of inspired revelation.**

We don't know much about what happened between Christ and John in those biblically obscure years, but one thing is certain. Something happened that became the single hinge from which hung all God would do through John. Sometime in those years John formed the identity of the beloved disciple. By the time he penned the Gospel, this iden-tity was intact.

John alone called himself "the disciple whom Jesus loved" (John 21:20). Do you find that peculiar? If we believe that John's Gospel was inspired, we must also accept that John's identity was inspired. Jesus' love for him didn't exceed His love for the others, but God wanted us to know how John saw himself.

At first we might be tempted to think John a bit arrogant for using such a term, but God would never allow a person who received such revelation to get away with self-promotion. I'd like to suggest that John's evolving identity over those years came from the opposite kind of heart. God is far too faithful not to have greatly humbled John before giving him such surpassing revelation. (See a parallel concept in 2 Cor. 12.)

Quite possibly, the heightened positions of Peter and Paul in the early church, coupled with their martyrdom, fed abasement in John rather than exaltation. Surely, fear that he too was doomed to martyrdom struggled with the fear that he wasn't. Does that make sense? When one person remains after all the others have died, yet no profound purpose has been revealed, all sorts of insecurities could arise. We don't even have to wonder whether Satan was after John.

Surely Satan saw the others' martyrdom as a victory, even though he was defeated through their willingness to die. John no doubt became the bull's-eye on hell's target of the New Testament church. Among plenty of other assaults, don't you imagine Satan taunted John with survivor's guilt? Believe me, I know how debilitating survivor's guilt can be. For more than 25 years I've been married to a man who lost his older brother and his younger sister and who suffered terribly with false guilt for a time. It's a powerful deception.

As the years went by and the virile, youthful fisherman grew old and gray, I am convinced that his weakening legs were steadied and strengthened on the path by the constant reassurance "Jesus, You chose me. You keep me. And above all else, You love me. You love me. No matter what happens or doesn't, Jesus, I am Your beloved."

> "No matter what happens or doesn't, Jesus, I am Your beloved."

Perhaps this theory is so plausible to me because without exception I most identify myself as loved by God during difficult times, not flourishing times. I went through a terrible time of loss and attack while writing *Breaking Free* that was almost unbearable. I survived two years of tremendous difficulty by repeating over and over, "O God, I am so thankful I am loved by You. You love me so much. I am Your beloved. The apple of Your eye."

Isaiah 54:10 became my absolute lifeline. What does it say to you?

_____

Psalm 90:14 began my mornings because I couldn't face the day without it. Read this verse. How could being satisfied in the morning with God's unfailing love make a profound difference?

_____

The lines of my journal through those difficult months are filled with confessions of love. Not so much my love for God, mind you, but God's love for me! I grabbed at His love like a starving refugee scavenging for food one day and like a selfish child snatching sweets the next. Not only was I desperate, but certain circumstances had also made me desperately insecure. I was so needy that all my loved ones could have done together was like throwing a bucket of water in a cavern. I needed more love than a person could spare. I needed the mammoth love of God.

How does Ephesians 3:19-20 indicate that we usually draw a measly cup

from a bottomless wellspring? _____

_____

Beloved, you and I are not on love rations! Are you desperate for a surplus of love and acceptance? If so, please try to tell why.

How are you are trying to get this extra measure of love and acceptance?

Have you discovered that your need exceeds mortal fulfillment? I've learned the hard way that when I am in a crisis of insecurity or pain, nobody has enough of what I need. The attempt to retrieve it from human resources will ultimately result in my despising them and their despising me. God is our only source. He will never resent us for the breadth, depth, and length of our need.

> God will never resent us for the breadth, depth, and length of our need.

I love Deuteronomy 33:12. What does it tell the beloved of the Lord to do?

We will all have seasons like the one I've described because their divine purpose is vital. Much of our identity develops right there. In the aloneness. In the search for purpose. In the fear of being passed over. In the terror that somewhere along the way we crossed the line of no return. Times when we're faced with the prospect, *If I am never greatly used by God in a way that I deem significant, can I still believe that I am loved like the apple of His eye?* Do we believe that He proves His love by His blatant use of us? If so, had any of us been John during the years conspicuously silent in Scripture, we might have given up. Or at least dropped into a lower gear.

Not John. He knew two things, and I believe he grabbed on to them for dear life. He knew that he was called to be a disciple. And he knew that he was loved. Over the course of time those two things merged into one ultimate identity: I, John, the seed of Zebedee, the son of Salome, the brother of James, the last surviving apostle am he—the one Jesus loves. The beloved disciple. Somewhere along the way John, that Son of Thunder, forsook ambition for affection. And that, my friend, is why he was poised and ready when some of the most profound words ever to descend from heaven to earth fell like liquid grace into his quill.

---

[1]James Stalker, *The Two St. Johns of the New Testament* (New York: American Tract Society, 1895), 148.

[2]R. Allan Culpepper, "John and Ephesus," *Biblical Illustrator*, fall 1977, 3.

[3]Lynn M. Poland, "The New Criticism, Neoorthodoxy, and the New Testament," as quoted in R. Alan Culpepper, *John, the Son of Zebedee: The Life of a Legend* (Minneapolis: First Fortress Press, 2000), 139.

[4]Lawrence O. Richards, ed., *The Revell Bible Dictionary* (n.p.: Fleming H. Revell Company, 1990), 775.

VIDEO RESPONSE SHEET
Group Session 4

Part 1: Grasping the Concept of Divinely Inspired Scripture

According to 2 Timothy 3:16, "All Scripture is _____-_____." The original Greek word is *theopneustos. Theo—God. Pneustos—breath* or *spirit.* Consider each of the following Scriptures.

1. Based on a comparison between 2 Peter 1:20-21 and 1 Chronicles 28:19, we might say the men God

   used to write Scripture served as neither the _____ nor the _____. They served as the

   _____. The author is God the Holy Spirit and the ink flowing through that pen is the

   Holy Spirit, the breath of God that He's pouring through.

2. The Word is _____, but God chose to give inspiration through _____ _____ (Ps. 119:89).

3. Compare Genesis 2:7. When God breathes, He breathes _____. Hebrews 4:12 tells us His Word is _____.

4. See Luke 1:1-3. We are told that _____ undertook writing accounts of Christ's life and fulfillment

   of God's plan; yet we don't have "many" of those accounts in the Bible.

Part 2: Grasping God's Primary Intention Through His Inspiration of John's Gospel
Read John 1:1.

1. One of the overriding themes in the Gospel of John is presented from the very first verse: Under the

   inspiration of the Holy Spirit, John wanted his reader to know and recognize the _____.

2. The Greek term for *Word* is _____. Basically it refers to the _____ of God

   _____ to man. God revealed Himself through His _____ and His _____.

3. The only way we will ever really know the Word, both the Person and the print, is to know His

   _____. Both of these verses (John 15:7; Eph. 6:17) employ the Greek word _____.

4. As we learn to receive and apply *rhema,* we are wise to remember that God's Word is written:

   _____ God about _____, _____ others about _____, _____ us about _____.

FUNDAMENTAL _____

VALID _____

PROVERBS 23:7 (KJV)

Hyper
_____
_____
(Romans 10:2)
All _____/No _____

Ways God
_____
_____ Speak

Hyper
_____
_____
(Matthew 23:4,15)
All _____/No _____

Conceptual
_____

SCRIPTURE

Concrete
_____

_____ _____ _____

_____ _____ _____

_____ _____ _____

RECEIVING HIS FULLNESS

Day 1

More Life

Day 2

More Belief

Day 3

More Wine

Day 4

More About the World

Day 5

More of Who He Is

I had a blast studying the highlights from the Gospel of John that you have before you for the next two weeks. When I first began my research for this journey, I knew we would consider John's Gospel, but I had no idea how I would ever choose what to emphasize. His Gospel is unique in many ways and provides endless insights. As I approached this part of the study, I felt overwhelmed by the task of picking and choosing one text over another. God mercifully and clearly spoke to me through His Word and told me exactly how to approach it to meet our study goals. I'll explain our approach in day 1. Every day of weeks 5 and 6 I learned something that I believe will mark my walk. I hope you do, too!

Principal Questions

Day 1: How does Hebrews 11:6 echo the idea of godly hedonism?

Day 2: According to John 20:30-31, what was John's purpose in the Gospel of John?

Day 3: What was the obvious and eternal significance of the wedding in Cana in John 2?

Day 4: What does Psalm 147:4 tell us about the estimated one hundred billion stars in our galaxy alone?

Day 5: What happened to the soldiers after Christ responded, " 'I am He' " in John 18:6?

Day One MORE LIFE

> **TODAY'S TREASURE**
> *"From the fullness of his grace we have all received one blessing after another."*
> —John 1:16

We have arrived at John's Gospel, the blood-pumping heart of our study. We will comprehend little about the man who wrote three brief epistles and the incomparable Revelation if we don't grasp the emphasis of the inspired apostle in his unique Gospel. John's Gospel is his electrocardiogram.

As I stated earlier, I am convinced by the evidence that John wrote during the reign of the Roman emperor Domitian, placing all his writings within the time line of A.D. 81–96. If I'm on target, the other apostles passed off the scene until John was the only one with feet still planted on planet Earth. His remaining was not without purpose. John's relationship with Christ grew in intensity over the obscure years. We learned something pivotal to us in our journey: John forsook ambition for affection. To love and be loved became his lifeblood.

The more I study John's life, the more I am convinced that intensity breeds extensity. The more intense John became in his relationship with Jesus, the more God extended the boundaries of revelation. God broke the sound and sight barriers for John and allowed him to experience a length, breadth, and depth that remain unparalleled. We will see proof of both John's intensity and extensity in his unique Gospel. Our purpose, however, is not only to marvel at John's beloved relationship with Christ but also to be indelibly marked in our own. The same Spirit, the same truth, and the same Lord also work in us for whom intensity will also undoubtedly breed extensity.

The more intense John's relationship became with Jesus, the more God extended the boundaries of revelation.

> **Carefully read John 1:14-16. Verse 16 introduces an overriding concept that will carry us throughout this vital two-week segment of our study. Write the verse on a note card and then memorize it!**

If you receive what this verse says to you, you won't be changed only for the course of this study; your entire life experience with Jesus will be transformed. The original word for *blessing* is *charis,* often translated *grace.* This explains the *King James* rendering: "Of his fulness have all we received, and grace for grace." *Charis* means "grace, particularly that which causes joy, pleasure, gratification, favor, acceptance, … a benefit, … the absolutely free expression of the loving kindness of God to men finding its only motive in the bounty and benevolence of the Giver; unearned and unmerited favor."

> **Based on John 1:14-16 and this definition, I believe we can accurately draw the following conclusions. Circle the phrase that means most to you right now.**
> - **Jesus is full of grace and truth, and He's the one and only.**
> - **All of us get to receive from His fullness! Not just John the apostle. Not just John the Baptist. Jesus is full and overflowing with everything any of us who believe could possibly need or desire, and we get to receive from His bounty!**
> - **These grace gifts flowing from Christ's fullness are not only beneficial but also expressions of God's favor that produce joy and pleasure!**

It's high time I made a blatant confession. I am a Christian hedonist. Have been for years, even before I knew what it means. I wish I had better words for it, but let me just say Jesus makes me happy! He thrills me! He nearly takes my breath away with His beauty. As seriously as I know how to tell you, I am at times so overwhelmed by His love for me, my face blushes with intensity and my heart races with holy anticipation. Jesus is the uncontested delight of my life. I never intended for this to happen. I didn't even know it was possible. It all started with an in-depth study of His Word in my late 20s and then surged, oddly enough, with a near emotional and mental collapse in my early 30s. At the end of myself I came to the beginning of an intensity of relationship with Christ that no one told me was possible. Now I spend my life telling anyone who will listen.

I thought I was just weird. I knew so many believers who wore Christ like a sacrifice that I thought I had missed something somewhere. Don't get me wrong. Plenty of believers in the world make huge sacrifices in the name of Jesus Christ, but I'm not sure American believers can relate—and we can be a little nauseating when we try. By far the biggest sacrifices I've ever made were times I chose to pursue my own will over Jesus and His. I'd be a liar to tell you that Jesus has been some big sacrifice for me. He is the unspeakable joy and love of my life. In crude terms, I think He's a blast.

> So many believers wore Christ like a sacrifice that I thought I had missed something.

While still in the closet, I began stumbling on other Christian hedonists. Perhaps Augustine is the most blatant historical example. Of his conversion in 386 Augustine wrote, " 'How sweet all at once it was for me to be rid of those fruitless joys which I had once feared to lose! … You drove them from me, you who are the true, the sovereign joy. You drove them from me and took their place, you who are sweeter than all pleasure.' "[1] My heart leaps as I read words that I too have lived!

Jonathan Edwards was another. In 1755 he wrote, " *'God is glorified not only by His glory's being seen, but by its being rejoiced in.* When those who see it delight in it, God is more glorified than if they only see it.' "[2]

C. S. Lewis was also a fine Christian hedonist. He wrote, " 'If there lurks in most modern minds the notion that to desire our own good and earnestly to hope for the enjoyment of it is a bad thing, I submit that this notion has crept in from Kant and the Stoics and is no part of the Christian faith. Indeed, if we consider the unblushing promises of reward and the staggering nature of the rewards promised in the Gospels, it would seem that our Lord finds our desires not too strong, but too weak. We are half-hearted creatures, fooling about with drink and sex and ambition when infinite joy is offered us, like an ignorant child who wants to go on making mud pies in a slum because he cannot imagine what is meant by the offer of a holiday at the sea. We are far too easily pleased.' "[3]

What do you think Lewis means that "we are far too easily pleased"?

_____

_____

Check any of the following that describe your attitude and heart about enjoying Jesus.
❏ I can't quite get over the idea that religion is supposed to hurt.
❏ I don't really feel that I'm worthy of so thoroughly enjoying Jesus.
❏ I'm having a hard time turning loose of the mud pies.
❏ I think Jesus is really becoming the number one love of my life.
❏ I love Him so much that I no longer care about toys or what people think.
❏ I really want Jesus to become the absolute passion of my life.

Grace is God's favor looking for a place to happen!

Meditate on John 1:14,16. Grace is God's favor looking for a place to happen! From His favor we receive multiple blessings! No matter who we are or how long we've known Jesus, we've hardly scratched the surface. So much more of Him exists! He's willing to give us so much more! Show us! Tell us! Oh, that we would spend our lives in furious pursuit!

John Piper is my favorite holy hedonist from the early 21st century. He concludes his position in one statement: "God is most glorified in us when we are most satisfied in Him."[4]

Write in your own words what you think Piper's statement means.

_____

_____

Don't get me wrong. Our motive for pursuing God is not strictly our delight and satisfaction. We pursue Him because He is the point and essence of existence; His glory is the sole purpose for our creation (see Isa. 43:7). However, when we pursue Him feverishly and desire to love Him passionately, we have an unexpected and stunning collision with joy and fulfillment. Not convinced? Just wait and see as we study together!

Long before Augustine graced the page with his confessions, inspired men like Moses, David, Paul, and Peter proved holy hedonists of sorts.

Read selections of their confessions below. Then describe the personal gain that came from their pursuits of God.

Moses in Exodus 33:13,15-18 _____

_____

David in Psalm 63:3-7 _____

_____

Paul in Philippians 3:8-10,14 _____

_____

Peter in 1 Peter 1:6-9 _____

_____

God's Word is full of godly hedonists who testified in one way or another that seeking God zealously and jealously was the best thing that ever happened—not to God but to them. God Himself said to Abram in Genesis 15:1, " 'I am your ... great reward.' "

How does Hebrews 11:6 echo the idea of godly hedonism? _____

_____

Is finding God not reward enough? Yet He superabounds in His giving! Many inspired men in Scripture confessed the glorious gain of pursuing God, but few can compete with

John. I plan to prove it to you. I'm no proficient Bible scholar, but I have learned to make use of a few study tools and have performed a little research of my own. John has more to say about the concepts of life, light, love, truth, glory, signs, and belief than anyone else in the entire New Testament. He has overwhelmingly more to say about God as Father. Of 248 New Testament references to God as Father, John wrote 120. In impressive balance John also has more to say about God and the world than any other inspired writer. John wrote 103 of 206 New Testament references to the world.

My point is certainly not that John's Gospel is better than others. God inspired each just as He perfectly intended. The point is that in length of life and depth of love, John discovered the concept of *more*. I'm convinced a nutshell explanation for John's entire experience and perspective is intimated in one of Christ's most profound statements.

" 'I have come that they may have life, and have it to the _____' "
(John 10:10).

We need to know by heart the Greek word for *full*. *Perisson* means "over and above, more than enough … generally, superabundant, … much, great." Do you realize that Christ wants you to have a great life? Am I making you nervous? Don't confuse *great* with no challenges, hardships, or suffering. In fact, the greatest parts of my life experience have been overcoming overwhelming challenges in the power of the Holy Spirit.

Christian hedonists don't discount suffering. They just don't give up until they find gain in the loss (see Phil. 3:8). When we lay down our lives, God wants us to be able to say we lived them fully. We didn't miss a thing He had for us. We had a blast with God just like John.

Jesus offered a lot of life; John took Him up on it. Jesus shed light; John chose to walk in it. Jesus revealed glory; John chose to behold it. Jesus delivered truth; John believed it. Jesus shed His blood; John was covered by it. Jesus lavished love; John received it. Jesus is full of all good things we could ever need or desire. Thankfully, many receive; others receive more abundantly. John was one of the latter. I want to be another.

Beloved, with all my heart I want to know God, and I want to experience one blessing after another flowing from His favor. I want more. That's all there is to it. I am convinced, Dear One, that He welcomes the approach that says, *God, You are the best thing that could ever happen to me, so happen indeed!*

Throughout weeks 5 and 6 we will concentrate on the overall invitation to abundance in John's Gospel. We'll meditate on the concepts he emphasized more than other writers. In other words, we're going to study the highest marks on John's electrocardiogram.

We have been too easily pleased. Along the way many of us formed a concept of Christ and settled with it. Few really grasp the invitation to great adventure. They try to reduce God to nothing but religion and then grow bored with the image they created. Far too many electrocardiograms are flat lining. As a result, hearts become accidents waiting to happen— for our souls were created to exult and dance in holy passion. If we don't find it in the Holy One, we'll search for it in the smoldering heaps of the unholy. I have burn scars to prove it.

THE HEART OF THE BELOVED

Jesus offered a lot of life; John took Him up on it. Jesus shed light; John chose to walk in it. Jesus revealed glory; John chose to behold it. Jesus delivered truth; John believed it.

Draw your spiritual electrocardiogram. I don't ask you to do this to provoke guilt or pride. Because they beat and don't hum, hearts don't beat at peak efficiency all the time. Let's not rest until ours pump passionately.

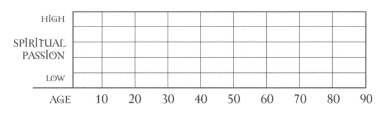

Day Two MORE BELIEF

TODAY'S TREASURE

"These are written that you may believe that Jesus is the Christ, the Son of God, and that by believing you may have life in his name."—John 20:31

The early church father Eusebius quoted Clement of Alexandria as saying, " 'John, last of all, conscious that the outward facts had been set forth in the Gospels, was urged on by his disciples, and, divinely moved by the Spirit, composed a spiritual Gospel.' "[5] If this is accurate, John was familiar with the Synoptic Gospels and had no desire or compelling of the Holy Spirit to repeat the biographical approach. John shares only about 10 percent of its content with the other Gospels. Clement did not mean all four were not equally inspired but that John can draw us even further into spiritual truths.

While Matthew and Luke begin with human genealogies, John begins with Jesus Christ, the preexistent, eternal Word. John's Gospel electrocardiogram begins with a peak off the page. Though his approach is vast and deep, my Greek teacher says John's Greek is the most easily read of all the New Testament books. Perhaps Augustine had these facts in mind when he wrote, " 'John's Gospel is deep enough for an elephant to swim and shallow enough for a child not to drown.' "[6] So whether we're elephants or children in our relationship to the Word, we can splash to our delight in the living water of this Gospel.

Like several other New Testament books, this Gospel explains at the end why the book had a beginning. John inscribed two insightful passages toward its conclusion.

According to John 21:25, how much did Jesus do? _____

_____

When I hear this verse, I think about my first guide in Israel, who told me that the ancient Hebrews often spoke in images. He said, "For instance, we would read John's intent in this final verse like this: 'If all the trees of the forest were quills and the oceans ink, still they could not record all Jesus did.' " Ah, yes! That's my kind of wording! We can conclude that John purposefully selected the elements in his Gospel.

What was John's purpose in this Gospel (see John 20:30-31)?

_____

_____

John wrote as an utterly convinced eyewitness.

No other Gospel writer shows more determination to express Jesus' absolute deity. John wrote his Gospel so that the reader would behold truth from an utterly convinced eyewitness that Jesus Christ is the uncontested Christ. The Messiah. The Son of God.

Why is this belief so important, according to John 1:12?
❑ **So that knowing the truth, we could be free**
❑ **So that we could have life more abundantly**
❑ **So that believing, we can become children of God**

Like no other Gospel or New Testament writer, John presents Jesus Christ as the Son of God. Of about 248 times in the New Testament in which God is deemed Father, approximately 120 are in John's Gospel. John was the consummate evangelist, and he knew that salvation could not be secured by those who do not acknowledge Jesus Christ as the absolute Son of the God. He made sure no one could miss the saving facts in his Gospel. Of course, the reader could see the facts and yet still miss the salvation because something vital is required of anyone who desires to become a child of God: belief!

In his book *Encountering John* Andreas J. Kostenberger wrote, "Apart from 'Jesus' ... and 'Father' ... there is no theologically significant word that occurs more frequently in John's Gospel than the word 'believe' (pisteuo; 98 times). John's ninety-eight instances compare to eleven in Mark, fourteen in Matthew, and nine in Luke. Thus Merrill Tenney seems to be justified in calling John 'the Gospel of belief.' Another interesting observation is that while John uses the verb 'to believe' almost a hundred times, he does not once use the corresponding noun (pistis, 'faith'). It appears therefore that John's primary purpose is to engender in his readers the act of believing, of placing their trust in Jesus Christ."[7]

Do you remember my telling you that God would transform our lives if we take Him up on the abundance He presents in John? If that transformation didn't begin in our previous lesson, you don't need to wait another moment. Through our study God calls us to believe Him more. John's Gospel does not just call us to belief as a past-tense experience. Christ calls us to be living verbs! He calls us to the ongoing act of believing! Yes, for many of us the belief that secures our salvation is past tense and complete. We have already trusted Christ for salvation. We are now and forever secured, but tragically, too many live in past-tense belief, believing God for little more from that time forward.

Is the scope of your belief in Christ in the past-tense security of salvation, or are you in the active, ongoing lifestyle of believing Christ? Are we simply nouns—believers? Or are we also verbs—believing? Believing in Christ and believing Christ can be two very different things. We begin with the former, but certainly don't want to end there! We want to keep believing what Jesus says about Himself, His Father, and us until we see Him face-to-face.

Take a look at Hebrews 11's hall of faith. In the margin list the names of the three or more faithful believers whose believing strikes you most.

As eternally vital as it is, none were commended for the initial faith that enabled them to enter a relationship with God. They were commended for ongoing acts of believing at times when their physical eyes could not see what God told them they could believe.

In our previous lesson we talked about John's use of the word *life* more than any other Gospel—over twice as many times, in fact, as Matthew, who falls in second place. By no coincidence the same Gospel that shouts life also shouts the act of believing. Any of those in the great cloud of witnesses in Hebrews 11 would tell us that really living the Christian life is synonymous with really believing the God who created it.

Who is your Jesus? In the weeks to come, we'll study John's Jesus, full of grace and truth, who offers us one blessing after another; but now who do we believe Jesus to be in our own lives? In reality, what we believe is measured by what we live, not by what we say.

If your life were a Gospel like John's, who could people believe your Jesus to be? Respond specifically and concretely.

_____

_____

FAITHFUL BELIEVERS

_____

_____

_____

_____

_____

_____

Based on your life, might people believe Jesus to be a Redeemer because He has obviously redeemed you from a pit? Or a Healer because He has healed you? Keep in mind that these kinds of questions are to provoke our deep meditations. They will either help us see progress and reasons for rejoicing or help us see where we want to go.

Throughout the Gospel John described his Jesus because he knew that the same Christ is meant to be ours: the preexistent, miracle-working, only begotten Son of the Father of all creation. Years ago God revealed to me that I believed in my childhood church's Christ, who thankfully was a Savior for sinners, but I had hardly begun to believe in the Bible's Christ. Although He is a Savior for sinners and so much more, we have derived many of our impressions of Christ from vastly incomplete if not totally unreliable sources, as sweet and respectable as they may be!

Who has best represented Christ to you? Why?

_____

_____

Either Jesus no longer does what the Bible says He did, or we don't give Him the chance.

We are blessed beyond measure for every time one of these human instruments extended us reliable impressions of Jesus. Most of my early impressions about Jesus were based more on what I saw than on what I learned at church. I certainly believed that Jesus saves; that belief led to my own salvation experience. But I believed Him for little more because I saw evidence of little more. The few marvelous exceptions marked me forever, but I wonder why so many believers believe so little of Jesus. I'm going to say it the way I see it. Either Jesus no longer does what the Bible says He did, or we don't give Him the chance.

John went out of his way to present us an all-powerful Son of God who speaks and His Word is accomplished. A Savior who not only saves us from our sins but can also deliver us from evil. A Great Physician who really can heal and a God of glory who reveals His magnificence to mere mortals. And yes, a God of signs and wonders. We've already seen John testify that one of his Gospel's chief purposes was to testify to the signs Jesus performed so that readers would believe—not in the miracles themselves, mind you, but in the Christ who performed them.

Many claim that the day of miracles has ceased. I don't doubt that God may employ miracles less frequently in cultures where His Word is prevalent, but I know that Jesus Christ still performs miracles. First, I know that He does because of the claims of Hebrews.

Read Hebrews 13:7-8. What can we conclude about the Jesus of the Gospels and the Jesus of the 21st century?

_____

_____

The second reason I know that Jesus Christ still performs miracles is because I'm one of them. I'm not being dramatic. I'm telling you the truth. The only excuse for an ounce of victory in my life is the supernatural delivering power of Jesus Christ. I was in the clutches of a real, live devil, living in a perpetual cycle of defeat. Only a miracle-working God could have set me free, then dare to use me. My friends Patsy Clairmont and Kathy Troccoli testify that they are nothing less than miracles, as well. You may remark, "Those are not real miracles," but Scripture suggests that no greater work exists.

According to Paul in Ephesians 3:20, where is this power at work?

_____

_____

Do you see? God's most profound miracles will always be those within our hearts and souls. Moving a mountain is nothing compared to changing a selfish, destructive heart.

Third, I know that Jesus Christ still performs miracles because I've witnessed them. I have seen Him do things most people don't even believe He does any more. Jesus healed a woman I know of liver cancer and a man I know of pancreatic cancer. I've seen women bear healthy children who were diagnosed inside the womb with debilitating conditions. I was in a worship service with a dear friend in his 80s who has been legally blind for years when God restored a remarkable measure of his sight. Hallelujah!

> Moving a mountain is nothing compared to changing a selfish, destructive heart.

How about you? Have you witnessed anything you'd consider to be an unquestionable miracle of God? If so, share it.

_____

_____

Like you, I have also seen many who have not received the miracles they hoped for. I can't explain the difference, except to say that God often defers to the greater glory. Sometimes the far greater miracle is the victory He brings and the character He reveals when we don't get what we thought we wanted. On the other hand, sometimes we see little because we believe little. That's the obstacle you and I want to overcome so that we can live in the abundant blessing of Jesus Christ. When my life is over, I may not have seen Jesus perform some of the miracles the Word says He can—but let it be because He showed His glory another way and not because I believed Him for so pitifully little that I didn't give Him the chance!

Through His work on the cross and His plan before the foundation of the world, Christ has already accomplished much for your life in heaven!

What does Ephesians 2:10 tell you? _____

_____

_____

If Jesus' work is going to be accomplished here on earth where your sweet feet hit the hot pavement, then you're going to have to start believing Him. When we received Christ as our Savior, you might picture that a pipe of power connected our lives to God's throne. Unbelief clogs the pipe, but the act of believing clears the way for the inconceivable! As much as John's Gospel has to say about believing, I'm not sure anyone recorded a more powerful statement than the writer of the second Gospel in Mark 9:23.

What did Jesus say in that verse?_____

_____

_____

Student of God's Word, the Jesus of some of our churches, denominations, family, and friends may not be able to deliver us, heal us, and stun us with amazing feats, but the Jesus of Scripture can. And He's the same yesterday and today and forever. It's time we start believing Him for more. When we've turned the last page of this Bible study, may we be found firmly embracing the powerful and believable Jesus of God's Word.

Day Three MORE WINE

> **TODAY'S TREASURE**
>
> *"When the wine was gone, Jesus' mother said to him, 'They have no more wine.' "*
> —John 2:3

Without a doubt, Jesus loves weddings. The preexistent, eternal Word began His divine thesis with the first one (see Gen. 2) and consummates it with the last one (see Rev. 19). Who can count the weddings He will attend in between? Jesus always officiates and signs the license—whether or not we ask Him. After all, marriage was His idea. His excitement over a simple wedding is because His heart floods with anticipation over His own— with us, His bride.

Take a good look at Ephesians 5:25-33. Read the verses aloud as if for the very first time. In what condition will Christ present His bride?

_____

Am I ever glad to know we're presented without wrinkles! Incidentally, take a good look at Ephesians 5:29. I'm almost positive that Scripture means husbands are supposed to do the cooking. One thing is certain: we're not going to have to do the cooking at our own marriage supper with the Lamb. Until then, every wedding He attends is a blessed rehearsal for the big one. We'll save our comments on that one until much later in our study. For now we have a wedding to attend in Cana, and I'd hate to walk in late.

Please read John 2:1-11. Name every player in this wonderful scene.

_____

We can readily assume the families involved in the wedding were people Jesus knew well. Don't miss the fact that Jesus was invited. We ordinarily don't invite strangers to our weddings. Furthermore, the wedding date caught Jesus at a critically busy time, just as His Father was launching His ministry. For Him to be intentional enough to attend this wedding tells us He had relationships and a divine purpose there. The hosts were probably good family friends, since Mary apparently helped with the wedding.

I believe Jesus didn't have to have His arm twisted to attend the wedding. I happen to think He loved a good party and still does! I'm convinced Jesus' basic personality in His brief walk in human flesh was delightful and refreshingly relational.

Jesus' basic personality was delightful and refreshingly relational.

Note what each of the following references suggests about Jesus' personality.

Matthew 9:14-17 _____

_____

Matthew 19:14 _____

Luke 5:27-31 _____

_____

I hope something caught your attention in the final verses. What common themes do they share with our focal reading today in John 2?

_____

_____

Bridegrooms. Jesus' presence. Disciples. New wine. Hmm. Push the hold button on these similarities while we reflect on the suggestions of the three earlier references.

For starters, children aren't drawn to cranky people. They are good judges of character, and they like people who are fun. The other references suggest that Jesus in our midst is reason enough to celebrate. Why in the world have we let partying become associated with licentiousness? God created humans with an authentic soul-need to feast and celebrate. In fact, God deemed celebration so vital that He commanded His people to celebrate at frequent intervals throughout the calendar year (see Lev. 23). Let me say that again: God commands us to celebrate His goodness and His greatness!

> God commands us to celebrate His goodness and His greatness!

It's time for us take back the whole idea of partying. I'm always mystified that many nonbelievers think Christians must be dull and wouldn't know a good time if it socked them in the noggin. Boy, do we have a secret! No one laughs like a bunch of Christians! My staff and I roll with laughter at times. They aren't my only fellow partyers. A week or so ago three of my dearest friends and I scrunched on one couch together all holding hands. One of us had lost a daughter several days earlier to a drunk driver. As we held on to one another for dear life, God gave us the sudden gift of the hardest belly laugh any of us have had in a long time. Unbelievers might be insulted to know that when we go to their parties, we wonder why they think they're having such a good time. Lean over here closely so that I can whisper: I think they're boring.

Celebrations around Christ's presence are wonderful; they are sparkling refreshment to a world-worn soul. We get to attend Christ's kind of parties without taking home a lot of baggage or getting a hangover. Christ-centered celebrations are all the fun without the guilt. That's real partying.

When was the last time you attended a party centered on Christ's presence? Briefly describe it.

_____

During weeks 5 and 6 we are studying the concepts of *more, fullness,* and *abundance* in John's overflowing Gospel. How fitting that the writer who had more to say about abundant life and effervescent living than any other Gospel penman was also the only one inspired to tell us about the wedding in Cana—an event where *more* became the very issue at hand. "They have no more wine. Son, You're the only one who can give them what they need." More.

John had unique insight into the wedding in Cana; he was the only Gospel writer there. The Gospels' chronologies suggest that Matthew hadn't been called yet and Luke and Mark didn't come into the picture until much later. Many scholars believe John was an adolescent when he followed Christ. A partying age if you'll ever find one! The last statement in John 2:11 intimates the wedding at Cana had a tremendous impact on him.

How did John and the other handful of disciples respond? _____

_____

It's one thing to follow Christ around the countryside. It's another thing to put your faith in Him. Never lose sight of the fact that Judas followed Jesus. Jesus is looking for true disciples who really place their faith—their trust—in Him. We can follow Jesus to Christian conferences all over the nation or down the aisles of every church in America and never put our faith in Him. John, the one who wrote what Merrill Tenney termed "the Gospel of belief,"[8] officially began his own great adventure of believing right there in Cana.

Yes, the wedding in Cana was a big day for John. It was also a big day on the kingdom calendar. What was its obvious eternal significance?

_____

Any first in Scripture is huge. How Jesus chose to perform His first miracle cannot be overestimated. The scene is replete with more applications than we have space to discuss. Because it's just the two of us, however, let's symbolically dip the ladle into the stone water jar and draw forth two cups of wine to share.

First of all, God ordained that Christ's first earthbound miracle would be filling empty jars. Praise God! Does any pain rival that of emptiness? Don't miss the significance of the kinds of jars these were.

What does John 2:6 tell you about them? _____

_____

I think this first miracle reveals a vivid picture of the condition God's chosen people were in at that time. Legalism soared during the four hundred years without a fresh word from God. As we discussed at the beginning of our study, the kind of Pharisaism Jesus found so revolting developed during the latter part of the intertestament silence. We too can substitute legalism for our lack of fresh involvement with God. The Jews' ceremonial rituals and washings left them as empty as those oversized jars and as cold as stone. Religious observances mean nothing apart from God.

Meaningless ritual and the self-helps of personal cleansings are not the only things that leave us empty. Jesus ran into a woman at Sychar's well who was as empty as the stone water jars ever thought about being. How do I know?

Read John 4:17-18. How had the woman tried to fill her life? _____

_____

We were never meant to live with emptiness! We were meant to be full!

Beloved, you can take this one to the spiritual bank: any compulsion for too much of anything is symptomatic of emptiness. Far too many people think that the good Christian thing to do about our gnawing emptiness is get a grip, stop whining, and live without for the rest of our lives. If that's what we do, we miss the very first miracle Jesus came to perform! John's Gospel came along to give us the best of good news. We were never meant to live with emptiness! We were meant to be full! God's children were meant to receive His fullness in one blessing after another!

Let me echo a precept continually underscored through this two-week segment. We were created to be full. When we're not filled with the good things Christ came to bring us, we will grasp at substitutes. An unsatisfied soul is a disaster waiting to happen.

Have you discovered this precept to be accurate? If so, how? _____

_____

Second, the first miracle brought new wine. To the woman at the well He brought the living Water. To the guests at the wedding He brought new wine. He gives us what we need. And what most of us need, Dear One, is some new wine!

Glance at John 2:11. What did Jesus reveal through His first miracle?

_____

The miracle performed in the physical realm was meant to reveal something far more glorious in the spiritual realm. Though Jesus certainly met an immediate need at the wedding, the wine represented something of exceeding significance.

Read Judges 9:13; Psalm 4:7; 104:15. With what is wine associated?

_____

Now let's release that hold button on the "hmm" passage (Matt. 9:14-17). One reason Christ came was to fill the emptiness created by the letter of the law, ritual religion, and earthly substitutes. What was the new wine? I believe it's beautifully implied in Ephesians.

> Christ came to fill the emptiness created by the letter of the law.

Read Ephesians 5:18. With what are we to be filled?
❏ **Cheer** ❏ **The Holy Spirit** ❏ **Good feelings** ❏ **Wisdom**

The passage also implies that the Holy Spirit's filling does in full measure what we try to accomplish when we desire to be "drunk on wine." One reason people drink much wine is because it changes the way they feel and the way they behave. So does the new wine, but its effects are always good. The three earlier passages suggested not the least of the effects. I hope you saw wine's association with joy and gladness. Jesus came to bring the new wine of the Spirit! Something from which we can drink our fill without the negative side effects of wine and the emptiness it leaves in the wake of the temporary fix.

Throughout the Old Testament only handfuls of people had the Holy Spirit in them or on them. The Holy Spirit was given for empowerment more than fulfillment. John's Gospel later reveals that one of Christ's primary purposes for coming and laying down His life was to send the Holy Spirit to us—not just to walk beside us but to dwell in us. At the first revelation of Christ's glory in Cana, they had no idea that the true New Wine was on its way! The Master of our banquet saved the best of the wine for last.

Beloved, did you realize that joy and gladness are among the many gifts and services Christ brought His Holy Spirit to grant? Check it out for yourself.

What are the side effects of this New Wine, according to Galatians 5:22-23?

_____

Just think! No matter how much you drink of His Spirit, against such things there is no law. Further, the more you drink, the more fully satisfied you are with love, joy, peace, and all sorts of side effects we're so desperate to achieve. To top off the goblet, instead of losing self-control, we gain it. You can't beat a drink like that!

When Melissa was a toddler, she was never satisfied with a little of anything. Every time I offered her a treat, she'd cup her plump little hand, thrust it forward, and ask, "Can my have a bawnch [bunch] of it?" The way she saw life, why bother with a little if you can have a bunch of it? Indeed! John would agree! Dear One, how tragic for us to continue with pangs of emptiness. What a waste! Christ came to bring us a bawnch of it! Stop feeling guilty because you crave lots of joy in your life. You were made for joy! You are a jar of clay just waiting to be filled (see 2 Cor. 4:7). May this lesson end with the clink of our cups as we toast to a life overflowing with New Wine!

You were made for joy!

Day Four MORE ABOUT THE WORLD

TODAY'S TREASURE
" 'God so loved the world that he gave his one and only Son, that whoever believes in him shall not perish but have eternal life.' "—John 3:16

Throughout weeks 5 and 6 we are studying what the apostle John seemed to want the readers of his Gospel to know more than anything else. We are searching the concepts he presented in greatest abundance. One distinctive of the Gospel of John is the frequency with which he uses the term *world*.

Based on a *New International Version* word-count comparison, Matthew mentions the world 10 times, Mark 5 times, and Luke 7 times. The Gospel of John? A whopping 73 times! In fact, John's New Testament contributions informing us about the world constitute almost half the mentions in the entire New Testament. Obviously, we would miss a very important concept in John's Gospel if we overlooked the world. Today do your own research and draw some conclusions. Following is a list of references in John's Gospel containing *world*. Don't worry! I didn't list all 73, but I did list several.

BASIC THEMES

_____

_____

_____

_____

Look up each reference. Write a summary statement for each Scripture and try to categorize what John wrote about the world by writing three or four basic themes in the margin.

John 1:9 _____

John 1:10 _____

John 1:29 _____

John 3:16 _____

John 3:17 _____

John 3:19 _____

John 9:5 _____

John 12:31 _____

John 14:27 _____

John 15:18-19 _____

John 16:33 _____

John 17:5 _____

John 17:18 _____

John 18:36-37 _____

Perhaps we've grown inordinately casual about the most overwhelming fact: God sent Jesus to the world. Let's try to get our arms stretched a little farther around that for a moment. I hope you didn't miss that the Father and Son had fellowship and shared glory before the world even existed. In fact, I am absolutely convinced that humankind exists because of the Trinity's holy passion to draw others into Their fellowship.

> We exist because of the Trinity's holy passion to draw others into fellowship.

The Father, Son, and Holy Spirit, though complete in Themselves, desired the overflowing and exceeding joy of additional relationship, so "in the beginning God created the heavens and the earth" (Gen. 1:1). Although distinctions exist in the Bible between the words *earth* and *world*, they are intertwined and virtually interchangeable where creation is concerned. Genesis 1:1 says that God created the earth, and John 1:10 tells us the world was made through Him. *Earth* tends to encompass the physical properties of our planet, while *world* encases more of the system on it and around it, social and otherwise. You might think of the distinction this way: our world exists on this earth.

Every time the word *world* is used in the NIV translation of John, the Greek word is *kosmos*. The word means: "World, with its primary meaning being order, regular disposition and arrangement. … The earth, this lower world as the abode of man."

God the Father, Son, and Holy Spirit desired the existence of humanity for fellowship. They wanted humans to have a will of their own so that they would choose God without being commanded. They knew that equipping people with their own will would necessitate a plan for redemption, because they would ultimately make some very poor choices. Thus, the plan of salvation was already completely intact before the creation of the world. When the holy Trinity was ready, each member participated in the astonishing six-day creation.

Consider Genesis 1:1 again.

"In the beginning God created the _____ and _____ earth."

Stay with me here. The Word of God delineates between one little planet He called Earth and the entire rest of the universe. We have no idea what is out there. What little science documents and hypothesizes makes Genesis 1:1 inconceivably impressive.

Our solar system is in a galaxy called the Milky Way. "Scientists estimate that there are more than 100 billion galaxies scattered throughout the visible universe. Astronomers have photographed millions of them through telescopes. The most distant galaxies ever photographed are as far as 10 billion to 13 billion light-years away. ... The Milky Way has a diameter of about 100,000 light-years. The solar system lies about 25,000 light-years from the center of the galaxy. There are about 100 billion stars in the Milky Way."[9]

An estimated 100 billion in our galaxy alone! What does Psalm 147:4 tell us?

_____

Impressive, isn't it? But this gets even more impressive: in the beginning God created the sun, the moon, every single star, all their surrounding planets, and the earth. You and I have no idea what God's activities may have been elsewhere in the universe, but according to the Bible and as far as He wanted us to know, He picked out one tiny speck on which to build a world. Our world. And He picked it out so that when the time had fully come, He would send His Son (see Gal. 4:4). Can you imagine the fellowship of the Trinity on the seventh day? As They rested and looked on the very good work They had accomplished, one planet had been tended like no other, to our knowledge. Perfectly placed in the universe with adequate distance from sun, moon, and stars to sustain human life, it was chosen for divine infiltration.

" 'God so _____ the world' " (John 3:16).

Scripture doesn't tell us He loved the sun, and it is the most impressive among visible elements. Nor are we told He loved the stars, even though He knows each by name. John went out of His way, however, to tell us not just that God loved the world but that He so loved the world. In a universe so vast, so incomprehensible, why does God single out one little planet to so love? Beloved, absorb this into the marrow: because we are on it. As despicable as humanity can be, God loves us. Inconceivably, we are His treasures. His prized creation. He just loves us. So much, in fact, that He did something I with my comparatively pitiful love for my children would not do for anyone.

As despicable as we can be, God loves us.

What did He do? _____

Dear One, let it fall afresh. I am overcome with emotion. _Elohim_ is so huge. We are so small. Yet the vastness of His love—so high, so wide, so deep, so long—envelops us as the endless universe envelops a crude little planet God called Earth.

Not long ago Keith had a bench with a simple covering placed in the corner of our small back yard. Almost every morning I light a candle and head out to that bench for a predawn worship service and quiet time. Sometimes I have to pull a big blanket out of a warm dryer to wrap around me in the cold. At that time in the morning the heavens are still as dark as the blackest night, and the stars as if God lit ten thousand candles of His own. In that morning hour I feel that He lit them just for the two of us. (And for the two of you.) I feel a million miles from the freeways of Houston. Blessed man that he was, David the psalmist was also besieged by the sight.

What did David seem to be feeling when he wrote Psalm 8:3-4?

_____

_____

In the midst of constant discoveries modern science hasn't even begun to discover the true wonder of God's universe. Yet even when I consider what they do know, I am overwhelmed with David's same question: "Who are we, God of all creation, that You would give a single thought to us? Let alone a mindful?"

Amanda was one of the dreamiest and most tenderhearted toddlers you can imagine. I often stooped down to talk to her so that I could look her right in those big blue-green eyes. Every time I squatted down to talk to her, she squatted down, too ... and there we'd be. The gesture was so precious I always had to fight the urge to laugh. I dared not, though, because she was often very serious about those contemplative moments between the two of us.

Of his God the psalmist wrote, "Your right hand sustains me; you stoop down to make me great" (Ps. 18:35). The *Amplified Version* says it this way: "Your gentleness and condescension have made me great." I don't think the Scripture intends the modern world's concept of greatness. I think it says of us, "You stoop down and make me significant." Yes, indeed. And when the God of all the universe stoops down and a single child recognizes the tender condescension and bends her knee to stoop as well, the heart of God surges with unbridled emotion. And there they are. Just the two of them.

As you conclude, please read John 1:10-12 aloud and thoughtfully with all this in mind. Much of the world carries on as if its Creator does not exist. Oh, but He does. Bow down, dear child of God. His love has made you great.

God's love has made you great.

> **Suggested prayer: Father God, it humbles me to realize that You stoop from the heavens to meet me where I am. Your love enfolds me like a warm blanket. I am not worthy to meet with You on my own, but I thank You that Christ in me gives me that privilege.**

Day Five MORE OF WHO HE IS

TODAY'S TREASURE
" 'I tell you the truth,' Jesus answered, 'before Abraham was born, I am!' "
—John 8:58

Much of the lost population and unbelieving world religions attempt a show of respect by claiming that although they don't believe Jesus Christ was the Son of God, they certainly esteem Him as a good man. A true prophet. They don't realize that their summation of this historical figure reveals that they are decidedly ill informed.

If Jesus is not the Son of God and Himself God, He was either a pathological liar or mentally ill. If at best Christ was a prophet, then He was a false prophet, because He unabashedly claimed messiahship. In reality, if the Christ who walked among men was not God's Son, then He grossly misled people, and nothing good is left to say about Him.

For years I've been aware of a group of scholars who meet annually to discuss and debate matters of Scripture. Of course, that is their right. The part that baffles and even somewhat amuses me is that they come to their final conclusions by popular vote. For example, they once voted on whether Christ would visibly return to earth in a second coming. (They voted it down.) They have also voted on matters such as whether Mary was really a virgin and the validity of certain biblically professed miracles.

If we voted on whether Jesus is the Son of God and not a single ballot was cast in His favor, He would still be the Son of God.

If they weren't people of influence, I would laugh my head off. Why? Because the vote of humans couldn't change Truth an iota if their lives depended on it! If the world's population took a vote on whether Jesus is the Son of God and not a single ballot was cast in His favor, He would still be the Son of God. Furthermore, when His Father says "Go!" Christ's feet will touch the Mount of Olives, and it will split from east to west (see Zech. 14:4). He doesn't need our permission or even our faith to be who He is. Aren't you thankful?

Today we will take a look at seven claims Christ made in the Gospel of John about who He is. These seven titles are by no means the totality of His claims. They simply share several common denominators in John's Gospel that we don't want to miss. As we remain with our theme of *more* through weeks 5 and 6, we will find that John tells us more about the self-proclaimed identity of Christ than the other Gospels.

Look up each reference below in the Book of John. Record Christ's claims of His identity on the lines provided. No matter how many times you've seen these titles, I pray that you will approach them with freshness.

6:35 _____

8:12 _____

10:7-9 _____

10:11-14 _____

11:25 _____

14:6 _____

15:1,5 _____

In fairly rapid succession Christ made a point of defining Himself with certain common denominators in John's Gospel a perfect seven times. Even hosts of scholars who do not heavily ascribe to an overriding significance of numbers in Scripture agree that seven appears to be the number of completion or perfection in the Bible. I see three basic common denominators in these seven titles. Consider each with me.

All seven titles are preceded by "I am." Of course, to make any sense, they must, but I want you to consider the impact of these two words from the mouth of Jesus Christ. Take a good look at John 8:48-59. Don't you love the inference of verse 56?

Read Galatians 3:6-9,14 and explain one way Abraham "saw" Christ's day.

_____

When God spared Isaac's life through a sacrificial offering (see Gen. 22), God preached the gospel in advance to Abraham! Now meditate on Christ's power-packed claim in John 8:58. Note the differing verb tenses.

What is Jesus' obvious point? _____
How did the Jews react to Christ's statement (see v. 59)? They—
❑ wanted to stone Him;   ❑ ran after Him;   ❑ ran from Him.

They reacted violently because they knew exactly what Christ implied. They wanted to stone Him for blasphemy because they understood the association of His reference to Exodus 3:12-15. Read these verses and concentrate on the last sentence in the passage.

By what name did God introduce Himself, and for what length of time is He to be called such?

_____

_____

Go back and meditate on Exodus 3:12. One of God's primary points to Moses is stated in this verse: " 'I will be with you.' " This great I Am That I Am, the completely self-sufficient, self-existent God of all creation, introduced Himself by this title in context with the promise to be with humanity. He did not need them. Rather, they needed Him, and He came in response to that need. Later in the lesson we will develop this concept further. For now you can safely conclude that the Jews listening to Christ in John 8 knew exactly what He meant by His "I am" statement. He was claiming to be God.

Dear One, we must consider His claims, as well. Either Jesus came as the incarnate great I Am, or He is a liar. He cannot be anything in between. You and I say that we believe Christ's words to be truth, and if we do, He is worthy of our most profound worship and followship.

Before we conclude this point, take a look at John 18:1-6. We've looked at the inference in these passages before, but I want you to see it in context with today's lesson.

What happened to the soldiers after Christ responded, " 'I am He' " (v. 6)?

_____

_____

The original language suggests the reason they fell to the ground—the Greek word we translate as _He_ is conspicuously missing. The _Interlinear Bible_ translates Christ's words like this: "Then when He said to them, I AM, they departed into the rear and fell to the ground."[10] The emphasis of the capital letters is theirs, not mine. You see, the rest of us could say, "I am," and it would be a common identification. When Christ speaks "I am," the words fall from the lips of the great I Am!

Our second common denominator is the inclusion of the word _the_ in each title. Go back and read each of the titles you supplied in your first interactive exercise on page 110, but this time substitute the word _the_ with the word _a._ What difference does "the" make?

The question may seem elementary scholastically, but nothing could be more profound theologically. For just a moment think about your approach to Jesus Christ. Is He "a" light to you? Or "the" Light? Is He "a" way for you to follow, or is He "the" Way you want to go? Is He "a" means to afterlife in your opinion? Deep inside do you think that several world religions probably offer a viable way to life after death and Jesus is one of them? Or is He "the" Resurrection and the Life? Be as honest as possible as you write your response to the following question. (You will not share this answer in small-group discussion.)

Beloved, is Christ an "a" to you among several other possibilities, or is He your "the"? Briefly explain how you've come to your conclusion.

_____

_____

When Christ speaks "I am," the words fall from the lips of the great I Am!

111

The third and final common denominator in today's lesson is that each of Christ's seven "I am" statements in John's Gospel is relational!

Find each reference. This time look for the way the title is associated with us. I've given you the first one so that you'll understand what I am asking.

6:35 *Those who come to this Bread of life will never go hungry.*

8:12 _____

10:7-9 _____

10:11-14 _____

11:25 _____

14:6 _____

15:1,5 _____

Christ is many things. He is truly the great I Am. He fulfills numerous titles in the Word of God, but I believe the spiritual inference of the seven "I am" sayings in the broad approach of John's Gospel is this: Jesus Christ is everything we need. He is each of these titles for us! Remember, He is the self-sufficient One! He came to be what we need. And not just what we need but what we desire most in all of life.

We will never have a challenge He can't empower us to meet. We will never have a need He can't fill. We will never have an earthly desire He can't exceed. When we allow Christ to be all He is to us, we find wholeness. One piece at a time, Beloved. Every time you discover the reality of Christ fulfilling another realm of your needs and longings, His name is written on a different part of you, and you are that much closer to wholeness.

> Jesus Christ is everything we need.

 What do the "I am" statements mean to you?

_____

Oh, the blessed simplicity of the pursuit and love of Jesus! "One thing have I desired …, that will I seek after"! (Ps. 27:4, KJV). In our harried times isn't the thought of becoming a "one thing" person refreshing and freeing? In one Savior we discover all things! Our Jesus is everything. That will never change, no matter how humans cast their vote.

[1]Augustine, *Confessions,* trans. R.S. Pine-Coffin (New York: Penguin Books, 1961), 181, as quoted in John Piper, *The Dangerous Duty of Delight* (Sisters, OH: Multnomah Publishers, 2001), 12.

[2]Jonathan Edwards, *The "Miscellanies,"* as quoted in Piper, *Dangerous Duty,* 19.

[3]C. S. Lewis, *The Weight of Glory* (Grand Rapids: Eerdmans, 1965), 1–2, as quoted in Piper, *Dangerous Duty,* 22.

[4]Piper, *Dangerous Duty,* 21.

[5]Eusebius, as quoted in Andreas J. Kostenberger, *Encountering John: The Gospel in Historical, Literary, and Theological Perspective* (Grand Rapids: Baker Books, 1999), 35.

[6]Attributed to Augustine, as quoted in Kostenberger, *Encountering John,* 19.

[7]Kostenberger, *Encountering John,* 56.

[8]Merrill Tenney, *The Gospel of Belief* (Grand Rapids: Eerdmans Publishing, 1997).

[9]*The World Book Encyclopedia* (Chicago: World Book Inc., 2001), s.v. "galaxy."

[10]Jay P. Green Sr., *A Literal Translation of the Bible,* as quoted in *The Interlinear Bible* (Peabody, MA: Hendrickson Publishers, 1986), 837.

VIDEO RESPONSE SHEET

Group Session 5

See John 3:5. One of the most often repeated phrases from the mouth of Christ is "____ _____

_____ ____ _____." In the NIV the phrase appears _____ times in the Gospels.

Jesus used the phrase …

1. For the sake of _____.

2. For clarity on issues of _____ _____ like _____ and _____.

3. For clarity on issues of _____.

   Christ tells us the truth. _____ _____ _____.

Take a good look at Psalm 31:1-5,13-16,21. Camp on the words in verse 14: "I trust in you, O Lord."
What makes a person able to trust God when the circumstances around him are screaming to disbelieve?
He has come to trust in the God of truth (v. 5).

1. Christ will tell us the truth even when we think we'd prefer a lie. Why?

   • Because He ____ _____ (John 14:6).

   • Because only the truth _____ _____ _____ (John 8:32).

2. Thankfully, Christ's truth always comes coupled with His _____.

3. Christ holds His _____ and His _____ responsible for telling not only

   His truth but His _____ truth.

Two extremes in unbalanced teaching or portraying:

⟵————————————————————⟶

God has nothing to do with anything we

could ever _____ as

_____ or _____

(2 Tim. 4:3-5).

God is always _____, never

_____, and usually _____

to _____ ____ (Luke 4:18).

See John 16:33. Christ Jesus came to us as the exact representation of the Father. He taught neither
of the above extremes. **See Matthew 18:4-7.**

LIFE MORE ABUNDANTLY

Day 1
More of the Spirit

Day 2
More Fruit

Day 3
More Revelation

Day 4
More Interaction with Women

Day 5
More About His Father

Are you enjoying our *mores* from the Gospel of John? I'm delighting in them. More life! More belief! More wine of gladness! More insight into the world! More of His fullness! I want more of everything God wants to give, don't you? This week we have five additional mores on our banquet table of God's Word. In Christ there's always more to know, to enjoy, to celebrate.

I can hardly believe we're at our journey's midpoint. Let's allow God to accomplish all He purposed when we turned the first page. I hope you'll commit not to allow the enemy to distract or discourage you from finishing. *Lord, You began a good work in us five weeks ago. You have nothing less in mind for each of us than inconceivable riches in Christ Jesus. We don't want to miss them! Empower us to complete what we've started and to reap every reward You graciously desire to grant us for seeking You (Heb. 11:6). Give us ears to hear and eyes to see! In Jesus' glorious name, Amen.*

Principal Questions

Day 1: According to 1 Corinthians 2:9-14, why is the Holy Spirit so vital in a relationship with God through His Word?

Day 2: In what ways does Christ love His own (see John 15:9)?

Day 3: Based on context and His response to Judas in John 14:19-25, what did Christ mean when He said that soon the world would not see Him but His disciples would?

Day 4: What were some of the encounters Jesus had with women in Scripture?

Day 5: What was the ultimate reason Jesus exercised restraint over His divine rights (see Matt. 26:53-54)?

Day 1 MORE OF THE SPIRIT

TODAY'S TREASURE

" 'The Counselor, the Holy Spirit, whom the Father will send in my name, will teach you all things and will remind you of everything I have said to you.' "—John 14:26

Throughout week 6 we will continue our emphasis on the concepts of *more* and *abundance*. John tucked them like priceless treasures into his Gospel. Again, our point is not that John's Gospel is superior to the Synoptics but that it is distinct. It also appears last in order, suggesting that God may have intended it to be the grand finale of a spectacular fireworks display showing forth the Light of the world!

Without exception John's Gospel equips us with more information about the Holy Spirit than any of the Synoptics. Today we focus on the Holy Spirit. I wish somehow I could write the next statement in neon lights to catch the eye of every reader: *the Holy Spirit is the key to everything in a believer's life!* Read that statement out loud! I have testified many times to my defeated Christian life through my teenage years and early 20s, even though I rarely missed a church service or activity. I take full responsibility for my own defeat, because I could have read for myself what the churches I attended did not teach me.

I received many wonderful treasures from the churches of my youth, but I did not learn two vital keys to a victorious life: how to have an ongoing, vibrant relationship with God through His Word and how to be filled with the power and life of the Holy Spirit. Both of these are vital concepts that the enemy does everything he can to make us miss. The Word and the Holy Spirit are by far his biggest threats. You may have been surprised that I would prioritize the Holy Spirit over the Word in my italicized statement. I don't think John would mind if his contemporary, Paul, launched our study today with an explanation.

> **Read 1 Corinthians 2:9-14 and explain why the Holy Spirit is so vital in a relationship with God through His Word.**

_____

_____

_____

Beloved, I hope you didn't miss that your own personal 1 Corinthians 2:9 is at stake in whether or not you start reaping the benefits the Holy Spirit came to bring you. Now we'll let John tell us what many of those benefits and activities are. John's primary truths about the Holy Spirit are compacted in chapters 14 and 16 of his Gospel. I want you to read both chapters thoroughly so that you can grasp the context.

> **On the chart on the next page, identify the theme of each chapter as it relates to the Holy Spirit. Then list all pertinent information recorded about Him.**

The Holy Spirit is the key to everything in a believer's life!

JOHN 14 Theme	JOHN 16 Theme
_____	_____
_____	_____
Pertinent Information	Pertinent Information
_____	_____
_____	_____
_____	_____
_____	_____
_____	_____

One of the most revolutionary truths Christ told His disciples is in John 14:17. He told them that the Spirit of truth at that time was living *with* them but would soon be *in* them. Think about the repercussions of that promise.

What difference could the Spirit of God make when living *in* a person, as opposed to *with* a person?

_____

Beloved, that very difference turned a band of fumbling, fleshly followers into sticks of spiritual dynamite that exploded victoriously on the world scene in the Books of Acts. The difference is enormous! Impossible to overestimate!

How would this era of the Holy Spirit begin (see John 16:7)?

_____

The fulfillment of Christ's critical promise to His disciples came to them in John 20:21-22, then filled them in a far more powerful expression in Acts 2:1-4. Read both of these passages and explain what happened.

_____

The Spirit of Jesus Christ Himself dwells inside you!

These glorious events unleashed a new, revolutionary era of the Holy Spirit for the church age. The Holy Spirit now indwells every person who receives Christ as personal Savior (see Rom. 8:9). Oh, that we would absorb the magnitude of that spiritual revolution! Dear believer in Christ, the Spirit of the living God—the Spirit of Jesus Christ Himself, the Spirit of truth—dwells inside your vessel! Have we heard these concepts so long that we've grown callous to them?

What is the greatest gift God gives His children (see Luke 11:11-13)?

_____

What does John 3:34 tell you about the Holy Spirit?

_____

Oh, Beloved, I hope you are getting this. I am about to hop out of my chair. Do we need to love an unlovely person? Do we need extra patience? Could we use a little peace in the midst of chaos? Do we need to show an extra measure of kindness? Could anyone stand a little more faithfulness to God or a strong dose of self-discipline? How about a heaping soul full of joy? All of these come with the fullness of the Holy Spirit! We don't just need more patience. We need more of the Spirit filling us and anointing us!

Now before anybody starts writing me letters, let me explain. I realize that the Holy Spirit is a person. When He comes into a believer's life at salvation, He moves in personally. We believers have the Spirit, but the infinite Spirit of God continues to pour Himself into our lives. Any given day I may enjoy a greater portion of His Spirit than I did the day before. He continues to pour out more of His Spirit from on high.

Does anyone need deep insight from God's Word? An added measure of understanding? Does anyone need the eyes of her heart enlightened to know the hope of her calling? Does anyone want to fulfill God's eternal purposes for her life and to think with the mind of Christ instead of the misleading mind of mortal flesh? All of these come with more of the Holy Spirit (see 1 Cor. 2)! Child of God, don't just absorb this truth! Get up and celebrate it! God gives the Spirit without measure! He has all that you need. Our fulfillment and greatest joy are in the flooding of the Holy Spirit of God in our lives!

> Our fulfillment and greatest joy are in the flooding of the Holy Spirit of God!

Here's a good one. Could anyone use a sharper memory? John 14:26 tells us that the Holy Spirit is the Blessed Reminder. Have you ever noticed that we have a sharp memory about destructive things but a far duller one about instructive things? We need more of the Holy Spirit! Recently, I had to memorize lines for a Christmas pageant at our church. I had never done anything like that, and I was a nervous wreck. Because I knew John 14:26, instead of just asking God to help me with my lines, I asked Him to fill me with more of His Holy Spirit so that the Blessed Reminder would manifest Himself to me—and He did! He is your key to memorizing Scripture or retaining biblical truth.

What do you need most from the Holy Spirit, based on the activities we've considered today?

_____

Are you actively praying for more of Him toward that end?   ❏ Yes   ❏ No

A deposit of the Holy Spirit dwells in each of us who has trusted Christ as Savior (see Eph. 1:14). We have each been sealed (see Eph. 1:13), and He will remain with us forever (compare John 14:16 and Heb. 13:5). But according to our level of cooperation, we can either quench/grieve the Holy Spirit within us, or we can be utterly filled and anointed by Him. The difference defines whether we live in victory or defeat.

Listen, Dear One, since I began to learn what God made available to me through His Holy Spirit and what He is not only willing but also anxious to do for me, the level of supernatural power in my life has skyrocketed. I want the same for you! I am so jealous with a godly jealousy for you, Believer, that I can hardly stand it! Beloved, every one of these Bible studies, as well as any book or message of value God has given me, has come directly from the power of the Holy Spirit! I know better than anyone else that I am incapable of any such thing. Years ago I came face-to-face with my own self-destructive humanity, surrendered my life to be crucified with Christ, and determined to live henceforth through the resurrection power of the Holy Spirit. I certainly don't always live my days filled with the Holy Spirit, but the rule (with obvious exceptions) has become the daily pursuit of the Spirit-filled, Christ-empowered life. The difference is night and day.

Do I ask for more and more of God's Holy Spirit? You bet I do! He gives Him without measure! The beauty of His endless supply is that my portion does not take an ounce away from yours! A word of warning: don't confuse asking for more of the Holy Spirit with asking for more manifestations of the Holy Spirit.

James 4:2-3 gives us two reasons we don't receive. What are they?

_____

One reason we may not have experienced the fullness of God's presence and power in our lives is that we haven't asked. James 4:3, however, adds an additional reason we don't receive: sometimes we ask with wrong motives.

What might be wrong motives for asking for more of the Holy Spirit?

_____

_____

I'd love to hear your list. Let me either agree or add to it with a few of my own examples of wrong motives. If I want more of the Holy Spirit so that people will be impressed with me or so that I will feel powerful, then my motives are self-glorifying and dishonoring to God. If I desire a manifestation of the Holy Spirit as proof that certain empowerments exist (and therefore God exists), then my motive is to prove (test!) God rather than glorify Him. A right motive for asking for more of the Holy Spirit is that God be glorified in us through our effective, abundant, Spirit-filled lives. Matthew phrased it best: " 'Let your light shine before men, that they may see your good deeds and praise your Father in heaven' " (5:16).

Remember what we learned from John Piper in our lesson on Christian hedonism? God is most glorified in us when we are most satisfied in Him. Our soul's satisfaction for His glorification is a wonderful motive for requesting more of the Holy Spirit. After learning many lessons the hard way, I want more and more of His Spirit because I want more and more of Him! The flooding of the Holy Spirit will manifest in all sorts of ways, but God and His glorification are our purest motives, not the manifestations themselves.

I am convinced that the essence of abundant life is simply put: an abundance of God in our lives. I don't just want to do the church thing. I want to experience Him every day of my mortal life and walk with Him as surely and vividly as I could walk with flesh and bone. I want to see His glory that the prophet Isaiah said fills the earth (see Isa. 6:3). I don't want just to be saved from destruction, as thankful as I am for the deliverance. I want to bask in the favor of His pure presence. I want God—a lot of Him! I think you do too.

Let's start asking for Him, Dear One. Every day of our lives. More of Your Spirit, Lord. More of Your Spirit!

> The essence of abundant life is simply put: an abundance of God in our lives.

Day 2 MORE FRUIT

TODAY'S TREASURE

" 'This is to my Father's glory, that you bear much fruit, showing yourselves to be my disciples.' "—John 15:8

I am so overwhelmed by all the Word has to say to us today that I am nearly paralyzed. I feel as if I've won a shopping spree and can have anything I can fit in my basket, but I want so much of what I see that I don't know where to start. Beloved, what we've won in Christ is so far beyond human thinking that if we don't learn to think with the mind of Christ through the power of the Spirit, we'll miss it! Unlike a woman who has won a basket full of goodies, we are never meant to pick and choose only what suits our fancy. Nor are we limited to one basket. God has chosen what He wants for us—treasures without measure—and all the baskets you could fit in your yard can't contain them.

God has chosen for us treasures without measure.

Read John 15:1-17. If it's familiar to you, approach every phrase as if you've never seen it before. What one jewel means the most to you? Explain why.

_____

_____

Remember that the chapter breaks and verse numbering in the Bible came much later than the inspiration of the Scriptures themselves. They are a huge help to us, but learn to consider each chapter in context with the Scriptures preceding and following it. In John 14:31 Jesus said, " 'Come now; let us leave.' " Obviously, the teaching that followed occurred en route. The next piece of geographical information is tucked in John 18:1.

Where were they heading? _____

Quite possibly, Christ's teaching on the vine took place as He and His disciples walked through a vineyard on their way to the olive grove. I want you to see yourself in this scene. You are a follower of Christ, a chosen disciple in this generation. Three sets of players appear in this vineyard scene. The labels and responsibilities of each are vital.

How did Jesus refer to the Father (see John 15:1)? _____

How did Jesus refer to Himself? _____

How did He refer to His disciples? _____

List everything you can about the Father, Jesus, and Christ's followers from John 15:1-17.

1. Christ's Father _____

_____

2. Christ_____

_____

3. His disciples _____

_____

What I'm about to say is not to your pastor, teacher, mentor, hero in the faith, best friend at church, or anyone else. It's to you. Beloved, the God of all the universe has ordained that your precious life bear much fruit. Do you hear what I'm saying? Are you taking it personally? This is about God, Christ, and you. Their eyes are on you this very moment. Hear them speak these words into your spirit loud and clear: *we want you to bear MUCH fruit.*

For the past 1½ weeks we've been talking about *more*. Today we'll talk about *much*. I will repeat it as many times as I must. God hasn't appointed you to mediocrity but to a life of profound harvest. Both yesterday and today I wept for the body of Christ I love so dearly because I am overwhelmed with Paul's godly jealousy (see 2 Cor. 11:2) that each of you receive, savor, and celebrate what God has for you. I am sick of the enemy's subtle scheme to convince the body of Christ that only a few lives in each generation are truly significant. Your life was set apart for significance! Get up right this second, look in the nearest mirror, and say it out loud to that image in front of you. And while you're at it, say, "God has chosen me, and He wants to be glorified by my bearing much fruit."

Were you obedient?   ❑ Yes   ❑ No

My friend, sometimes what you and I need is a good fussing! We are not yet fully believing God! If we were, we'd be so astounded and delighted in Him and living so far beyond ourselves that we wouldn't be able to contain our joy.

What kinds of things hold us back from immensely productive lives? Give this question some thought.

_____

_____

I hope we clear a few of those obstacles out of the way through the course of our lesson, but I'd like to address one right away. Many think that the sins of their pasts exempt them from tremendously fruit-bearing lives. First, if that were true, I would not be writing to you right now. Second, if we haven't repented and allowed God to restore us and redeem our failures, we will tragically fulfill some of our own self-destructive prophecies. God is not the one holding us back from much fruit. In tandem with the devil, we are the culprits.

God's primary concern is that He be glorified. Few unmistakable evidences glorify Him more than powerfully restored lives that humbly and authentically proclaim His faithfulness to the death. The Father is so adamant that we bear much fruit that He extends practically inconceivable offers to us. Pardon my excitement as I share some of the blessings God offers.

A love we can live in. When will we get through our heads how loved we are? Take a look at perhaps the most astounding verse in this entire segment of Scripture.

The Father extends practically inconceivable offers to us.

In what way does Christ love His own (see John 15:9)? _____

_____

Try to grasp this truth as tightly as you can: Christ Jesus loves you the way the Father loves Him. He loves you like His only begotten! As if you were the only one!

Christ follows His statement with a command: " 'Now _____ in my love.' "

I love the *King James Version's* word *abide*. The term means exactly what it implies: *dwell in His love, remain in it, tarry in it, soak in it.* For heaven's sake, live in it! How do we do such a thing?

Let me paraphrase what I think Christ is saying in this passage. Please write your name in the following blanks.

My love for you, _____, is perfect, divine, and lavish beyond your imagination and far beyond your soul's cavernous needs. In fact, I love you the way my Father loves Me, and I am the only begotten Son and the uncontested apple of His eye. _____, My love for you is as constant as an ever-surging fountain, but you don't always sense it because you move in and out of the awareness of My presence. My desire is for you to park your mobile home so intimately close to Me that you are never outside the keen awareness of My extravagant love.

Why is a constant awareness of God's love for us so vital in a profusely fruit-bearing life? One reason is that Satan does not want us to bear much fruit. He will do everything he can to discourage, accuse, and condemn us. Even the most steadfast among God's servants make mistakes and foolish decisions along the way. None is worthy to serve the holy God of all creation. We will always give Satan plenty of ammunition to discourage us. If we don't literally camp in Christ's love, we will talk ourselves out of untold fruit by dwelling on our own unworthiness. Accept the facts that we are unworthy and that we are lavishly loved by a God of redemptive grace. God also provides something else.

A source we can draw from. When I asked what kinds of things hold us back from immensely fruit-bearing lives, you may have responded, "A lack of talent or ability." Any such reference to ability is conspicuously missing in this Scripture. To bear much fruit, we must abide in Christ as a branch remains physically attached to the vine.

Apart from Him we can do _____ (see John 15:5).

Christ tells us that we must embed ourselves in Him and let the power source flow. He will do the work through us. That's the secret!

Picture the attachment between the vine and the branch. One of the most important elements of the branch is that it remains open to the flow of the vine's life. If the branch were simply wound around the vine tightly, it would still die without producing any fruit. The branch must be attached to the vine with an openness to receive from it. Do you see the parallel? So often we have our own agendas about how we want to serve God. We spend untold energy and never produce lavish, God-glorifying fruit. We must be open to the power flow and the purposed work the Vine wants to accomplish.

> Accept the facts that we are unworthy and that we are lavishly loved by God.

We've got to be open to the life, agenda, and timing of the Vine.

Often we fall into the trap of making up our own minds about how we want to serve Christ, based on human reasoning and personal preferences. Trying to force our own ministries is a frustrating waste of time. I spent the first half of my adult life trying my hardest to make something—anything—work for God. After all, He had called me! Nothing worked until I gave up in exhaustion and failure and let Him work. We can't force fruit. We can only abide in the Vine. If we're going to produce much fruit, we've got to be open to the life, agenda, and timing of the Vine.

Have you ever tried to force a ministry for your life? If so, explain.

_____

_____

Christ is a Gardener we can depend on. We've heard of personal trainers—our Gardener is so determined that fruitful lives bear even more fruit that He commits Himself as our personal Pruner! Notice verse 2. I believe this verse suggests that God works hard on a child who is producing fruit so that she or he will produce even more. If you are a true follower of Jesus Christ, you may feel as if God is picking on you. Have you ever exclaimed in exasperation, "God never lets me get away with anything"? Have you ever noticed that God seems particularly jealous with you? That He refuses to allow you mindless and meaningless activities that He seems to tolerate in other believers? He does so because you have proved to be a cooperative, fruit-bearing child. He knows that you are His prime branch through whom He can be glorified.

Do you see the progression suggested in verses 2 and 5? God desires for those who bear fruit to bear more fruit and for those who bear more fruit to bear much fruit! As nervous as the thought may make us, God can be trusted with a pair of shears.

The following exercise is strictly for your benefit and between you and God. Don't let Satan use it to condemn.

Based on an abiding sense of God's presence and pleasure, as opposed to numbers and notoriety, plot where you think you are in the process represented below.

No apparent fruit   Some fruit   More fruit   Much fruit

If you've made it past "No apparent fruit," jot phrases on the diagram to describe what your personal Pruner did to take you to the next level. The pickier we let Him be with us, the more productive He will be through us. Beloved, when all is said and done and we are living in heaven, all that will matter is whether our lives glorified God. Let's let Him prune to His heart's content. Let's surrender to a life that will matter more than a hill of beans when we've drawn our last breath. There's one more thing He offers us.

A joy we can revel in. A surrendered life will produce joy. We are called to lives of obedience. Yes, God's grace covers our sins as we trust in Christ's finished work on the cross, but we will not bear much fruit without obedience to our Father's will. According to John 15:10, if we don't walk closely to Him in obedience, we will never draw near enough to abide in His love. He loves us no matter what we do, but we will not be able to pitch our spiritual tents in His presence when we're disobedient. Does all this sound like a life of just serving and sacrificing? Then you'd better read John 15:11 again.

What is the result of the obedient, abiding, fruit-bearing life?

_____

_____

Whose joy will be in us? _____

What an amazing thought! The sovereign God of the universe could have rigged the plan to serve Himself only. He could have demanded our obedience and service—or else. But He didn't. Our Heavenly Father is the giver of all good gifts (see Jas. 1:17). God longs to bless us with abundant life and joy—and not just any joy. Christ's joy! Perfect, full, magnetic, and contagious! The joy of Jesus comes to the believer only one way: transfusion—an intravenous drip from Vine to branch! Let's receive the Son-sweetened sap of the Vine. God doesn't just have more for you. He has much—much love, much fruit, much joy. The God of the universe derives much glory from one measly mortal. Who can beat a deal like that?

> God longs to bless us with abundant life and joy.

Day 3 MORE REVELATION

TODAY'S TREASURE
" 'Whoever has my commands and obeys them, he is the one who loves me. He who loves me will be loved by my Father, and I too will love him and show myself to him.' "—John 14:21

What fun I've had studying the concepts of *more* and *abundance* with you through John's Gospel! My spiritual life—particularly my prayer life—has already been marked by what we've discovered. Today we will study another Scripture in John with such implications that I am relying on God to help me do justice to the topic. In day 1 we read today's segment of Scripture, but I waited until now to examine it.

Read John 14:19-25. Based on the context and Christ's response to Judas' question, what did Christ mean when He said that soon the world would not see Him but that His disciples would see Him?

_____

_____

Now read again verse 21. What promise can we draw from this verse?

_____

_____

Throughout today's research we're going to focus on the words "show myself" and try to determine what Christ meant. The original word, *emphanizo,* means "to make apparent, cause to be seen, to show … of a person, to manifest oneself meaning to let oneself be intimately known and understood." Comparing several translations of the Bible can be helpful when trying to understand a term or concept. Read the following renderings of the phrase "show myself to him."

- *The King James Version:* "will manifest myself to him"
- *The New American Standard Version:* " 'will disclose Myself to him' "
- *The Amplified Bible:* "will show (reveal, manifest) Myself to him. [I will let Myself be clearly seen by him and make Myself real to him.]"
- *The Contemporary English Version:* "show you what I am like"
- *The Message:* " 'make myself plain to him' "

In Christ's response to Judas' question, He clearly stated that this particular disclosure, manifestation, or making plain would not occur in heaven but on earth. " 'We will come to him and make our home with him' " (John 14:23). This statement is in perfect context and beautiful contrast with Christ's promise in John 14:2-3. Christ promised that one day He would come to take His followers back to be with Him. The assumption is that they (and we) would dwell in the many rooms Christ is preparing. I believe this is what Christ was saying to them: "I am going to leave you so that I can prepare rooms for you where you will one day dwell and indeed make yourself at home where I live in heaven. Until then, I have built a room in each of you where I can make Myself at home with you. This way I am at home with you in Spirit until you are at home with Me in heaven."

Christ is making heavenly rooms for us while making earthly room in us. Glory to God! During this period of time, while Christ and His Father come to Their obedient followers, Christ's promise was to disclose Himself to us (see John 14:21). Certainly Christ revealed Himself at the resurrection (see v. 19) and then at Pentecost, but I believe John 14:21 implies spiritual revelation as well.

R. C. H. Lenski offers this explanation of the wording in John 14:21: "The future tenses refer to the day of Pentecost and thereafter. This appears especially in the last verb; for the appearances during the forty days were only preliminary manifestations to be followed by his constant presence, help, and blessing in the spirit (v. 18)."[1]

God and Christ reveal themselves in several different ways. First and foremost, They reveal Themselves through the Bible. In fact, Scripture is our only totally reliable source of revelation, because it is clearly written rather than subject to our feelings. Scripture is also clear, however, that God reveals dimensions of Himself and His glory to human beings through other sources.

Write the sources of revelation from the following references.

Psalm 19:1 _____

Acts 14:17 _____

Romans 1:20 _____

God has revealed Himself to me neither in flames of fire from a bush as He did to Moses nor in chariots of fire as He did to Elisha, but I have often beheld God's glory through nature. My soul is drawn to a certain chain of mountains in the Northwest. At least several times a year I feel God wooing me to come and meet Him there. I confer with Him every day at home, but our souls sometimes crave a display of His glory that can best be seen against a less common backdrop, don't they?

A few months ago I stayed by myself in the national park overlooking "my" mountains. Every night when I got into bed, I reminded myself that I came for rest as well as inspiration. I'd try to talk myself into sleeping past dawn, but I never could. I rose every

Christ is making heavenly rooms for us while making earthly room in us.

morning long before light, threw on a heavy coat, and drove to find a front-row seat to behold the sunrise. I rolled down my window to hear the mighty beasts of the field bugle their presence. In perfect covenant consistency, every morning God caused the rays of sunlight to illuminate the tips of the mountain. Then I watched until He bathed the valley as well. I was so overcome by the majesty such awesomeness suggested that I thought my heart would leap from my chest. At such a moment Habakkuk 3:3-4 invaded my thoughts: "His glory covered the heavens and his praise filled the earth. His splendor was like the sunrise; rays flashed from his hand, where his power was hidden."

Do you have a favorite place where you've seen God reveal His glory through nature? If so, describe it.

_____

Scripture suggests that God reveals Himself in many ways, but His ultimate revelation was through His very own Son. Jesus came to show us God in an embraceable, visible form. I believe a very important part of Christ's promise in John 14:21 is that after His departure He would continue to reveal, manifest, or make Himself known to His followers here until they join Him in heaven. Now that His Spirit has come and His Word is complete, I believe the Holy Spirit and the Word are the primary means by which Jesus discloses Himself to His followers.

Having built what I pray is a solid foundation for Christ's continued revelation to His followers, let's celebrate the enormous ramifications for our lives.

John 14:21 is bulging with conditions to its promises. What are they?

_____

Let's diffuse any upset over Christ's statement " 'He who loves me will be loved by my Father.' " Aren't we told in John 3:16 that God so loves the world? Absolutely! Aren't we also told in 1 John 4:19 that we love because He first loved us? No doubt! John 14:21 does not suggest that God's love for us is conditional and responsive to our love for Him. I believe the phrase is best interpreted by a deeper understanding of the nature of God's love.

Fill in the following blank according to Romans 5:8.

"God _____ his own love for us in this: While we were still sinners, Christ died for us."

One of the most significant qualities found in God's brand of love is that it is demonstrative. Christ directed His followers to love as He loved them.

Although we'll look more closely at 1 John 3:18 in our study of John's letters, how does this verse direct us to love?

_____

Do you see the concept? One of the most important dimensions of _agape_ love is that it is demonstrative. I believe John 14:21 implies that the more we obey and love God, the more vividly we may see, experience, and enjoy demonstrations of His love. Mind you,

> The more we obey and love God, the more vividly we may enjoy demonstrations of His love.

Romans 5:8 says His most profound demonstration of love was while we were still sinners, but like His disciples, we are often unable to recognize the demonstration until we obey the wooing of the Spirit in repentance and sprout the firstfruits of love. Like you, I have always been loved by God, but I have been more aware of the demonstrations of His love (what we might call His favor) when I've been loving and obedient—especially through painful circumstances. I've lived an illustration that might help.

God brought a darling young woman into my life who had been through untold turmoil. Abused and misused, she didn't trust anyone. She needed love as badly as anyone I had ever known, but she was terribly suspicious and hard to show love. God kept insisting that I show her the love of Jesus. One day I said to Him, "Lord, I'm trying to be obedient, but it's like trying to hug a porcupine!" Over months and years God turned my beloved porcupine into a puppy. I loved her throughout our relationship, but the softer and more loving she became, the more love I was able to show her. On a much greater scale, I believe the principle applies to God's demonstration of love to us.

What about you? Are you more like a porcupine or a puppy in terms of receiving the demonstrative love of God (whether through His Word, through His Spirit bearing witness in your inner being, or through a human vessel)? I'm more like a … ❑ porcupine; ❑ puppy. Explain.

_____

_____

I am convinced that John 14:21 suggests that the more we obey and love Christ Jesus, the more He will disclose Himself to us. The eyes of the Spirit within us see these manifestations or ways He makes Himself known and understood. Isaiah 6:3 tells us that the earth is full of His glory.

According to John 12:41, to whom does Isaiah 6:3 refer? _____

Christ perpetually surrounds us with His worth, providence, and presence.

Beloved, I don't believe I stretch the text when I say the glory of our Lord Jesus surrounds us constantly. Christ perpetually surrounds us with means through which He can show us His worth, His providence, and His presence. We don't want to miss them!

Describe a few ways Christ could disclose Himself to us.

_____

_____

Perhaps some of the same examples occurred to you and me. I'll share a few.
- Christ sometimes discloses His forgiving nature by empowering someone to forgive us for something that seems unforgivable.
- Sometimes Christ manifests His activity in our lives so strongly through a Bible teacher or a preacher that we feel as if we're the only ones in the audience.
- Often when we read a portion of Scripture, our eyes suddenly open to see an astounding, transforming understanding of Christ.
- Many of us have attended a dying loved one who is a believer and have seen Christ so manifest His presence that we were overwhelmed by His care and comfort.

- Christ sometimes makes His nearness and omniscience known by working through a detail no one else knew anything about.
- Sometimes an impending disaster is suddenly averted, and we're covered by chills as we sense Him as our Deliverer.
- Sometimes in worship we sense His powerful presence and sweet pleasure.

I've experienced each of these demonstrations, but I want to see more. I want Jesus Christ to manifest Himself to me! I want to know Him on this earth as well as a mortal can know Him. Don't you? Then let's pray toward that end!

At this point in our journey I am persuaded that the truth God inspired in John 14:21 became John's virtual philosophy and approach to life. We have already concluded that John forsook ambition for affection. Love became his absolute center. As we continue our journey, we will also discover that John pursued obedience even when no one was watching. With his whole being, John lived the divine conditions of John 14:21. Is it any wonder our immortal Savior and Lord handpicked John to deliver the incomparable Book of Revelation? How fitting. John himself represents the ultimate human example of his own penmanship.

> ### THE HEART OF THE BELOVED
>
> With his whole being, John lived the divine conditions of John 14:21. Is it any wonder our immortal Savior and Lord handpicked John to deliver the incomparable Book of Revelation?

Day 4 MORE INTERACTION WITH WOMEN

TODAY'S TREASURE
"Just then his disciples returned and were surprised to find him talking with a woman."—John 4:27

Begin by reading Today's Treasure. You might even read it aloud. You know something? Some of His followers are still surprised to find Jesus talking with women. Today's lesson supports the biblical fact that Jesus Christ talks to and highly esteems women.

Before we take another step, please hear me say that the farthest thing from my mind is disrespecting men or downplaying their biblical roles in leadership. I have never been and will never be a male basher. I was reared with two brothers and two sisters, so I tend to get along with men as easily as women (though understandably differently). I have a good, solid marriage with a man I deeply love and treat with respect. I am delighted that I have healthy, respectful relationships with my brothers in Christ and have rarely been in conflict with any. I strongly believe in the biblical roles designed for men and women and am convinced that our churches are rarely stronger than the men of our churches. I do not want women to take men's places. I just want to see women take their own.

Occasionally, someone asks me if I wish I could have a church of my own and be a pastor. My answer? "Are you out of your mind?" Frankly, I like passing the proverbial buck to my pastor and my husband. If women realized how directly God holds men responsible for so much, we'd pray unceasingly for them. I treasure the memory of a service one night at my church when the men were called to kneel at the altar and the women formed a shield around them and cried out in intercession on their behalf. Our hearts were bound together with a unity that could only accompany a fresh realization of distinct but equal purpose.

Hear me clearly: I am pro-men. And (not but) I am also pro-women. What may come as a news flash to some is that these pros are not exclusive. The biblical roles and responsibilities of men and women sometimes differ to complement and complete each other. Our places in the heart of God, however, are the same. I am very comfortable in my womanhood in the body of Christ, but not every woman is. Sometimes a spiritual inferiority complex stems from having been exposed to steady doses of inaccurate representations of Christ and His Word.

Not long ago someone handed me the book *When Life and Beliefs Collide* by Carolyn Custis James, and I began reading it without knowing anything about the subject matter. The author explained that God birthed the entire concept of the book from an unsettling statement a seminary professor made to her years earlier. "With more than a hint of mischief in his eyes, he said, 'You know, there have never been any *great* women theologians.' "[2] He had no idea how God used him to propel her to study the Word of God and prove him wrong! Like the disciples, he might have been surprised to find that Jesus talks to women.

My purpose today is not so much to prove the tie between women in the Bible and theology as to prove an unmistakable tie between several women in the Bible and Christ. Ties, I might add, from which Christ knitted some very deep theology. Yes, Jesus speaks to women who listen—He always has, and He always will. Anyone who wants to believe that Christ didn't have profound encounters with women might want to skip the Gospel of John. Let me again be clear that the New Testament bulges with encounters and relationships between Christ and men. We're not taking away one iota from those. Our goal today, however, is to study His interaction with women. Once again, John's Gospel supplies *more* detailed accounts *abundant* in meaning.

> Jesus speaks to women who listen—He always has, and He always will.

Each of the following passages records an important encounter with a woman. Before you become frustrated with such varied reading, keep in mind that we want to draw conclusions based on all of the snapshots rather than to stare intently at one picture.

Read John 4:1-39. What is the general story line? _____

_____

How would you describe Christ's overall approach to her? _____

_____

What did she need? _____

What did He give her? _____

What was the outcome? _____

Read John 8:1-11. What is the general story line? _____

_____

How would you describe Christ's overall approach to her? _____

_____

What did she need? _____

What did He give her? _____

What was the outcome? _____

Read John 11:17-44. What is the general story line? _____

_____

How would you describe Christ's overall approach to Martha and Mary?

_____

What did they need? _____

What did He give them? _____

What was the outcome? _____

Read John 12:1-8. What is the general story line? _____

_____

How would you describe Christ's overall approach to her? _____

_____

What did she need? _____

What did He give her? _____

What was the outcome? (Matt. 26:13 wraps up this scene best.)

_____

Read John 19:25-27. What is the general story line? _____

_____

How would you describe Christ's overall approach to her? _____

_____

What did she need? _____

What did He give her? _____

What was the outcome? _____

Read John 20:10-18. What is the general story line? _____

_____

How would you describe Christ's overall approach to her? _____

_____

What did she need? _____

What did He give her? _____

What was the outcome? _____

Based on these passages, four things about Christ astound me and make me fall even more in love with Him.

Jesus was not ashamed to be seen with a woman. At first glance this point may not seem like a big deal, but how many of us have dated or even married someone who seemed ashamed at times to be seen with us? Beloved, Jesus Christ isn't ashamed to be seen with you. In fact, He wants nothing more! He's also not ashamed to talk to you. I meet so many women who are timid about sharing what they've gleaned in Bible study because they "don't have much education" and they're "probably wrong." Listen here, young lady, the One who spoke the worlds into being has chosen you for a bride! Study His Word like someone being spoken of and spoken to! He wants your life to radiate proof that He's been talking to you. He's proud of you!

Not long ago I was approached by a woman whose husband shoots sporting clays with my husband. She said, "I thought you'd be touched to know that my husband said, 'Keith Moore sure loves his wife. You can hear it in the way he talks about her.' " If only we could hear Jesus talking behind our backs!

Though very much a man, *Jesus understands women's needs.* I despise ridiculous feminist "theology" that tries to make a woman out of God or at least make Him feminine so that we can feel as if we have an advocate, Someone who understands. Beloved, Christ understands us better than we understand ourselves! Of course, He has a decided advantage over every other man. He wove us together in our mothers' wombs. Still, I'm relieved to know that I am never too needy for Christ—particularly when I'm feeling a tad high-maintenance. Did you notice how personal Jesus got in almost every scene? He was totally unafraid of intimacy then—and He still is.

> Christ understands us better than we understand ourselves!

In the readings you completed, did Jesus leave any of those women without acting on behalf of their deep needs? ❏ Yes   ❏ No

In every case *Jesus looked beyond the woman's actions and into her heart.* He's looking into yours at this very moment and knows what you need even more than you do. Jesus even knows what motivates you to do the things you do. All He requires to meet our needs is that we allow Him to draw near to us, talk to us, and change us.

To which of the women in today's reading do you most relate? Why?

_____

Without exception *Jesus honored women and gave them dignity.* Do you see a single hint of second-class treatment? In any stretch of the imagination can you make a woman-hater out of Jesus? Not on your life. A woman-ignorer? No way. How about a womanizer? The mere thought is absurd. Jesus is stunningly personal, intensely intimate, and completely proper. He replaces her shame with dignity. He brings resurrection life to her loss. And, Dear One, He appoints and approves her good works. No, Mary of Bethany wasn't called to preach, but Christ said her story would be preached throughout the world. Mary Magdalene? She was the very first to spread the good news! The adulterous woman? Surely she got her life together. Maybe even married a fine man and had a family. After all, that's what happened to Rahab, who appears in the genealogy of Jesus. And Martha? Personally, I think she invented air freshener.

Day 5 MORE ABOUT HIS FATHER

TODAY'S TREASURE
"Jesus said to them, 'My Father is always at his work to this very day, and I, too, am working.' "—John 5:17

One of the first passionate words out of a toddler's mouth is "Mine!" I'm not even sure this word has to be taught. I don't know many moms and dads who stomp their feet exclaiming, "Mine!" No one will argue where two-year-olds get the word *no,* but where in the world do they get *mine?* Possessiveness seems to be intrinsic. No one has to learn a *my* orientation. It's intertwined in every stitch of our DNA.

A large part of what we call maturity is gaining some kind of respectable control over our *my* orientation, and rightly so. The inmost desire to have something we can call our own, however, does not make us bad or even selfish. In fact, I think it's fundamental to our personhood, but as usual, our flesh natures etch their doctrines from basic human rights that are wigged out of control.

People are created with a need to know that something belongs to them. Toddlers test what is theirs by process of elimination. Everything is "mine" until they learn what doesn't belong to them. "No, that's not yours, but here's this blanket. It is yours." In fact, perhaps we could say that maturity is not so much disregarding our *my* orientation as learning how to appropriately recognize and handle what is and isn't ours.

Maturity is learning how to recognize what is and isn't ours.

I don't know about you, but I need to know that a few things really do belong to me. I might tell you to drop by my house this afternoon, but even after 18 years that stack of bricks really belongs to the bank. For most of us, so do our cars. And speaking of banks, the bank account I call mine could disappear in some unforeseen financial disaster tomorrow, and so could yours. When we really consider the facts, each of us can call very few things in life "mine." Like the toddler, we often learn by the process of elimination. I have insisted that a few things were mine until God found very creative ways to show me otherwise.

What are a few things you would like to have called "mine," but life experiences proved otherwise?

God is protective enough of our hearts not to encourage a death grip on things we can't keep.

I am convinced that a certain need to possess is so innate in all of us that if we could call nothing our own, our souls would deflate with hopelessness and meaninglessness. Please hear this: ours is not a God who refuses us all possession. He's simply protective enough of our hearts not to encourage a death grip on things we cannot keep. He's not holding out on us. He's not dangling carrots in front of our noses and then popping us in the mouth when we lunge to bite the bait. Contrary to much public opinion, God does not play some kind of sick "I-created-you-to-want-but-will-not-let-you-have" game with us. Quite the contrary, the Author of life will only encourage us to call "mine" what is most excellent. Most exquisite. To those who receive, God gives Himself.

God called the psalmist David a man after His own heart. What are a few ways David freely exercised his *my* orientation in Psalm 18:1-2?

_____

_____

Life is replete with boundaries and no-trespassing signs. To live in any semblance of order, we confront a never-ending influx of no's. In the midst of so much we cannot have, God says to His children, "Forsake lesser things and have as much as you want … of Me." Remember, John 3:34 says that God gives His Spirit without measure. While God is the owner and possessor of all things, He freely invites us to be as possessive over Him as we desire. He is my God. And your God. He's the only thing we can share lavishly without ever lessening our own supply.

Christ gave up His divine rights to accomplish His earthly goals. Philippians 2:7 says, "[He] made himself nothing, taking the very nature of a servant, being made in human likeness." John 1:3-4 tells us, "Through him all things were made; without him nothing was made that has been made. In him was life, and that life was the light of men." Yet Christ didn't walk around saying, "Hey, Bud, do you see that dirt you're walking on? Who do you think made that? In fact, what do you think I made you out of? It's on the bottom of your shoes. And that's what you'll be again one of these days if you don't watch your step!"

To our knowledge, Christ didn't sit with the disciples in the moonlight and tout His ownership over the heavens by giving them the proper names of all the stars in alphabetical order. When we consider that Jesus Christ came to earth as the fullness of the Godhead bodily, He actually showed amazing restraint in exercising His divine rights.

What was the ultimate reason Jesus exercised restraint over His divine rights (see Matt. 26:53-54)?

_____

Another reason Christ exercised such restraint was because He had nothing to prove to Himself. John 13:3 says, "Jesus knew that the Father had put all things under his power, and that he had come from God and was returning to God." He knew. Jesus made a point of fully exercising one right, however, to the constant chagrin of the Jewish leaders. That right became the apex of the argument recorded in John 5:16-18.

Why did the Jewish leaders try all the harder to kill Him? _____

_____

Take a look at the context of John 10:31. What similar claims made the Jews so angry that they wanted to stone Jesus?

_____

_____

For two weeks we've drawn _more_ out of the Gospel of John. Based on the previous nine days, in the margin write as many of the concepts John either presented _more_ or with greater emphasis in his Gospel. Try to do this exercise from memory. I'll get you started with one: more belief.

None of the comparative statistics among the Gospels staggers me more than the number of references to God as Father. Approximately 120 of the 248 references to God as Father in the New Testament appear in John. No other book comes close. Coincidence? Not on your life! I have become increasingly convinced that God inspired John's Gospel to be intentionally more relational than the others.

Never lose sight of the fact that relationship came to mean everything to John. From now on, when you think of him, immediately associate him with one wholly convinced of Jesus' love. In turn, John had much to say not only about reciprocal love but also about love for one another. We will see the concept swell over the remaining weeks of our study. I don't believe we're off base in assuming that the priority of relationship with Christ is exactly what fitted John to receive the great revelation. To John, identity came from association. He very likely absorbed this philosophy from tagging along with Jesus.

Read the following Scriptures from the Gospel of John and describe how each underscores identification by association.

John 6:38 _____

John 14:9 _____

John 14:28 _____

John 14:31 _____

John 15:9 _____

John 15:26 _____

John 16:15 _____

John 16:32 _____

JOHN PRESENTED MORE IN HIS GOSPEL

_____

_____

_____

_____

_____

_____

_____

_____

Christ knew His constant references to God as His Father incited the Jews; yet He persisted. He had to be making a point. Through His actions and expressions Christ seemed to say, "I've set aside My crown, My position, My glory, and soon I'll set aside My life for all of you, but I will not lay down My Sonship. God is My Father. Deal with it."

The Son of Man had no place to call His own. He had no wife or children. He had no riches, though the diamond and gold mines of the world belonged to Him. He laid claim to nothing. He laid aside everything to descend to earth and wrap Himself in our injured flesh. Taking on our humanity, He also took on our most intrinsic need. In all the loss and sacrifice, He needed something He could call "Mine." Christ came to earth with nothing but His Father, and that relationship was nonnegotiable.

The revolutionary message Christ told Mary to extend to His disciples (present and past) can be grasped only in context with Jesus' magnificent obsession with His Father.

Read John 20:17. Record your fresh impressions about our study today.

_____

How do the following verses echo Christ's glorious announcement?

Romans 8:15 _____

Galatians 4:4-6 _____

Dear Child of God, if you and I were as unrelenting in exercising our rights of sonship or daughtership, our lives would be transformed. Satan would never be able to dislodge us from God's plan and blessing. You see, Christ had to make the decision to lay aside many rights, but because He retained the most important one of all, His right of Sonship, Satan could not win. Christ led many sons to glory and got to once again pick up every right He had laid aside.

God may ask us to lay down the right to be acknowledged in a situation, to give our opinion, to take up for ourselves, or to be promoted as we think we deserve. The right to leave a spouse, even though we might have biblical grounds; to withhold fellowship when the other person has earned our distance; to be shown as the one who was right; to maintain our dignity in earthly matters; to exercise our basic human rights. But let this truth be engraved on your heart: you will never be required to lay aside your rights as God's child—nor must you ever fall to Satan's temptation to weaken your position. As long as you exercise your rights of sonship, constantly reminding yourself (and your enemy) who God is and whose you are, Satan will never be able to defeat you or thwart any part of God's plan for your life. Any loss or other right God permits or persuades you to lay aside is temporary. You will ultimately receive a hundredfold in return.

Hold your position! Never let anything or anyone talk you out of exercising your rights of sonship! Satan targets us because we are the children of God. He is defeated when we refuse to back off from our positional rights. The last thing he wants to hear from you is, "I am a born-again, justified child of God, and I exercise my right to rebuke you! You, devil, are defeated. You can't take me from my Father nor my Father from me."

No matter what you may lose or lay aside, you can call the Father of life "mine!" As His child, you have 24/7 direct access. God will never turn a deaf ear to you or look the other way when you are treated unjustly. You aren't left to hope He hears you, loves you, or realizes what's going on. Know it, Sister. Never view your situation in any other context than God as your Father and you as His child.

As we conclude, carefully think about your current challenges. Are there ways you may be trying to hold on to all sorts of rights that are completely secondary yet not exercising the most important right you have?

> Never view your situation in any other context than God as your Father and you as His child.

---

[1]R. C. H. Lenski, _The Interpretation of St. John's Gospel_ (Columbus, OH: Wartburg Press, 1942), 1008.
[2]Carolyn Custis James, _When Life and Beliefs Collide_ (Grand Rapids: Zondervan Publishing, 2001), 18.

VIDEO RESPONSE SHEET

Group Session 6

Our previous lesson concluded the written focus on the concepts of "more" and "abundance" in the Gospel of John. Today we will pick up and expand on an important principle for the believers life that

was established in week 6, day 5: _____ _____ _____. No other chapter in all four Gospels has "more" to say about this wonderful principle than the incomparable John 17.

In contrast, man's natural life principle is: _____ _____ _____.

"Identification by association" is beautifully illustrated in John 17.

1. Between _____ and _____. Read John 17:1-5.
   A. Traces of Intimacy

   - In _____ (the time has come …)

   - In the essence of _____ _____

   - In reference to relationship _____ the _____ began

   B. Terms of Intercession

   - "_____ your _____, that your Son may _____ _____."

   - Identification by association for _____.

2. Between Father, Son, and _____ God _____ _____. Read John 17:6,20.
   A. Traces of Intimacy
   - The revelation of the Father received through …

     1) Obedience to His _____ (*logos*)

     2) Acceptance of His _____ (*rhema*)

   - Christ's insistence that _____ had come to Him through them

   - Christ's passion for the _____ God has for Him

   B. Terms of Intercession

   - "protect them by the _____ of your _____."

   - "protect them from the _____ _____"

   - "that all of them may be _____ … brought to _____ _____"

LETTERS FROM THE HEART

Day 1

Koinonia

Day 2

A Love Letter

Day 3

Loving Through Us

Day 4

Love in the Truth

Day 5

Body and Soul

This week we will consider the epistles John penned under the inspiration of the Holy Spirit. As we gain insight into the fires that fueled the passion of our protagonist, we will discover a man who could express great depth in few words. I could use a couple of lessons, don't you think? I hope John's terms of endearment will bless you this week. Somehow he had a way of approaching his recipients as "little children" without talking down to them. Reap the wisdom of age this week as you consider the letters of the apostle John. You will undoubtedly recognize the concepts he prioritized most as he matured.

Principal Questions

Day 1: According to 1 John 1:9, what is the secret to sharing a life of fellowshipping with Christ and walking in the light?

Day 2: How did Paul describe God's love in Ephesians 3:18-19?

Day 3: Why do we love, according to 1 John 4:19?

Day 4: What do John's words "love in truth" in 2 John mean?

Day 5: How did Paul describe the participation of labor between a believer and God in Colossians 1:29?

Day 1 KOINONIA

> ## TODAY'S TREASURE
>
> *"We proclaim to you what we have seen and heard, so that you also may have fellowship with us. And our fellowship is with the Father and with his Son, Jesus Christ."—1 John 1:3*

Years passed. His beard grayed. The skin once leathered by the sun's reflection off the Sea of Galilee bore the deeper creases of age. His voice rasped the telltale signs of a fiery evangelist. The calluses on his feet were thick with age and country miles. The wrinkles around his eyes folded and unfolded like an accordion as he laughed and mused. While some scholars believe that John's Gospel and his letters were written within just years of one another, few argue that the epistles emerged from the pen of anything other than an aging man. First John was probably written around A.D. 85–90.[1]

John had celebrated many Passover meals since the one at which he leaned his head against the Savior's strong shoulder. So much had happened since that night. He'd never get the picture of Christ's torn frame out of his mind, but neither would he forget his double take of the resurrected Lord. The last time John saw those feet, they were dangling in midair off the tip of the Mount of Olives. Just as quickly, clouds covered them like a cotton blanket. The fire of the Holy Spirit fell. Then the blaze of persecution seared. One by one the other apostles met their martyrdom. People changed, and landmarks vanished. Just as Christ had prophesied, Herod's temple, one of the wonders of the ancient world, was destroyed in A.D. 70.

The winds of the Spirit whisked John away from all that was familiar and to the city of Ephesus. Decades separated him from those early days of water-turned-to-wine and fishes-turned-to-feasts. For most of us age means sketchy memories and vague details, but not for John. Read 1 John 1:1-4 aloud if possible.

Unlike the writings of the apostle Paul, who often started his epistles with his name, John signed neither his Gospel nor his letters.

Compare 1 John 1:1 with John 1:1-2,14. If you were a Scripture analyst, what evidence would you offer to support the same authorship of both works?

John didn't gradually climb to a pinnacle in his writings. He started at one. His letters seem to open with a crescendo as if he had waited until he was about to explode to write it all down.

> John didn't gradually climb to a pinnacle in his writings. He started at one.

Based on your previous comparison between John's Gospel and his first

letter, who is the Word of life? _____

What kind of certainty did John have about Jesus Christ (see 1 John 1:1)?

I love to remind believers that our faith is based on fact. Beloved, decades had passed. Each of the disciples hoped Jesus would return before they died, but even with the promise yet to come, not one of them wavered! You would think John's certainty might have waned or weakened with time and distance, but listen to his unrelenting witness!

Why did they proclaim what they had seen and heard (see 1 John 1:3)?

_____

With whom is this fellowship? _____

The Greek word for fellowship is _koinonia_. The _Amplified Version_ describes the concept well: "What we have seen and [ourselves] heard, we are also telling you, so that you too may realize and enjoy fellowship as partners and partakers with us. And [this] fellowship that we have [which is a distinguishing mark of Christians] is with the Father and with His Son Jesus Christ (the Messiah)" (1 John 1:3).

Both the concepts of partnership and partaking are wrapped up in the wonderful word _koinonia_. My husband is a partner in business, but his partnership can as easily translate into deficit as profit. If the company doesn't do well, he loses. If it does well, he gains. As partner, he always partakes of the work but not necessarily the profit. We fellowship with God the Father and His Son, Jesus Christ, and our partnership in the kingdom never translates into a deficit. The kingdom of God operates only in surplus—inconceivable riches and more than we could ask or imagine!

> The kingdom of God operates only in surplus!

Dear Partner, do you more actively partake in the works involved in partnership or the profits involved in partnership?

_____

Perhaps you're beginning to see why both concepts are critical. Our partnership involves responsibilities, but what a shame to miss partaking in the lavish surplus of riches!

The _Amplified Version_ explains fellowship as "the distinguishing mark of Christians." How does Moses say the same thing in different words in Exodus 33:15-16?

_____

_____

Beloved, you and I can be saved to the bone and yet blend in perfectly in our workplaces and neighborhoods. Goodness knows, carnal and ineffective Christianity is rampant. I can say that without condemning others because I've practiced both. Our fellowship with the very presence of God is the only thing that sets us visibly apart.

If you agree, explain why. _____

_____

I love 1 John 1:4. At this point in John's life, he began to sound a lot like his Teacher.

Read John 15:11 and then look at the context. Do you see any similarities between the catalysts for complete joy?

———————————————————————————————

I'm experiencing one of those times when I want to stand up to type. In fact, I believe I will. Based on our previous discussions of John 15 and John 17, do you grasp that Jesus so thoroughly enjoyed His relationship with His Father and with His followers that He wanted everyone else to enjoy it, too? Perhaps the most distinguishing mark of a true partaker of the riches of God and Christ is that the partner cannot hoard the treasures. He wants everyone else to enjoy them, too. Authentic partners and partakers of *koinonia* simply cannot be selfish. Their joy is complete only as others share in it.

Beloved, my *koinonia* with the Father and Son is light years from the apostle John's, but I know what he's talking about. In fact, it's my fever and my total passion. I so thoroughly love and enjoy seeking and finding the living, breathing Son of God that I cannot stand for others to miss it. That many have diluted the dance of true *koinonia* to the dirge of stale religion drives me crazy! He's so thrilling and adventurous that I can't keep Him to myself. I want others to fellowship with me as I fellowship with Him! Do you hear 1 John 1:3-4? Read it again. That's what I believe John was trying to say. From receiving many letters along the way, I believe many of you feel exactly the same.

What have you experienced through your *koinonia* relationship with the Father and the Son that you almost cannot stand for others to miss?

———————————————————————————————

The next verses in 1 John 1 describe some of the reasons this *koinonia* is so precious to me. Please read verses 5-10. Fill in this sentence: "God is

light; in him _____" (v. 5).

What does that mean to you? _____

———————————————————————————————

Dear One, I've seen such a dark side of life. I have seen darkness in people of light. I then nearly despaired of life as I faced the dark side of my own self. We can run from the reminders of the dark side of this world, but we cannot hide … for we'd find them in ourselves. If we stick our heads out of our shells at all, the newspapers and magazines are full of reminders. In the time it takes you to complete this day's study, a father has been murdered, a woman has been raped, and a child has been abused. At times I read specific accounts and feel as if I can hardly bear to stay on this planet another minute. Only knowing that God has not forsaken this world and that He is light and in Him is no darkness at all keeps us hoping and believing.

God has no dark side. Hear that! Absorb it to your marrow! No matter how many theological questions remain unanswered to you, of this you can be sure: God has no dark side at all! You see, that's why He can purify all of us, no matter how dark our lives have been. He is utterly, perfectly pure. Oh, don't you just want to stop right now and tell Him how much you love Him? Do you see that His total lack of darkness is also why you can trust Him? He is incapable of having impure motives.

> God has not forsaken this world. He is light and in Him is no darkness at all.

The safety I find in Christ and the pure blast He is to me make me desperately want to stay in fellowship with Him. Don't you?

First John 1:9 tells us the secrets to sharing a life of fellowshipping with

Christ and walking in the light: "If we _____ our sins."

The Greek word for *confession* is *homologeo*, derived from *homou*, meaning "at the same place or time, together," and *lego*, meaning "to say." Confession is agreeing with God about our sins. The portion of the definition that holds the key to remaining in *koinonia* is the expediency of "the same place or time." I have confessed and turned from sins that profoundly interrupted *koinonia*. Why? Because I waited too long to agree with God about them and turn. I still found forgiveness, but *koinonia* was broken through delay. As God taught me to walk more victoriously, I learned to respond often to the Holy Spirit's conviction at the "same place or time," thereby never leaving the circle of fellowship or the path of light. Some of us think fellowship with God can be retained only during our perfect moments.

How does 1 John 1:8, in the context of a chapter on true fellowship, refute that philosophy?

_____

You might ask, "How can a person grievously sin and still remain in fellowship?" Please understand, all sin is equal in its demand for grace, but not all sin is equal in its ramifications (see Ps. 19:13). A person who commits robbery, adultery, or vicious slander departed *koinonia* when he or she refused to agree with God over the sin involved in the thought processes leading up to the physical follow-through. Think of *koinonia* as a circle representing the place of fellowship. We don't just walk in and out of that circle every time a flash of critical thinking bolts through our minds. I don't even think we leave that circle if a sudden greedy, proud, or lustful thought goes through our minds.

If we're in *koinonia* with God, the Holy Spirit's conviction will come at that place and time and tell us those thoughts or initial reactions aren't suitable for saints of God. If we respond something like the following, we never depart *koinonia*: "Yes, Lord, You are absolutely right. That's not how I want to think. I don't want to entertain destructive thoughts. Forgive me and help me have thoughts that honor You and that don't harm me." Confession without delay not only helps keep us in *koinonia*, but it is also part of our *koinonia*!

I have had many conversations with people who can't imagine being that honest and out front with God over their thought lives. If we don't learn to get honest with God over our thought lives, we will never allow Him to teach us new ways to think. If we never develop renewed minds, consistent victory and glorious *koinonia* will tragically elude us. Dear One, God already knows! Our conviction tells us not only that He knows but also that He wants to apply His grace to the problem and correct it. By agreeing with God, we bring our thoughts or initial actions straight from our minds or mouths into the light! "But I'd rather keep them hidden in the dark. I'm too humiliated," some might say.

Agreeing with God brings our thoughts or initial actions into the light!

We're not keeping anything hidden from God. Psalm 139:11-12 tells us why. Explain in your own words.

_____

We open a door for Satan to further tempt us when we leave our sins in the dark. Ultimately, his goal is for us to heap sin upon sin. Our joy and protection are in the circle of *koinonia* light, but we can expediently respond to conviction and agree with God over our sin and still inadvertently exit the circle of *koinonia*. How? By refusing to accept and believe God's forgiveness and our fresh purification. Agreeing with God over our forgiven state is just as important as agreeing with God over our sin! If Satan can't tempt us to hide our sin and refuse to confess, he'll tempt us not to accept our forgiven and purified state. If we persist in feeling bad, we will think destructively and ultimately act it. Don't let the devil get away with that! *Koinonia* is your right in Jesus Christ! Make His joy complete.

Day 2 A LOVE LETTER

TODAY'S TREASURE
"How great is the love the Father has lavished on us, that we should be called children of God! And that is what we are!"—1 John 3:1

I can hardly type for wanting to rub my hands together and say, "Hot dog! Let's get to the love!" (Am I not scholarly?) One of the most important transitions we've seen is John's abandonment of ambition for affection. If we get any one-liner out of this Bible study, let that be it! Let's go further than the issue of ambition and abandon any number of dead works for affection. Ambition may not be your issue, although I am convinced we can possess it without realizing it. Secretly and subconsciously wanting to make a name for ourselves—while rationalizing that God can share the glory, too—is frighteningly common in the body of Christ. We either glorify God or ourselves. Never both. Somewhere along the way, John chose God alone, engaging heart, soul, mind, and strength.

The beauty of choosing to glorify God alone and to pursue a love for Him beyond all else is that every other thing of authentic value comes in the package. Remember Matthew 6:33? " 'Seek first his kingdom and his righteousness, and all these things will be given to you as well.' " One of our greatest needs is simplicity. God offers us the privilege of surrendering to the one thing that ensures everything else of great value. You can't beat that deal! We see a perfect example of this concept in John, who chose to believe and fully receive Christ's love above all else. Like Solomon, who asked for wisdom and became the wisest man in history, John prioritized love and became a flooding wellspring of affection. When God esteems our prayers, we get what we ask and far more.

I wish we had the time and space to study all five chapters of 1 John. Remember, our purpose in studying John's writings is to glean insight into the man himself and to learn what he most wanted us to know. We don't have to be scholars to quickly ascertain that John's focus in his first epistle was relationship. In our previous lesson we targeted *koinonia*. For the remainder of our focus on 1 John, we'll cut straight to the heart and study his favorite subject: love. Today we'll hear John's heartbeat on God's love *for us*. Tomorrow we'll hear from John about God's love *through us*.

> ### THE HEART OF THE BELOVED
>
> John chose to believe and fully receive Christ's love above all else. John prioritized love and became a flooding wellspring of affection.

Read the following verses from 1 John and record everything you can know and apply about God's love for you.

3:1-3 _____

3:19-22 _____

_____

4:13-18 _____

_____

I originally learned 1 John 3:1 in the *King James Version:* "Behold, what manner of love the Father hath bestowed upon us"! Keep in mind that all major Bible translations must trace back to the Greek for conceptual accuracy. By "behold" I think John was saying, "Can't you see it? Don't you perceive it? The love of God surrounds us with evidences! Just look!" The original word for *manner* speaks of "disposition, character, quality." If we asked God to help us more accurately grasp the true disposition, character, and exquisite quality of His love for us, our lives would dramatically alter! Because John chose to prioritize love, God opened his eyes to behold it and his soul to perceive it in ways others couldn't imagine. Paul discovered something similar and prayed for us to do likewise.

Read Ephesians 3:18-19. How did Paul describe God's love in these verses?

_____

Paul's prayer that we might "know this love that surpasses knowledge" thrills me. I think Paul may have been saying, "Experience a width, length, depth, and height of love that far exceeds the experience itself." In other words, experience God's love to the full measure of your capacity through the Spirit of God within you; then try to comprehend that its true measure and nature are far beyond that experience. We've had just a taste, just a glimpse. We are invited to know a love that is beyond human comprehension.

God's love for you exceeds all reason. I'm not talking about your pastor, your Bible study leaders, or anyone else you greatly admire in the church. I'm talking about *you.* "We know and rely on the love God has for us" (1 John 4:16). The word for *know* in this verse is the same one Paul used in Ephesians 3:19. We can't define God's love, but we can behold, experience, and rely on it.

We can't define God's love, but we can behold, experience, and rely on it.

Is 1 John 4:16 a reality for you? Have you come to experience and rely on God's love? His love for us is an absolute reality, but we can be so emotionally unhealthy that we refuse to experience and absorb it into our hearts and minds.

The *NIV* translates 1 John 3:19-20 powerfully: "This then is how we know that we belong to the truth, and how we set our hearts at rest in his presence whenever our hearts condemn us. For God is greater than our hearts, and he knows everything." Many people resist God because they imagine Him to be very condemning. In reality, we are more condemning and emotionally dangerous. I am intrigued by John's statement about Christ.

What is the basic thrust of John 2:24? _____

_____

I can almost imagine Christ saying to humanity, "I am perplexed with all your talk about whether or not you can trust Me. Actually, your heart can be at complete rest in My presence. My love is perfectly healthy. The greater risk is in My entrusting Myself to you." You see, our unhealthy hearts not only condemn us, but they also condemn others. I have seen marriages destroyed because one spouse refused to accept the reality of the other's love. Our hearts sometimes even condemn God as we decide for ourselves that He can't be trusted and that He doesn't love us unconditionally. Our natural hearts are very deceitful and destructive on their own. We may have a condemning heart without ever facing it.

Picture a condemned house with the sign Keep Out: This Property Condemned. Describe how you imagine the property looks.

_____

_____

Is that your heart? Is in it shambles? Beyond proper living conditions? Are broken pieces of glass scattered all over it? Has it not only been endangered but become dangerous? As most of us know, hurt people hurt people. My heart used to resemble a condemned property. Oh, I kept a fresh coat of paint over it so that no one would know, but I knew it was a wreck on the inside. I even turned the sign over on the other side and wrote: Fun Person Who Has It All Together … As Long As You Keep Your Distance and Don't Look Closely.

What might your sign have said? _____

Some of us may think our hearts aren't unhealthy because we assume they all look alike. Nothing could be further from the truth. Unhealthy hearts come in all shapes and sizes. Some are cold, others indiscriminate. Some have thick walls around them; some, no boundaries at all. Some are forthright and angry. Others are passive and self-disparaging. Some are completely detached. Others are so attached that the object smothers.

I am convinced that few people possess a virtually whole heart who have not deliberately pursued it in Christ. We don't have to be raised in severely dysfunctional homes to develop unhealthy hearts. All we have to do is expose ourselves to life. Life can be heartless and mean. Purely and simply, life hurts. However, we can't check ourselves out of life. Instead, God hopes that we'll turn to Him to heal us from the ravages of natural life and make us healthy ambassadors of abundant life in an unhealthy world. I asked you earlier what your heart is like. I hope you've had a little time to think.

> Few people possess a virtually whole heart who have not deliberately pursued it in Christ.

Between you and God, are you able to know and rely on His love? Explain.

_____

_____

Besides God, what are a few things you really rely on and why?

_____

Let me suggest two sure signs of an ailing heart: (1) You're convinced that nothing in life is reliable. Code name: Jaded. (2) You keep trying to convince yourself you can rely on something that has proved unreliable over and over again. Code name: N. Denial.

In case you have a heart like the one I had, please know that God can heal your heart, no matter what got it in such a condition. First John 3:20 tells us that God is greater than our hearts! And He knows everything! Even the thing we secretly believe makes us

God can heal your heart, no matter what got it in such a condition.

unlovable and unloving. Knowing all things, God loves us lavishly. Perfectly. Unfailingly. If He can heal my shattered, self-destructive heart, He can heal anyone's.

Perhaps you've allowed the enemy to hang a Condemned sign on your heart, and you've almost given up on authentic love. Perhaps he's even talked you into becoming a cynic. Beloved, Satan is a liar! He knows if we take this thing about God's love seriously, we might become a John or a Paul in our generation. Oh, let's glorify God, spite the devil, and do it! It's not too late. Take your pulse. If your heart is still beating, it's worth healing! Here's the catch, however: God's method of healing a condemning heart is to love it to death, then create in us a new heart. A healthier heart. A heart filled with faith instead of fear. His perfect love is the only thing that will drive out our fear.

 Deep in your heart, what are you most afraid of?

_____

_____

Fears are fillers—mind, heart, and soul fillers. Satan fuels them because they leave little space for the filling of the Holy Spirit and the welcome flood of divine love. "God hath not given us the spirit of fear; but of power, and of love, and of a sound mind" (2 Tim. 1:7, KJV).

Based on this verse, why would Satan want to do anything possible to supply us with fillers other than the Holy Spirit?

_____

_____

Satan doesn't want us to know who we could be or what we could do. Lives full of God's power, love, and soundness of mind are a terrible threat to the kingdom of hell. After all he's done to me and to so many others, I want to be a threat, don't you? Let's begin by allowing God's perfect love to start driving out our destructive fears and condemning natures like an 18-wheeler plowing through a cornfield!

Wholeness begins by deliberately and daily receiving the lavish, unreasonable, unfailing love of God all the way into our marrow. When life is too foggy to see the evidences of His love around us, behold it in His Word, Dear One! Know it until you feel it.

Day 3 LOVING THROUGH US

TODAY'S TREASURE
"If anyone says, "I love God," yet hates his brother, he is a liar. For anyone who does not love his brother, whom he has seen, cannot love God, whom he has not seen."
—1 John 4:20

I am convinced that virtually everything in an individual believer's life hinges on his or her deliberate belief and active acceptance of the lavish, unconditional love of God. I'm not sure we can be reminded too often of God's absolute priorities for our lives.

What are His priorities, according to Mark 12:28-31? _____

_____

No matter how different our personalities, gifts, styles of worship, or denominations, God's chief priority for each of us is that we love Him with everything in us. Like two chambers in one heart, the lifeblood of His first priority cannot flow apart from the second: that we love others as ourselves. What does the fulfillment of God's unparalleled priorities for us have to do with deliberately believing and actively accepting His lavish, unconditional love? Everything!

Why do we love, according to 1 John 4:19? _____

_____

One of the biggest problems many believers have in loving God and others is distrust or unwillingness to accept God's love! Everything begins there. To love God and others, we need to consider all God has said and done to prove His love through His Word and His Son. Then, we can confess the sin of unbelief and choose daily to act on what God says and does, regardless of the ebb and flow of our emotions.

> We need to consider all God has said and done to prove His love.

What do the following passages in 1 John teach about love?

3:11-15 _____

_____

3:16-22 (Don't miss the context of the verses we considered in our previous lesson on condemning hearts.)

_____

_____

4:7-12 _____

_____

4:16-21 _____

_____

5:1-5 _____

_____

Admit it. Loving is a mammoth challenge. Because He is invisible, loving God can be difficult. John the apostle said so himself under the inspiration of the Holy Spirit. Developing what Saint John of the Cross called an "answering love" requires the active participation of faith and the willingness to learn to "live by the Spirit" (Gal. 5:16), no matter how awkward the process. Based on my experience, let me assure you that God is very patient! He wants us to desire to follow Him even if the process isn't pretty. How is a person with spiritually and emotionally broken legs supposed to walk pretty? Take it from me on this one. Keep taking another step in His direction, no matter how ugly—and if you fall, fall forward and not back. Eventually and miraculously along the way, He will heal those legs. That's much of what makes loving Him so irresistible.

I don't find loving God as challenging as loving some others. I fear they'd say the same thing about me. We use "Oh, Brother!" as an expression of frustration with good reason. Our most serious challenges are usually not with circumstances. They're with people.

My younger daughter recently called from college on a rampage about someone she "just cannot stand." She is a God-seeking young woman with a fiery passion for His Word, but she agrees with most of us who feel we could serve others more successfully if others weren't so—otherly! I reminded her of a difficult challenge she had with a relationship the year before. Then I assured her that she'd have another next year—and the next. Why? Because our loving people we find difficult is important to God. Just about the time we get one challenging relationship under the Spirit's control, God supplies another.

 Without details or the least hint of dishonoring another person, have you found this principle to be true? ❑ **Yes** ❑ **No If so, estimate how many persons you've been very challenged to love in the past five years. _____**

If any of those relationships became some of your dearest, please explain.

_____

I intended to use the phrase *loving difficult people* in today's lesson, but under the Holy Spirit's direction, I changed it to *loving people we find difficult.* Just because we find some individuals difficult to love doesn't make them difficult persons. The difficult person in my challenging relationship may be me! I'll never forget when someone who had just completed *Breaking Free* told me that I was her stronghold! Another who just completed *Jesus, the One and Only* told me she could hardly stand the way I taught, but she toughed it out, received a blessing, and "likes [me] better now." Sometimes two persons just don't make an easy mix. What a perfect combination for the practice of *agape!*

That we exercise and strengthen weak muscles of otherly affection is paramount to God. It's why we're still here. So what's a believer to do with all the challenges to love people we find difficult? Forget faking it.

Romans 12:9 already blew our cover on that one. What is the first sentence

of this verse? _____

Sincerely loving others forces the issue of heart change.

You and I are called to the real thing. God knew that commanding us to love others sincerely would force the issue of heart change in those who truly desire to obey and please Him.

While loving others God places in our paths will never cease to be challenging, the key is learning to draw from God's own *agape* rather than our own small and selfish supply of natural *phileo* or fondness. *Agape* is many things we imagine as love, but two primary elements set it apart. *Agape* begins with the will. It is volitional love. In other words, the beginning of true love is the willful decision to agree with God about that person and choose to love. Also, when *agape* and *phileo* love are distinguishable, *agape* love is based on best interest, while *phileo* love is based on common interests.

Both kinds of love are biblical and are wonderful expressions in the body of Christ, but *phileo* love often originates through preference and taste as in a naturally developed friendship or sisterly relationship. Based on my limited biblical understanding, *agape* tends to be the more expensive love, because the element of sacrifice is part of its nature. God's directive to love our enemies involves *agape* (such as in Luke 6:27), which is simply harder and often requires exercising will over emotion.

The key to love is drawing from God's resource of *apape*. Love comes from God and not from our own determination (see 1 John 4:7). Our will is involved in choosing to receive and exercise God's love, not our own. Romans 5:5 displays the concept beautifully.

Love comes from God and not from our own determination.

Read Romans 5:5. How does God's love get into human hearts? _____

_____

What is the first quality of the fruit of the Spirit in Galatians 5:22?

_____

Based on these verses, how can we love others more effectively and sincerely?

_____

God's chief goal is to deepen our relationships with Him. He knows if we don't see our need for Him, we will never understand how sufficient and wonderful He is. Therefore, He challenges us to live beyond what we are naturally able. God knows that challenges such as loving someone we find difficult will prompt us to come to Him for a constant supply of His love. We have to pour out our toxic and preferential affections so that our hearts can be filled with His affections. As we ask for our cups to overflow with *agape*, the living love of God will surge through our hearts and splash on anyone nearby!

So did John practice what he preached? I thought you'd never ask! Did you hear the gush of affection in John's constant endearments?

Glance over the entire letter of 1 John. How often do you find terms of endearment for his readers, and what are they?

_____

The original word for *children* is *teknion,* meaning "a little child."[2] The seriousness of the subject matter tells you John didn't write to young children. He was an older man by this time, and his flock was as dear to him as flesh and blood. Jerome, one of the early church fathers (approximately A.D. 340–420), "tells the story that John lived to an advanced age in Ephesus. So feeble was he that only with difficulty could his Christian disciples carry him to the church building. He could hardly speak, but when he did he said the same words: 'Little children, love one another.' Eventually his disciples grew weary of hearing the same phrase, so they asked him why he always spoke it. 'It is the Lord's command,' he replied, 'and if this alone be done, it is enough.' "[3]

My favorite account from the early church fathers about John was preserved by Clement. It begins with the statement "Listen to a story which is not a story but a true tradition of John the apostle preserved in memory." While visiting a new bishop and his congregation in Smyrna, John "saw a young man of strong body, beautiful appearance, and warm heart. 'I commend this man,' [John] said, 'to you with all diligence in the face of the church, and with Christ as my witness.' " John returned to Ephesus and, as promised, the bishop took the young man under his wing and baptized him. Time passed, and the bishop "relaxed his great care and watchfulness. … But some idle and dissolute youths, familiar with evil, corrupted him in his premature freedom." Before long the young man gave himself entirely to a life of sin, committed crimes, and even renounced his salvation. Eventually, John was summoned back to Smyrna and asked for a report of the young man. Somewhat taken aback, the bishop answered, " 'He has died.' "

John inquired, " 'How and with what death?' " When the bishop described the young man's abandoned faith as death, John replied, " 'Well, … it was a fine guardian whom I left for the soul of our brother. But let me have a horse, and some one to show me the way.' " (Sounds a bit like the old Son of Thunder, doesn't it?) When the elderly John found the young man, he started to flee. John called out to him, " 'Why do you run away from me, child, your own father, unarmed and old? Pity me, child, do not fear me! You have still hope of life. I will account to Christ for you. If it must be, I will willingly suffer your death, as the Lord suffered for us; for your life, I will give my own. Stay, believe; Christ sent me.' " (These figures of speech meant that John would give his life to see the young man return to Christ. John knew better than anyone that only Christ could ransom someone's life.)

The young man wept bitterly, embraced the old man, and pled for forgiveness. The account says that John led the young man back and "baptized [him] a second time in his tears. … He brought him to the church, he prayed with many supplications, he joined with him in the struggle of continuous fasting, he worked on his mind by varied addresses and did not leave him, so they say, until he restored him to the church, and thus gave a great example of true repentance and a great testimony of regeneration, the trophy of a visible resurrection."[4]

Yes, John practiced what he preached. How many baby Christians might never leave our pews empty if we practiced what he preached?

> How many baby Christians might never leave our pews if we practiced what John preached?

Day 4 LOVE IN THE TRUTH

TODAY'S TREASURE
"The elder, to the chosen lady and her children, whom I love in the truth— and not I only, but also all who know the truth."—2 John 1:1

I'm having a really bad day. I can either lose a writing day over it or write about it. I inherited a strong work ethic from my father, Major Dad, so brace yourself. I'm having the kind of day when I may do something rash like eat nothing but sweets. I may go back and see if that woman who told me to have a nice day is still in the elevator. If she is, I'm going to push all the buttons at the same time and see if I can get her stuck between floors for a minute. Then when the door opens, I might just say something mature like, "Same to you and more of it!" This day takes my husband by surprise every year. He's not accustomed to my beginning a day bawling out loud. Then when he says, "Please don't cry," I reply (loudly), "I'll cry if I want to. And I want to!" He even called to check on me when he was halfway to work. He knows I'll be OK. This happens every year. I don't plan it. It just happens. I have a bad case of anniversary grief.

The silly thing is, the day isn't the anniversary of anything tragic. It was one of the sweetest days of my whole life: the day our son of seven years came to live with us. The calendar day is of importance only to Keith and me. And God. He knows. My head was so full of dreams that night. I had never seen a more beautiful little boy. He looked so much like Keith—only tiny, almost fragile. He played with Keith's plastic fishing worms while I planned his whole future in my head. He would be my man-child. The one I always wanted. One day his wife would say, "I hope he loves me someday as much as he loves you." And I would think, *He won't. Not really.*

I just feel fussy today. I really like the song "Trading My Sorrows," but I have absolutely no intention of trading them today. For now this pain in my heart is all I have left. Although I'm aware of the loss every day, I rarely give it permission to shift to the gear of full-throttled pain. Today's the day. So for now, it's my party, and I'll cry if I want to.

For reasons known to God, the dreams spun in my head that night were not to be. The whole situation has been difficult to understand and impossible to explain. God, however, has gone out of His way to clearly state that we are not to interfere. We were on temporary assignment. He will let us know if and when He has further need for us. Period.

Every other day of the year I can look at my life through a telescope and sit in utter amazement. God has fulfilled dreams I couldn't have had sense enough to dream. He has done the unimaginable. He delivered me from a life of recycling defeat and deeply embedded bitterness. He saved my marriage. Had anyone told me 25 years ago that I'd still be wild about my husband a quarter century later and have two young-adult daughters who are crazy about Jesus, I might have thought they were dreaming. Not to mention God's scandalous love to allow such a former pit-dweller like me to serve someone like you. Oh, He has been indescribably gracious to me … just as He has to you. On difficult days we just need to pull back the lens a touch and look at the wider picture.

From a wider lens on your life, what do you see? _____

_____

But on those microscope days when we determine to slap the most upsetting thing we can think about on a slide and stare at it for hours, we throw a pity party and resent any loved one who refuses to come.

What do you tend to focus on during a microscope day? _____

_____

Let me warn you, Satan rarely refuses to attend a good pity party. I appreciate the way David exposed the opportunism of an enemy. Of God David wrote, "He rescued me from my powerful enemy, from my foes, who were too strong for me. They confronted me in the day of my disaster, but the Lord was my support" (Ps. 18:17-18). Don't think for a moment that Satan won't confront you on the day of your disaster—whatever that may be. Sometimes we give him credit for having a heart and respecting when something should be off limits. After all, fair fighters don't hit a person when she's down.

Satan doesn't fight fair. He confronts us on our worst days and approaches us with his specialty: lies. You can't imagine the lies he tries to tell me on my microscope day. Lies like "You didn't love him enough. You failed him. You failed God. If you had just tried this … or that. If you had waited a little longer." Other times he tries a different approach: "Never take that kind of risk again. Taking someone into your heart like that isn't worth

Don't think that Satan won't confront you on the day of your disaster.

it. You will always get hurt. Love will fail you. Here's your old hammer, and I even saved the nails. Rebuild that fortress around your heart. Don't let anybody hurt you again."

Just about the time I want to default back to my old coldness, the Spirit of God within me whispers warm breath on my cooling heart: "My little child, love comes from God. Whoever does not love does not know God, because God is love."

Be still, my soul. Set your heart at rest in His presence. Don't let your heart condemn you. God is greater than your heart, and He knows everything.

> Don't let your heart condemn you. God is greater than your heart.

Read 2 John. Let's stay with our microscope a moment. My favorite words in this letter are "love in the truth" (v. 1). What do you think those words mean?

_____

We've talked about the paramount importance of truth and found biblical evidence to support the phrase "Truth breeds trust." We considered that trust is often developed more deeply through truth than love. We discussed that many of us have been loved by unhealthy people who proved deceptive, leaving us injured and confused. Incidentally, if we didn't let God heal us, we likely became one of them. Unhealthiness is contagious; deceived people deceive people. Truth sets us free. God, the great I Am, is the totality of wholeness, completeness, and self-existence. He is truth and love! While Satan approaches us with hate and lies, we can be loved in the truth by God and those His Spirit fills. God will tell us only truth; one of His chief truths is that loving is always worth doing.

I feel much better now. Sometimes I just have to talk it out. I'm ready to put up my microscope and go back to my bifocals, because 2 John has a few other things to say. I love trying to figure out a good mystery, and this small piece suggests a marvelous one.

Who is the recipient of John's second letter? _____

Scholars admit that 2 John may have been written to an actual woman and her children. Many, however, believe that the address was more likely metaphoric to hide the identity of New Testament believers in a time of fierce persecution. If the letter fell into the wrong hands, no one could be singled out. The letter may well have been written to a church.

Read Ephesians 5:25-27. What do these verses describe? _____

_____

What metaphorical gender does the Word give the church in these verses?

_____

John's reference to "the chosen lady" (2 John 2:1) could certainly have spiritual implications. How does 1 Peter 2:9 refer to believers in Christ?

_____

Look again at the greeting in 2 John 1:1. A hint could be John's proclamation of love for "the chosen lady and her children, ... and not I only, but also all who know the truth." What individual would be loved by "all who know the truth"? Yet all who know the truth love the church (corporate body) and "her" children (individual believers). John's reference to "we" in 2 John 1:5 may suggest another hint. In exhorting us to love one another, he wrote, "I am not writing you a new command but one we have had from the beginning." Don't miss that he doesn't mention the father. Individually, these suggestions may not strongly support "the chosen lady" as the church, but considered together, I lean toward the idea.

After calling the chosen lady and her children to walk in love, what warning did John give them?

_____

No sooner was truth revealed than Satan popped onto the warpath with lies. Deception is his specialty, and his goal is to get us to believe the lies. They can't be blatant, or we'd recognize them. Notice nothing is said about these false teachers refuting all Christian doctrine. Some of the false teachers did not refute that Jesus was divine. They simply said He wasn't man as well as God. John focused on this false teaching in his first letter.

Read 1 John 4:1-3. Why is the issue of Christ coming in the flesh so vital?

_____

Carefully read Hebrews 10:19-20. Exactly how have we gained access to the most holy place, meaning the very presence of God?

_____

Satan always tries to undermine the issue of salvation. Think about this with me.

God created humans in His image. John 4:24 says, " 'God is _____.' "

We were created in three parts: body, soul, and spirit. I believe the spirit part of us is created most in God's image. Then what is the soul? When distinguished from spirit, the soul or psyche constitutes who we are immaterially but naturally—our personalities, emotions, and the ways we think. The spirit—when distinguished in Scripture from the soul—is the part of each human being that has the capacity to know and have a relationship with God. Our Maker literally equipped us with an inner longing to find Him.

> Our Maker literally equipped us with an inner longing to find Him.

What does 1 Corinthians 6:17 say? _____

_____

When we receive Jesus as Savior, our spirit (the part of us with the capacity to know God) unites with the Holy Spirit, and they become one. Because I believe in Christ, when I refer to the spirit within me, I am talking about the Holy Spirit. Satan does all he can to keep us lost and blinded to truth. He knows we are created with a longing for God that we often confuse with a longing for spiritual things. The good news of Jesus Christ was running rampant over the Middle East in John's day. Jesus was a hot topic of conversation. Satan couldn't squelch spiritual hunger or stop the talk about Christ, so he supplied a story that used both. He suggested through false teachers that Christ came—but not in the flesh. Therefore, the spiritually hungry could still have a belief system involving God but remain, as my relatives would say, as lost as a goose. Why? Our access to God is through Jesus Christ's torn flesh. To deny His incarnation is to deny our only means of salvation. You may know someone who is spiritual but who doesn't believe in Christ's incarnate death and resurrection as the means to salvation.

If so, without labeling the belief system, briefly describe it. _____

_____

Satan tries to feed our need for the spiritual yet keep us blind to the truth.

Satan tries to feed people's need for the spiritual yet keep them blind to the truth. Clever and terribly destructive, isn't he? Don't judge them. Pray for them! Pray for the veil to be removed and the torn veil of Jesus' flesh to be made clear! Pray for those who teach such false doctrines. John warned "the chosen lady" not to take any such teacher into her house. In those days most gatherings of believers met in homes. Though John's directive is certainly important for any individual believer, you can imagine how vital it is for an entire church gathering. Traveling teachers were common. I think John was saying, "Don't consider giving anyone who teaches such false doctrine freedom to speak in your gatherings!"

Recently I spoke in a denominational church I rarely have the privilege to serve. The pastor stood in the back of the sanctuary and listened to every word I taught. Someone asked if I were bothered by his presence. I assured them I had nothing but respect for a pastor who watched over his flock so carefully. I was also quite relieved when I passed his test!

Pastors aren't just shepherds of the men of the church; yet I have met pastors who are totally unconcerned about what their women study or to whom they listen. Some think we all just sip tea and talk girl talk. I find myself thinking, *Mister, with all due respect, if your women catch a fire of false doctrine, they can burn down your whole church!* Watch who you take into your house! Watch me, for heaven's sake! Watch all of us! Many would never knowingly teach deception or distortion, but we are all dreadfully human.

In his second letter John certainly said volumes in so few words. If only I could do the same. One of the things I like best about John is his balance. "Love one another"! And while you're at it, "Test the spirits"! Now, that's a fine teacher.

Day 5 BODY AND SOUL

TODAY'S TREASURE
"Dear friend, I pray that you may enjoy good health and that all may go well with you, even as your soul is getting along well."—3 John 1:2

Today we will conclude our brief look at John's letters. While you and I may still have much we'd like to explore in these rich epistles, we've peeked further into the heart of the apostle John and centered on the elements he most wanted us to explore: *koinonia*, love, and truth. I enjoyed the mysterious elements involved in trying to identify "the chosen lady and her children" in our previous letter. In contrast, John's third letter leaves no doubt that he addressed a specific individual. In fact, John drops several names in this one-chapter letter.

Read 3 John. List each person identified and write a brief description.

_____

_____

_____

Imagine being named in a letter that turned out to be inspired Scripture for all the world to see! Whether in commendation or criticism, having your name immortalized in Scripture is a heavy thought! When I see a portion of Scripture with brief testimonials similar to the segment we're studying today, I almost shiver.

Write what you think a one-sentence description of your life would say. Then describe what you would want it to say.

_____

_____

_____

At times I would have been anywhere from devastated to humiliated over what might have been written in my life's theoretical one-sentence statement. I love knowing that as long as we're kicking and breathing, we can change the course of our testimonies. God hasn't put a period at the end of our sentences yet, but that tiny little dot doesn't take long to jot. We may think we're only midsentence when we're not. Attending as many funerals as I do is a constant reminder to me. Let's not put off working toward what we hope God's testimonial for our lives will state. As the writer of Hebrews said, " 'Today, if you hear his voice, do not harden your hearts as you did in the rebellion' " (3:15).

I love the insight we're gaining into John's lifestyle and practices today. We're getting to see him engaged with people—which I believe was his specialty. As we determined yesterday, nothing is more refreshing than Christian leaders' practicing what they preach. Obviously, you can see that John also had people in his life who were difficult to love. Poor Diotrephes. You'd think with a name like that, he wouldn't have wanted to be first. Can you imagine such a one-sentence testimonial? "Beth loved to be first and didn't like to have anything to do with the common folks." The very idea makes the hair on my neck stand up!

Notice that John didn't say the man was lost. He was obviously a member of the church. Though his actions weren't loving, he could easily have been a Christian. If gossip and divisiveness were unquestionable signs of lostness, the few folks that go to heaven would probably have considerable elbow room. Thank goodness we won't have hard feelings and conflict in glory. Otherwise, I could almost imagine Diotrephes saying to John, "Did you have to go and write it down? Why couldn't you have just gossiped as I did?"

Gaius, on the other hand, was obviously easy for John to love. The original word translated my dear friend is _agapetos,_ meaning beloved. Gaius wasn't only John's dear friend. He was John's dearly loved friend. The Gaius to whom John's third letter is addressed could very likely have been the one by the same name mentioned several other times in Scripture.

As long as we're kicking and breathing, we can change the course of our testimonies.

153

Read the verses referenced below and note what you learn about Gaius.

Acts 19:28-31 (Check the context of this passage, and note the city where this uproar occurred.)

_____

Acts 20:4-5_____

_____

1 Corinthians 1:13-15 _____

_____

The fact that Paul's Gaius and John's Gaius can both be traced to ministries in and around Ephesus suggests it could be the same individual. If so, I love to imagine the conversations that took place between them. John was old. Gaius couldn't have been young. Paul had been in the presence of his beloved captor for years. Don't you know that John and Gaius had a big time talking about the great apostle? What a character he was! Surely John and Gaius laughed their heads off about him. (Sorry about the head joke, Paul. But it all turned out well, didn't it?)

You'll laugh when I tell you I'm sitting here with a lump in my throat. You see, I love these guys! I've spent months getting to know Paul and now John from the pages of Scripture. They were real men with real relationships. They agreed and disagreed just as we do. Imagine all of them knowing, loving, appreciating, and getting aggravated with one another. The stuff of real life. Every time Jesus Christ touches the hard hearts of human beings, a divine drop of rain hits the carnal sod of earth, and it is refreshed.

Refreshed. What a wonderful word! It just happens to be a word I'd like to target for the remainder of our lesson. I hope you didn't miss John's desire for Gaius to be as healthy in body as he was in soul. The _Amplified Bible_ writes, "Beloved, I pray that you may prosper in every way and [that your body] may keep well, even as [I know] your soul keeps well and prospers" (3 John 1:2).

The Spirit of God dwelling in each redeemed person is linked to our physical bodies.

My Beloved, you and I need to do what we can to watch after our health! Certainly, our spiritual health is paramount, but while we're on this earth, the Spirit of God dwelling in each redeemed person is linked to our physical bodies. In our previous lesson we talked about God creating us as one entity made up of three parts.

What are the three parts? _____, _____, _____

Read 1 Thessalonians 5:23. Most believers instinctively know that the health of their souls and spirits is vitally important, but notice Paul's plea that we would allow God to sanctify us through and through, meaning our entire soul, spirit, and body. (You may wonder why the heart isn't mentioned, but in this context the soul encompasses everything immaterial in a person apart from the spirit. The emotions and the will fall under the category of soul in this verse.)

God has taught me serious lessons about the impact my physical body has on both my soul and my spirit. Think about the soul for a moment. If my body is completely exhausted, my soul is deeply affected. Over time it can absorb physical weariness and translate it into depression or feelings of hopelessness. If we eat poorly, we can fuel untold anxiety and fear. Most of us know that stress is linked to heart problems, high blood pressure, and many digestive problems. As long as our souls and spirits are imprisoned in these physical bodies, they are greatly affected by their condition.

You and I live stressful lives. I've heard many of your testimonies, and I am astounded at some of your challenges. Some of you work all day and then tend a sick loved one all night. Others of you hold down several jobs as you try to keep your children in college. I often hear from young mothers who have three or four children under five years old. Now that's stress! I can't even imagine some of your challenges. I never dreamed I would have the challenges I face today. I am so grateful and humbled by God's present calling on my life to minister to women, but I will not kid you. It is work! Yes, God does most of it all by Himself, but the little He requires from me is everything I've got!

In your own words, how does Paul describe the division of labor between a believer and God in Colossians 1:29?

_____

_____

My dear collaborator, you and I can't effectively fulfill our callings if we don't watch after our health. Our bodies are temples of the Holy Spirit. Each of us faces a life beyond our natural capabilities. My calendar is overwhelming, and I take each scheduled date very seriously. If I end up with a virus and can't make a conference scheduled a year earlier, I am devastated. If I'm going to be faithful to you, I've got to cooperate with God and do my part. I take a handful of vitamins every day and then pray to stay well. When I get sick, I know either my schedule is out of control again, Satan is on the warpath, or God is checking me out of the loop for a while. All of us deal with illness, but I think God's expectation is for us to do everything reasonable to avoid poor health. Meanwhile, we've got to keep our heads on straight about our motivation. Satan simply wants us in bondage. He loves the bondage of poor health, but he also delights in the yoke of excessive, compulsive fretting over the physical body. Ecclesiates' directive to avoid all extremes speaks volumes to me about this subject (see Eccl. 7:18).

Note what each of the following verses suggests about practices that tremendously influence our physical health.

Psalm 127:2 _____

Matthew 11:28 _____

Mark 6:30-32 _____

Beloved, I am convinced that one of our most serious needs is pure rest. Not only sleep but refreshment and recreation. Recently, God spoke to me about capturing what He and I are calling Sabbath moments. Like many of yours, my schedule right now is particularly tough, and I see no time in the near future for a number of days off. God spoke to my heart one Saturday morning while I was preparing for Sunday School: "My child, in between more intense rests, I want to teach you to take Sabbath moments." I wasn't certain what He meant. Just that morning God confirmed His desire for me to drive all the way to the other side of Houston to the Medical Center to visit a patient with brain

One of our most serious needs is pure rest.

cancer. I was very thankful for the privilege of visiting this patient, but I knew in advance it would be tough emotionally and far from restful.

I fought the traffic across Houston and visited with my new friend and her husband while choking back the tears. They have two young sons, and unless God performs a miracle, their mother will go home to be with the Lord before they are grown. I got in my car and prayed. I pulled out of the parking garage, fighting the tears. A few blocks later, as if on autopilot, I turned my steering wheel straight into the parking lot of the Houston Zoo! Christ seemed to say, "Let's go play!" And that we did. I hadn't been to the zoo in years. I heard about all the improvements, but I never expected the ultimate: Starbucks Coffee! (OK, so I don't have all my health issues down pat.) Can you imagine watching a baby koala take a nap in a tree on a rare cold day in Houston with a Starbuck's grande cappuccino in your hand? Now that's a Sabbath moment! God and I had a blast.

A few weeks later I kidnapped my hard-working staff for a few hours to go play a practical joke on another staff member who was running an errand. We hid in the store and had her paged to our department where we—grown Christian women—were hiding in the clothes rounders. We rolled all over the carpet with laughter at the look on her face. After we made complete fools of ourselves, one of the sales ladies walked up to me and said, "Don't I know you from somewhere?" We went to pieces. And then we went back to work … the better for it, I might add.

Sabbath moments! We live in a hard world. If you have guts enough not to disconnect and hide from the overwhelming needs out there, you need some Sabbath moments to help you keep your head on straight. Start taking them!

> You need some Sabbath moments to help you keep your head on straight.

"Beloved, I wish above all things that thou mayest prosper and be in health, even as thy soul prospereth" (3 John 1:2 KJV).

Concludest with thine own example of a Sabbath moment thou hast taken. If thou canst not remember one, get thy rest-rebellious self out of thy workplace before thou collapseth.

_____

_____

[1] Spiros Zodhiates, Warren Baker, and David Kemp, *The Hebrew-Greek Key Study Bible* (Chattanooga, TN: AMG Publishers, 1996), 1437.
[2] Spiros Zodhiates, "Lexical Aids to the New Testament," 5448, in Zodhiates, Baker, and Kemp, *Hebrew-Greek Key Study Bible*, 1677.
[3] "John: A Last Word on Love," *Biblical Illustrator*, summer 1976, 26.
[4] R. Alan Culpepper, *John, the Son of Zebedee: The Life of a Legend* (Minneapolis: First Fortress Press, 2000), 142–43.

VIDEO RESPONSE SHEET

Group Session 7

Our journey with the apostle John will take us now over the waters of the Aegean Sea to a small island called Patmos. In week 8, day 1 we will look more closely at John's arrival and the introduction to the Book of Revelation. Today, however, we're going to consider to the best of our understanding the vision of Christ that John recorded in **Revelation 1:9-18.**

While we understand that John received a one-time-only vision of Christ, I believe we can draw some important parallels about becoming the kind of people to whom Christ can reveal Himself.

1. Though a prisoner in exile, John remained spiritually _____ and _____.

   Revelation 1:10, "On the _____ _____ I was in _____ _____."

2. John was faithful with what he "_____," and God invited him to "_____" (Rev 1:10,12).

   The original word for *hear* often used in Scripture is *akouo,* meaning "not only to hear but to

   _____ and _____."

3. John came to the startling realization that the immortal Christ _____

   _____ he could have _____ his _____ to imagine (v. 17).

4. John encountered the _____ _____ wrapped in the complete

   unfamiliarity of _____ "_____-_____" (v. 17).

5. Conspicuously _____ in the record of John's staggering encounter with the

   immortal Christ is a _____ _____ from the _____ _____ (Eccl. 5:1-2).

AMONG THE LAMPSTANDS

Day 1
Banished to Patmos

Day 2
The Church in Ephesus

Day 3
The Church in Smyrna

Day 4
The Church in Pergamum

Day 5
The Church in Thyatira

This week we take a turn with the apostle John that he couldn't have expected. We can be quite sure he never sketched Patmos on his personal itinerary. Surely the old man was horrified as he was shipped like a criminal from his loved ones in Ephesus to a remote, unfriendly island in the Aegean Sea. He had no idea what awaited him. God's ways are so peculiar at times. The greatest privilege of John's life waited for him in the gravest circumstances. Have you ever noticed how Christ suddenly seems to reveal Himself to us in the places that seem most remote? Our brief overview of the study of Revelation will remind us afresh that Jesus will never send us anywhere He will not meet us.

Principle Questions

Day 1: What does Jeremiah 32:17 say about God?

Day 2: What does Christ pinpoint about Himself to the church in Ephesus in Revelation 2:1? What is the corresponding verse in the Revelation 1 vision?

Day 3: According to 1 Peter 1:6-9, how are believers able to be faithful in suffering?

Day 4: Based on Hosea 11:3-4, what does God say about healing?

Day 5: What was the promise, and to whom would it come (see Rev. 2:26-28)?

Day 1 BANISHED TO PATMOS

TODAY'S TREASURE

"I, John, your brother and companion in the suffering and kingdom and patient endurance that are ours in Jesus, was on the island of Patmos because of the word of God and the testimony of Jesus."—Revelation 1:9

The rest of our journey will be both sobering and elating. We will join John in exile on the island of Patmos (PAT-muhs) in the Aegean Sea. Don't bother packing a swimsuit. This irregularly shaped island that will fit in a 6 by 10-mile rectangle is not exactly paradise. In John's day its rocky, barren terrain attracted the eye of the Romans as a perfect place to banish criminals. Under the rule of the Roman emperor Domitian (A.D. 81–96), Christianity was a criminal offense, and John was fiercely guilty.

We don't know the exact reason for John's confinement on the island. The only absolutes we have are those explained by John himself in Revelation 1:9.

What do you think John meant by the reasons he gave for being on Patmos?

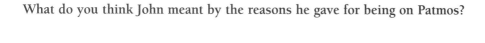

_____

_____

I am curious why John, an undeniable Son of Thunder, was exiled rather than killed like the other apostles. Scholars agree that we can safely assume he was harshly treated, even at his age, and was forced into hard labor in the mines and quarries on the island. I still wonder why the Romans bothered, since they publicly and inhumanely took the lives of so many other Christians. Ultimately, God wasn't finished with John's work on earth, and no one was taking him without his Father's permission. I wonder whether the stories from the early church fathers are true that the Romans tried to kill him but couldn't.

John may have journeyed to Rome for at least a brief stay. Tertullian, often called the "father of Latin theology," lived during the generation closely following that of the apostles (A.D. 150–225).[1] Tertullian wrote a work called *On Prescription Against Heretics* that included a stunning claim about the apostle John. He wrote that "the apostles poured forth all their doctrine along with their blood!" He said that "the apostle John was first plunged, unhurt, into boiling oil, and thence remitted to his island exile!"[2]

Few scholars question the reliability of Tertullian's word about Peter's death on a cross. Yes, Peter endured a passion like his Lord's; yet because he felt unworthy to die in exactly the same manner, early tradition holds that Peter requested to be crucified upside down. Likewise, I've never read a commentary that cited a reason to question the traditional information that Paul was beheaded like John the Baptist. Therefore, we are left to wonder whether Tertullian's account about John the apostle was simply fiction. I certainly don't know whether the account about John's plunge into boiling oil is reliable, but if you ask me whether I think such an event is possible, I could only answer yes! In Acts 12 God wasn't ready for Peter's work on earth to end, so He loosed his chains and caused him to walk right out of the prison where 16 soldiers had been left on guard. I can't even count the times the apostle Paul narrowly escaped death. Beloved, don't let the modern church make you cynical. Ours is a God of wonders, and don't you forget it!

God wasn't finished with John's work on earth.

159

What does Jeremiah 32:17 say about God? _____

_____

If Tertullian's account has any accuracy, the Romans may have tried to take John's life and, in their foiled efforts, banished him to exile on Patmos. His charge may have been failing to die when told. Though a number of chronological orders are proposed for John's stays outside Jerusalem and Judea, I lean toward the following:

- John first lived and ministered in Ephesus. At some point he made a trip to Rome, where he encountered persecution.
- Then John was banished to Patmos, where most scholars believe he remained for about 18 months. Though I used to believe differently, I am now most convinced by the commentators and early teachers who say that John returned to Ephesus, where he stayed until he died.

With these thoughts in mind in pencil rather than permanent marker, let's read our introduction to the mysterious and wonderful Book of Revelation. Keep in mind that our approach to the last book of the Bible will be general and not primarily with an attempt to explain Last Things. The goals we established from the beginning will carry us all the way to the end. We will search Revelation for insight into the apostle John himself and for the facts and concepts he most wanted us to know.

Please read Revelation 1:1-10. The Book of Revelation is unique in its inspired promise of blessing (see v. 3). To whom will blessing come?

_____

_____

> The most profound revelation in Revelation is that of Jesus Christ Himself.

Even though our approach to the Book of Revelation will not include verse-by-verse exposition, I believe we can expect a measure of blessing as a direct result of our study. I'm going to be looking for mine, and I hope you will look for yours, too. The most profound revelation in Revelation is that of Jesus Christ Himself, not only in visions but also in authority.

List every title or description of Jesus Christ in verses 4-8.

_____

_____

The word _revelation_ (from the Greek word _apokalupsis_) means _unveiling_. Thrown on a boat transferring criminals, John had no idea what God would unveil to him on the island of Patmos. Imagine John's frail, aging frame as he held on tightly while the sea vessel tossed its long way across the Aegean. He probably pushed his gray hair out of his face to look at the few other prisoners sharing his destination. Don't picture a bonding experience. No one would likely carry him through a small group of worshipers while he said, "Dear children, love one another." Exile was intended not only for overwork and overexposure to elements but also for crazing isolation. The tactic was wasted on John, just as it can be wasted on us when Satan tries to force us into isolation.

John most likely would have preferred death. His long life may have frustrated him. If forced to remain on earth, exile from ministry and isolation from those he loved was certainly not the way he intended to spend his senior years. I can imagine that in the labors forced on him, John slipped on the jagged, rocky surfaces and ripped his thinning skin like paper. He had no bedding for his aching body at the end of a day. I also cannot imagine him thinking, *Finally! A little peace and quiet for writing a new book!* John couldn't have expected to meet Jesus on that island the way he did. Beloved One, how many testimonies do we need to hear before we accept that sometimes the places and seasons in which we expect Him least, we find Him most? And oddly, sometimes the places we expect Him most, we find Him least.

> Sometimes the places and seasons in which we expect Him least, we find Him most.

If you agree, why do you think this paradox is true? _____

_____

When was the last time one or the other of those scenarios proved true to you personally?

_____

Revelation 1:7 says, "Look, he is coming with the clouds, and every eye will see him." Christ described this event in Matthew 24:26-30,36. What else do these verses tell about His return?

_____

Indeed, when Christ returns to this groaning soil in His glorious splendor, every eye will see Him. Until then, He sometimes comes with clouds. The concept isn't original. I pondered it because Oswald Chambers did, and I will share his thoughts momentarily. However, the concept didn't originate with him, either.

What does each of the following tell you about the Lord and clouds?

Exodus 16:10 _____

Exodus 24:15-16 _____

Leviticus 16:2 _____

1 Kings 8:10 _____

Luke 9:34 _____

God's glory is so inconceivably brilliant to the human eye that He often shrouds His presence in a cloud. One day the clouds will roll back like a scroll, and He will stand before us revealed. He has much to disclose to us in the meantime, and we'll be greatly helped when we accept that clouds are not signs of His absence. Indeed, within them we most often find His presence.

In the July 29 entry of *My Utmost for His Highest* Oswald Chambers wrote figuratively of clouds, "In the Bible clouds are always connected with God. Clouds are those sorrows or sufferings or providences, within or without our personal lives, which seem to dispute the rule of God. It is by those very clouds that the Spirit of God is teaching us how to walk by faith. If there were no clouds, we should have no faith. 'The clouds are but the dust of our

Father's feet' (see Nahum 1:3). The clouds are a sign that He is there. ... Through every cloud He brings, He wants us to *unlearn* something. His purpose in the cloud is to simplify our belief until our relationship to Him is exactly that of a child—God and my own soul, other people are shadows. ... Unless we can look the darkest, blackest fact full in the face without damaging God's character, we do not yet know Him."[3]

Is your life covered in dark clouds? Or perhaps the clouds aren't dark. They simply obscure clarity and tempt you to be confused by your circumstances.

 What kinds of clouds—if any—are in your life? _____

_____

THE HEART OF THE BELOVED

Would John the Beloved love Christ all the more and seek Him with his whole heart amid the rock and wasteland? His answer rises like a fresh morning tide lapping the jagged shore: "On the Lord's Day I was in the Spirit."

I've been on Patmos, and the clouds that settled on the island obscured what might otherwise have been a beautiful view. I wonder whether clouds covered the island as Domitian thought he left John at its mercy. I wonder how the old apostle viewed his circumstances. I wonder whether he ever imagined getting off that island. Or what he'd see while he was there.

John had a critical decision to make while exiled on the unkind island. Would he at least relax his walk with God and at most resist? After all, no one from his church or ministry was watching. Would he lie down and die? Goodness knows he was weary. Or would John the Beloved love Christ all the more and seek Him with his whole heart amid the rock and wasteland? His answer rises like a fresh morning tide lapping the jagged shore: "On the Lord's Day I was in the Spirit" (Rev. 1:10). And there He was: the Alpha and Omega. The first and last Word on every life. Every trial. Every exile.

When darkness seems to hide His face, I rest on His unchanging grace;
In every high and stormy gale, my anchor holds within the veil.
On Christ, the solid Rock, I stand; all other ground is sinking sand.[4]

Day 2 THE CHURCH IN EPHESUS

TODAY'S TREASURE
" 'I hold this against you: You have forsaken your first love.' "—Revelation 2:4

Our task in our brief three-week overview of the Book of Revelation is to gain further insight into the apostle John and to draw out truths he wanted us to know. In every book or letter he wrote, John was most adamant that we know Jesus Christ Himself. Let's pour a proper foundation before we build on it with today's subject matter. Please refresh your mind with the vision of Christ that John received.

Read Revelation 1:11-20. To whom was the message to be sent?

_____

_____

To the chagrin of many, most of the proposed symbolism in Revelation is beyond our attempts at dogmatic interpretation. However, Christ does identify certain characters and events in the book.

How did Christ identify the seven stars and the seven lampstands?

Scholars are divided over the exact interpretation of the angels of the seven churches. Many believe they are literal celestial beings assigned to each church. Since the basic meaning of the word is *messenger,* however, others think that the messenger is a man, perhaps the pastor or overseer at each church. Thankfully, the message is the same no matter who Christ appointed as the messenger. We will focus much of our time in Revelation on the messages to the seven churches. The fact that God included the communication in Holy Writ tells us they have something to say to us. In fact, Christ Himself pointed out their relevance to others as He drew all seven letters to a close with a broad invitation.

Christ's invitation is first recorded Revelation 2:7. Whom does Christ invite to hear?

Now feel the side of your head. Do you feel an ear? You need only one. "He who has an ear." If you have one, Jesus would like you to hear what the Spirit says to the churches. I have one, too, so I'm in with you. The reason is obvious. You and I are people of His church today, and we have much to learn from the successes, failures, victories, and defeats of the early churches. The generations may be far removed, but basic human nature and the concepts of Scripture remain consistent.

Actually, Christ had more in mind than talking to people who had at least one physical ear. I certainly had ears throughout my young years, but I'm not sure how well I used them to listen to God. For the most part, my ears were important hair accessories. "Will I put my hair behind both my ears today? One ear? Or shall I let my hair hang over both ears?" I was so deep.

The messages to the seven churches are for people with a little more depth than that. Christ's broad invitation was more like this: "What I've said to them will speak volumes to anyone who really wants to hear and respond."

The future portions of Revelation are going to occur just as God wills, according to His kingdom calendar. Our thorough study may increase our knowledge and understanding of future events, but their personal application in our daily lives is a little more challenging. On the other hand, Christ's messages to the seven churches can be applied by the Holy Spirit to change us and to affect the condition of Christ's church today. So let's each grab an ear and hear! We will study the first message today and each of the remaining messages in the next six days of study.

Please read Revelation 2:1-7. The letters have several repeated components that I want you to identify from the very beginning. I'll ask you to pinpoint these where they appear in each letter. (An asterisk [*] will mark the components that don't appear in all seven letters.) In His messages to the churches ...

Christ identified Himself in a specific way that corresponds to an element of John's first vision in Revelation 1:12-18. The fact that each letter contains a different description of Christ may further imply that the hearer who applies himself to only a few of

The Holy Spirit can apply Christ's messages to change us and to affect the condition of Christ's church today.

them may receive an incomplete message. I believe God has something very important to say through all seven letters.

What does Christ identify about Himself to the church in Ephesus in Revelation 2:1? What is the corresponding verse in the Revelation 1 vision?

_____

_____

As Christ walked among the first-century churches, He walks among our churches.

Christ issued a commendation* based on intimate acquaintance. Although not every letter contains a commendation, all seven include the phrase " 'I know your ...' " I practically shudder every time my eyes settle on the Scripture that tells us that Christ " 'walks among the seven golden lampstands' " (Rev. 2:1). We already know they are the seven churches. The verb tense suggests a continuous action. I believe that as surely as Christ walked among the first-century churches and knew them intimately, He walks among our churches today. We would be tragically amiss to think Christ is uninvolved and unmoved by the conditions, activities, and inner workings of His present churches. He walks among us. Nothing is more important to Christ in any generation than the health of His church because through it He intends to reach the lost and minister to the hurting.

Based on His intimate knowledge of the church of Ephesus, what commendations did Christ issue (see vv. 2-3)?

_____

_____

Also based on His intimate knowledge, *Christ issued a rebuke.**

What is His rebuke to the church in Ephesus? _____

_____

John was most involved in the church in Ephesus. Knowing what we've learned about him, how do you think he felt when he heard this rebuke?

_____

Christ issued an exhortation.

Christ instructed each church to do something specific. What did Christ exhort the church in Ephesus to do (see v. 5)?

_____

Last, *Christ issued an encouragement to overcome.* Celebrate the fact that no condition was utterly irreversible! In each case the church (made up of individual believers) was invited to overcome, but we must also be aware that time was of the essence!

Read Revelation 2:5. Christ told the church in Ephesus that if it did not repent and " 'do the things' " it " 'did at first,' " He would come to them and

_____

That doesn't mean they would lose their place in heaven. We lose our lampstand when we lose our godly influence on earth. In other words, we lose our light in the world. Keep in mind that a church is no stronger than its people. A church is the people of God, not brick and mortar. God confronted a church I was in that had sins of division and cynicism. Though individuals repented and did not lose the light of godly influence, the church as a whole refused to go face to the ground, as I call it, in corporate repentance. For an excruciating time, we completely lost our viable influence in the community. The church's sins were serious but not hopeless! Nor are ours! Let's repent so that we can overcome!

> We lose our lampstand when we lose our godly influence on earth.

What was Christ's message to the overcomers in the church in Ephesus?

_____

Notice that the church in Ephesus received tremendously noble commendations from Christ and yet somehow let go of the most important thing of all: her sacred romance with Jesus Christ. We spent much of week 7 discussing the priority of love. Beloved One, you and I can work hard, persevere through extreme difficulty, refuse to tolerate wicked people, and accurately discern false teachers—yet still forsake our first love.

Ironically, many believers don't view an absence of fiery, first love for Jesus Christ as sin. They view it simply as something they lack. This misunderstanding may be part of the holdup. If God's absolute priority for all followers of Christ is love—for Him first and others second—then the absence of such love is sin. I don't pound this point to condemn. Remember, it's not an irreversible condition! I pound the point so that we can do what we must do to get on to the business of loving! God says, "Repent!" _Repent_ means _turn_. I believe God told them and is telling us to turn from whatever we have given a higher priority than our sacred romance with Christ. He tells us to pour our lives back into the first things.

Keep in mind that with the first things rightly established, all other things of value come to us as well. The church in Ephesus very likely allowed spiritual busyness and stalwart religiosity to displace love. Because everything else hinges on the laws of love (see Matt. 22:40), over time all things of eternal value would have crumbled in Ephesus. Christ exhorted them to go back to the first priority of love so that all their works would flow from a boundless wellspring of _agape_. Surely this exhortation speaks to each of us.

How does the command to return to your first love speak to you?

_____

Somehow in my previous studies of this letter, I have overlooked the original meaning of a critical word in the phrase "forsaken your first love." I am astonished to find that the original word for _forsaken_ is the same word often translated _forgive_ in the New Testament. The word _aphiemi_ means "to send forth, send away, let go from oneself."[5] The word is used in the phrase describing Christ's physical death when He "gave up his spirit" (Matt. 27:50). _Aphiemi_ is employed in many contexts and simply means _giving up or letting go of something_. The word is translated _forgive_ both times in the familiar words of Matthew 6:12 (KJV): "Forgive us our debts, as we forgive our debtors."

How many times has Christ watched His beloved ones let go of intimacy with Him to hang on to unforgiveness?

I could sob. How often we give up our first love—our indescribably glorious sacred romance—because we refuse to give up our grudges and grievances. How many times has Christ watched His beloved ones let go of intimacy with Him to hang on to unforgiveness? Believe one who has been there: we cannot hang on to both our sacred romance with Jesus Christ and our bitterness. We will release one to hang on to the other.

Release the one that is nothing but bondage. Life is too short. The room unforgiveness takes up in your life is cheating you of the very thing you were born (again) to experience. Send it into the hands of the faithful and sovereign Judge of the earth. Grab the neck of Jesus Christ and hang on to Him instead with every breath and every ounce of strength you have. Pray to love Him more than you pray for blessing, health, or ministry. Unless our lampstands are lit with the torch of sacred love, they are nothing but artificial lights. Fluorescent, maybe. But sooner or later, the bulb burns out.

Day 3 THE CHURCH IN SMYRNA

TODAY'S TREASURE
" 'Be faithful, even to the point of death, and I will give you the crown of life.' "
—Revelation 2:10

Today we have the privilege of focusing on the second of seven messages Christ sent to churches in Asia Minor. Smyrna (modern Izmar) was an exceptionally beautiful city about 40 miles due north of Ephesus. The people of Smyrna placed a high premium on learning. Science and medicine flourished, contributing to great wealth in the metropolis during the early New Testament era in which John received the revelation.

With this picture of Smyrna in mind, read Revelation 2:8-11. Fill in the characteristic components of Christ's messages to the church.

• **Christ's self-identification that coincides with the Revelation 1 vision:**

_____

• **Christ's commendation based on intimate acquaintance:**

_____

How were they (and how are we) rich, according to 2 Corinthians 8:9?

_____

• **Christ's rebuke: Is one issued to this particular church?**   ❏ Yes   ❏ No

• **Christ's exhortation: (see v. 10)** _____

_____

• **Christ's specific encouragement to overcome (see v. 11):** _____

_____

We won't always be able to link Christ's specific self-identification to something note-worthy about the recipient, but we are probably wise to assume that a link existed. In the letter to the believers in Smyrna, Christ identified Himself as the " 'First and the Last.' " Almost every book and commentary I studied mentioned the ancient inscription on the coins in first-century Smyrna: "First of Asia in beauty and size."[6] As Christ addressed His letter to humble believers surrounded by arrogant pagans, I can picture Him implying, "I am the First in Asia, Africa, and everywhere else. In fact, I spoke them into existence. What's more, I am also the Last. I am the inescapable One, the Judge of the living and the dead, and I have come to commend you."

You no doubt noticed the missing rebuke to the church in Smyrna. As Christ walked beside this lampstand, He found no fault. Impressively, the church didn't pass her tests because her exams were easy. On the contrary, no other church is characterized by greater depths of suffering. Christ didn't mince words when He described her afflictions and poverty. Christians were despised and terribly mistreated in Smyrna, primarily because no other city in Asia Minor held more allegiance to Rome.

"As early as 195 B.C., Smyrna foresaw the rising power of Rome and built a temple for pagan Roman worship. In 23 B.C., Smyrna was given the honor of building a tem-ple to the Emperor Tiberius because of its years of faithfulness to Rome. Thus, the city became a center for the cult of emperor worship—a fanatical 'religion.' "[7] The obsessive allegiance of the people of Smyrna became deadly for Christians. Anything the emperor reviled, the people of Smyrna hated, too. For emperors like Domitian, Christians were on the top of the list.

" 'I know … your poverty.' " Surrounded by wealth, those known to be Christians were persecuted in many ways, not the least of which was economically. They were often refused decent jobs, and many merchants withheld goods from them. Against a sparkling backdrop of opulence and affluence, Christians in Smyrna were invited to take their poverty personally. _Voice of the Martyrs_ contains bone-chilling accounts of Chris-tians today who are forced to live in horrendous poverty because of their faith. A single mouth never goes unfed without God's notice. No government or people group gets away with a lack of compassion or with outright oppression. God feels so strongly about the poor that I believe He may withhold blessings from cities and nations that neglect or oppress them.

> No government or people group gets away with a lack of compassion or with out-right oppression.

> **Read God's strong words of exhortation in Isaiah 58:5-12. We can observe all the religious fasts and ordinances in Christendom and yet fall under God's chastisement because of our lack of compassion and our unwilling-ness to see. What kind of fast has God chosen?**

_____

Christ commented about the slander of those who falsely claimed to be Jews but instead were a synagogue of Satan. This statement may imply that the Jews in Smyrna identified Christians to the government and greatly heightened their persecution.

Imagine God's derision for a people who not only look the other way but also actively enforce poverty and affliction. They had no idea the King of the earth walked through the perfectly paved streets of their fair city, checking on those who called themselves by

His name. The people of Smyrna took great pride in the beauty of their city. I found the following quotation ironic: "The hills and the sea added to the picturesque quality of the city. The city itself nestled under the hill Pagos, which made an ideal acropolis. This beauty was marred, however, by a drainage problem in the lower city which resulted in the silting up of the harbor and an accumulation of unpleasant odors."[8]

Try as they may to build the most impressive city in Asia, Smyrna just couldn't do anything about that putrid smell. Don't think for a moment their unrelenting persecution of innocent people didn't rise up to the nostrils of God. Interestingly, the name *Smyrna* means *myrrh*.[9] The ancient extract by the same name was used in Scripture for anointing oil, perfume, purification, and embalming. Myrrh was among the gifts offered by the Magi to Jesus. Nothing but stench ascended to the heavens from the arrogantly pristine, highly educated, and wealthy of Smyrna. From the hidden slums, however, rose a fragrant incense of great value. No perfume is more costly and more aromatic to God than the faithfulness of believers who are suffering.

> No perfume is more costly and more aromatic to God than the faithfulness of believers who are suffering.

Do you know a believer in Christ whose faithfulness astounds you in the midst of his or her suffering? If so, describe him or her.

_____

_____

A few nights ago I served on a team with a pastor whose son will soon die of a malignant brain tumor unless God miraculously intervenes. I stood near him during praise and worship. This precious father did not deny his immense pain. His tears fell unashamedly, but his worship rose just as unashamedly. I can hardly hold back my own tears as I picture his face. Many of us felt God's favor over our prayer gathering that night. Somehow I believe in the midst of much praise, a fragrance of greater price and exceeding sweetness ascended to the throne from one grieving servant of God.

How are people like my pastor-friend and the believers in Smyrna able to be faithful through such terrible suffering? First Peter 1:6-9 implies one primary reason.

What do these verses describe? _____

_____

Those who are faithful in the midst of immense suffering somehow allowed their fiery trials to purify rather than destroy them. If we've never suffered like some of the saints we know or have read about, we tend to indict ourselves with failure before our trials ever come. We must remember that God grants us grace and mercy according to our need. No, I don't have the strength or character to be faithful under such heart-shattering conditions, but the Holy Spirit will impart a power and grace I've never experienced when my time comes. The challenge is whether or not to accept them.

Why do we sometimes refuse God's grace during our times of suffering?

_____

The believers in Smyrna did not refuse grace. They inhaled it like air because they were desperate. As much as the church in Smyrna had suffered, Christ warned them of more to come. He wanted them to be aware, but He did not want them to be afraid. I believe much of the Book of Revelation was written to believers for the same purpose.

If you were addressing a new Christian, how might you explain why we don't need to fear but need to be aware?

_____

_____

Mind you, imprisonment and death awaited some of those in the fragrant church of Smyrna. We don't know what Christ meant by the time segment of 10 days. Some scholars believe it was literal. Others think it represented 10 years. Still others assume it is a figure of speech for a segment of time known only to God. Whatever the length of trial, Christ called the church of Smyrna to be faithful unto death. His self-identification as the One who died and again came to life reminded them of the absolute assurance of resurrection life. He also promised to reward them with a *stephanos,* or victor's crown. They would not be touched by the second death, a term referring to the final judgment for all unbelievers.

Father, how desperately we, Your children, need the renewing of our minds! In our human ways of thinking, overcoming a life-threatening situation always means staying alive! **Add your prayer to mine. Use verse 10 if you like.**

_____

_____

_____

We inhale the sweet fragrance of the church of Smyrna today, Dear One, to learn another option under the heading of overcoming. Sometimes Jesus defines overcoming as dying well—dying with faith and spiritual dignity. Beloved, dying is the one thing each of us is going to do unless we are chosen to meet Him in the air (see 1 Thess. 4:17). We need to learn more about the glorious overcoming of faithful, spiritually dignified deaths.

> Sometimes Jesus defines overcoming as dying well—dying with faith and spiritual dignity.

At least one of the saints in Smyrna left us a profound and wonderful example of an overcoming death. His name was Polycarp. Having studied directly under John's tutelage, he was alive at the time Revelation was written. He became the bishop of the church in Smyrna and served the generation that followed John's heavenly departure.

Foxe's Book of Martyrs recounts Polycarp's arrest and martyrdom. After serving a meal for the guards who apprehended him, Polycarp asked for and was granted an hour in prayer. He "was so full of the grace of God, that they who were present … were astonished, and many now felt sorry that so venerable and godly a man should be put to death." Nevertheless, Polycarp was carried before the proconsul and condemned. The proconsul said to him, 'Swear, and I will release thee;—reproach Christ.' Polycarp answered, 'Eighty and six years have I served him, and he never once wronged me; how then shall I blaspheme my King, Who hath saved me?' " Sentenced to be burned alive, he was then tied, not nailed as usual, to a stake having assured them that he would stand immovable.[10]

His persecutors tried to fight fire with fire, but they failed. Polycarp's faithfulness to the death only heightened the flames of godly passion, carrying the costly fragrance of

Death gave way to life, and faith gave way to sight.

myrrh past the jeers of the crowd to the throne room of God. He had overcome. Perhaps crucifixion is the only slow death with pain that exceeds the fires of a stake. As long as those moments must have been, nothing could have prepared Polycarp for the sight he beheld when death gave way to life and faith gave way to sight. The only Jesus he had ever seen was in the face and heart of John the Beloved. That day the old bishop of Smyrna saw the One he loved and served for 86 years. Face-to-face. With a victor's crown in His hand.

When I get to heaven and meet him, I'm going to try to remember to ask Polycarp if he thought his suffering was worth it. Oh, I already know the answer ... but I want to see his expression.

Day 4 THE CHURCH IN PERGAMUM

TODAY'S TREASURE
" 'To him who overcomes, I will give some of the hidden manna. I will also give him a white stone with a new name written on it, known only to him who receives it.' "
—*Revelation 2:17*

Today we'll travel farther north in the cluster of the seven churches to Pergamum. About 65 miles above Smyrna, Pergamum was the legal center for the district and administrative capital city of Asia until the close of the first century. You may still have Smyrna pictured in your mind. Imagine a city with exceeding grandeur as we make our way through the city gate of Pergamum. I was stunned by the pictures of the ornate ruins. Not only did the city boast imposing gymnasiums, theaters, and government facilities, its two-hundred-thousand-volume library was second only to the library in Alexandria.

When word of the plans for such a library circulated, an Egyptian papyrus importer was so offended by the thought of a rival that he stopped Pergamum's shipments. The deficit forced the development of parchment (Greek, *pergemene*) from Pergamum.[11] We have more to learn about the architecture and personality of Pergamum, but let's go straight to Scripture to pour the concrete.

Please read Revelation 2:12-17 and fill in the characteristic components of Christ's messages to the church.

• **Christ's self-identification coinciding with the Revelation 1 vision:**

_____

• **Christ's commendation based on intimate acquaintance:** _____

_____

• **Christ's rebuke:**_____

_____

- **Christ's exhortation (see v. 16):** _____

  _____

- **Christ's specific encouragement to overcome:** _____

  _____

Christ identified Himself to the church in Pergamum as He who has the sharp, double-edged sword. This word picture could mean many things. A primary purpose of a double-edged sword is to divide. As Christ walked among the people of this lampstand, He obviously found those who were true to His ways and those who were not. Likewise, as He walks among our lampstands today, Christ sees us as individuals who together compose a church. The faithfulness or rebelliousness of any given individual never gets swept up in the corporate whole. How I wish at times it did!

In defense of the young church in Pergamum, we can only imagine what kind of warfare they experienced. Christ referred to the city as the place " 'where Satan has his throne.' " Because Satan is not omnipresent, Christ's claim is hair-raising. We can't be certain what He meant, but historical evidence from the first century tells us that Perga-mum was the uncontested center of pagan worship in Asia Minor. Keep in mind that Satan's primary goal is to keep people blinded to truth while providing something that momentarily seems to assuage their spiritual hunger. Pergamum delivered. Christ spoke about the church in Pergamum remaining true to His name. Goodness knows, inhabitants had plenty of names from which to choose. Within its walls were temples to Dionysus, Athena, Asclepius, and Demeter; three temples to the emperor cult; and a huge altar to Zeus.

> Satan provides things that momentarily seem to assuage our spiritual hunger.

Although the philosophy of the city seemed to be "Pick a god, any god," two primary religions exceeded all others in Pergamum: the worship of Dionysus, considered the god of the royal kings (symbolized by the bull), and the worship of Asclepius, called the savior god of healing (symbolized by the snake). Does that second title make your skin crawl as it does mine? I know the Savior God of healing, and I assure you He isn't the snake. God heals in many ways, but He alone is God our Healer.

I'm reminded of Hosea 11:3-4. What did God say about healing?

_____

_____

All healing is meant to reveal the Healer. Satan will do anything he can to block the connection. The first psalm I memorized was Psalm 103. I still love it.

Read the first five verses of this wonderful psalm. List God's benefits.

_____

_____

When given the opportunity, Satan gladly supplies a counterfeit savior providing a dandy benefit package. Any world religion or brand of humanism will do. Because humanity was created to seek God's benefits, Satan works most effectively when he is able to offer alternatives. For instance, he is sly to suggest other ways for people to unload their guilt. One way is to convince them they haven't sinned. He also needs to address health issues.

Worship of the body works nicely as a preoccupation. He has all sorts of means of providing counterfeit redemption. Not long ago I received a letter from a loved one with whom I shared my testimony about the transforming power of God's Word. A practicing Buddhist, he wrote me his own testimony about how life had improved since he changed his karma. My heart broke over the inevitable disillusionment of self-worship. At some point surely a self-worshiper looks in the mirror and thinks, *If I am as good as God gets, life stinks.* What about love and compassion? Counterfeits can be sold or manufactured on any corner. And the renewal of youth? It's one of the hottest money-makers in the world economy. Keeping people preoccupied is big business to the devil.

 How have you personally seen the enemy counterfeit one of God's benefits?

Christ's commendation tells us that many believers in Pergamum, though surrounded by counterfeits, remained true and did not renounce their faith, even when Antipas was put to death. Several sources say that Antipas was publicly roasted in a bowl-like vessel. Others claim we have no dependable information on him. Perhaps all we know for certain is the meaning of his name, "against all."[12] Sometimes I travel to countries alone. One was particularly dangerous, and the thought occurred to me that I could find myself in trouble without a local ally. The odds of one-against-all can be overwhelming.

We don't have to cross an ocean to feel those kinds of odds. All some of us have to do is go to work. Or go home! At times when we realize we're against all in a given environment, we are wise to ask God to confirm whether we are right. Sometimes I've been out on a limb when God confirmed that I wasn't even in the right tree!

Name a time when God had to show you that your position was wrong.

If God confirms our positions, we accept them as opportunities to display His glory.

On the other hand, if God confirms our positions, we are challenged to gracefully accept them as opportunities to display His glory. Romans 8:31 becomes our watchword: "If God is for us, who can be against us?" The day Antipas died, God was for him. Like Polycarp, Antipas stood against all, and he overcame. You and I are going to learn something vital from our study of Revelation: death doesn't always mean defeat.

Not every member of the church in Pergamum was a faithful witness like Antipas. Christ rebuked an undesignated number for holding to the teachings of Balaam and the Nicolaitans. If Christ commanded the repentance of the whole church, the number had to be significant. Although God esteems repentance of the faithful on behalf of the unfaithful, He doesn't require it from people who haven't sinned. Look back at His commendation to the church in Ephesus in Revelation 2:2. I suspect the church in Pergamum may have tolerated wicked men and false apostles more than the church in Ephesus.

We can't dogmatically identify the teaching of the Nicolaitans, but they are closely associated with the teachings of Balaam. The account of Balaam and Balak is found in Numbers 22—24. In a nutshell, Balak, the king of Moab, greatly feared the Israelites as they settled in the promised land. He hired Balaam the soothsayer to curse Israel, but he blessed them instead. Balaam did, however, instruct Balak in how to defeat the Israelites. He told Balak to seduce them into idolatry through the harlotry of the Moabite women. Based on all I've read, I believe the basic concept of Balaam's teachings is this: if you can't curse them, try to seduce them!

The whole idea makes my blood boil. You see, Satan is waging war on our generation with Balaam's weapon (see 1 Tim. 4:1!). Satan can't curse us, because we are blessed (see Eph. 1:3) children of God, covered by the blood of the Lamb. If the devil can't curse us, then how can he defeat us! He can try to seduce us! How does seduction differ from temptation? All seduction is temptation, but not all temptation is seduction. Many temptations are obvious. The aim of seduction is to catch the prey off guard. That's why Satan's best henchmen (or women) are often insiders. Some in the church of Pergamum were enticed into sin by others among them. Whether or not the seducers were truly saved is unclear. Either way, Christ expected the church to jump to action.

If the seducers were true believers, they needed to be confronted properly and restored when repentant. Some may wonder how believers could be used by Satan to seduce. Beloved, seduced people seduce people. If the devil's scheme is not exposed and the chain broken, it perpetuates. Without a doubt, some of Satan's most effective seducers are within the church. We must develop discernment and jealously guard our hearts without becoming fearful and suspicious. Authentic godliness, rather than religiousness, is our best defense against seduction.

Christ's letter to the church in Pergamum must have hit hard, but the tenderness and encouragement of the conclusion spared their hearts.

What two things did Christ promise to those who overcame (see Rev. 2:17)?

_____

The hidden manna contrasts beautifully with the food sacrificed to idols. Jesus Christ is the Bread of life sacrificed on the altar before the one true God. Now His Spirit falls like manna from heaven to all who hunger. Jewish tradition holds that the ark with the pot of manna in it was hidden by order of King Josiah and will be revealed again during the earthly reign of the Messiah.

The most probable meaning of the white stone in verse 17 is remarkable. In an ancient courtroom jurors voting to condemn the accused cast their votes by tossing a black stone or pebble. In contrast, jurors voting to acquit the condemned cast their votes by tossing a white stone or pebble. Scripture actually records this ancient practice, but our English translations don't portray it.

Take a look at Acts 26:10 and its context. What does this verse describe?

_____

Carefully look at the phrase "cast my vote." The original wording is *katenegka psephon*. The Greek word *katenegka* means *to deposit or cast*. The Greek word *psephon*, meaning *pebble* or *stone*, is only used in Acts 26:10 and Revelation 2:17.[13] In Acts 26:10 Paul testified that he formerly deposited or cast his pebble to vote against the saints.

The terminology Christ used was perfectly fitting for Pergamum. Do you remember one of the first facts we learned about the city? It was the district's legal center. How I praise God that the Judge of all the earth pitches a white stone to acquit us—not because we're innocent but because Someone has already served our sentence. And the new name on the stone? It could be Christ's, but I also think we each have an overcoming name as Abram had Abraham, Simon had Peter, and Saul had Paul.

I'll be honest with you. I'm glad to leave Pergamum. I'm not crazy about the food, and I'm petrified of seducers. But the manna and the stone? Those were worth the trip.

The Judge of all the earth acquits us because Someone has already served our sentence.

Day 5 THE CHURCH IN THYATIRA

TODAY'S TREASURE
" 'I have this against you: You tolerate that woman Jezebel, who calls herself a prophetess.' "—Revelation 2:20

Today we'll take the inland route about 45 miles east of Pergamum to Thyatira. Few ruins can be explored today because the modern city of Akhisar in Turkey stands atop its ancient history. Perhaps we're better off. It has a shady past. We'll learn as much as we need to know and be thankful that God spared further details. As we walk through the ancient city gates, we won't find the splendor and opulence we witnessed in Smyrna and Pergamum. Thyatira is known not for beauty but for commerce.

Please read Revelation 2:18-29 and fill in the pertinent information.

- **Christ's self-identification coinciding with the Revelation 1 vision:**

  _____

- **Christ's commendation based on intimate acquaintance:** _____

  _____

- **Christ's rebuke:** _____

  _____

- **Christ's exhortation (see v. 25):** _____

  _____

- **Christ's specific encouragement to overcome:** _____

  _____

Christ described Himself with fire and bronze.

Thyatira found significance in two identities, both of which Christ intimates. During the Greek epoch, the city was originally an important military headquarters. Thyatira unfortunately suffered the fate of one conqueror after another but never relinquished its military identity. Its legacy continued under Roman rule, but the city evolved into one of the most thriving commercial centers in all Asia. The city walls bulged with wool and linen workers, dyers, leather workers, potters, tanners, bakers, slave dealers, and bronzesmiths. Many scholars believe that Christ described Himself with blazing fire and burnished bronze because inhabitants of Thyatira took such pride in their metal works. Thyatira's dual identity was honored in a commemorative coin struck by the Roman government. The coin depicted "a metalworker seated at an anvil hammering out a helmet in the presence of the goddess Athena, who stands ready to receive it."[14] A metal worker representing commerce, a helmet representing military government, and a goddess representing feminine influence. Don't forget those three inscriptions. They tell the story of Thyatira.

The New Testament mentions the ancient city of Thyatira one other time. Not coincidentally, the two references fit as contrasting puzzle pieces inviting us to reflect on the best and worst of womanhood. This lesson is one in which this female author will act on the right she reserves to completely single out women. Ladies, this one's entirely for us.

The two references invite us to reflect on the best and worst of womanhood.

> **Please read Acts 16:11-15 carefully. Discern everything you can about Lydia from Thyatira, based on the biblical facts and the elements they might suggest. Then write a brief paragraph describing the way you picture her.**

_____

_____

_____

Scripture associates Thyatira with two different women: Lydia and Jezebel. Some scholars interpret Jezebel as a reference to a false doctrine, a type of demonic spirit, or a behavioral concept. Others believe she was a flesh-and-blood woman who played havoc in the church at Thyatira. I am strongly inclined to agree with the latter, but I am also thoroughly convinced she represents a kind of woman none of us want to be.

> **Reread Revelation 2:20-21. Discern everything you can about Jezebel from Thyatira, based on the biblical facts and the elements they might suggest. Then write a brief paragraph describing the way you picture her.**

_____

_____

_____

Jezebel could have been the woman's actual name, but Christ was far more likely drawing the parallel between the woman in Thyatira and King Ahab's brazen wife. The account of the original Jezebel can be found in bits and pieces from 1 Kings 16 to 1 Kings 21. She was raised in Sidon, a commercial city not unlike Thyatira, known for idolatry and licentiousness. She married Ahab, a King of Israel, and moved to Jezreel. The city served the one true God, but she determined to turn it into a center of Baal worship. "The wicked, idolatrous queen soon became the power behind the throne. Obedient to her wishes, Ahab erected a sanctuary for Baal and supported hundreds of pagan prophets."[15] She massacred the prophets of the Lord when they opposed her. Many of those who escaped her hid in caves. Elijah remained and became a thorn in her flesh. He was a man who witnessed the majestic wonders of God, defeating Jezebel's prophets as God sent fire from heaven. Yet she wielded such power and intimidation that when she threatened Elijah, he ran for his life and fell into deep depression for a time.

After Ahab was killed in battle, Jezebel retained her imposing authority for the next 10 years through her sons Ahaziah and Joram. After their bloody deaths Jezebel was thrown from a window just as Elijah predicted, was trampled by horses, and was eaten by dogs (see 1 Kings 21:19). A gruesome death, indeed.

Fast-forward to the New Testament to meet a woman who bears her predecessor's name. The ancient city of the Bible's Thyatira tells the story of women and power. It's a story we may not want to hear, but we need to hear it. Surrounded by a male-centered culture, in tired 20th-century terms, Thyatira was liberated. Women could be quite successful, which was—and is—admirable. Just leave it to someone to give it a bad name. Because the fabric of the ancient city was practically woven in military green, the bigger the stick someone carried, the better. Authority was everything. You can even hear Christ address the authority issue in His promise to overcomers.

What was the promise, and to whom would it come (see Rev. 2:26-28)?

_____

Under Roman rule the evolution of Thyatira's commerce shifted from military authority to successful merchants. Almost every commentary I researched talked about the powerful trade guilds that ran the city like the mob. Clubs and societies, some of which were underground, were not only social but also highly political. They were strangely religious because they entrenched their members in all sorts of idolatrous practices. Much pressure for membership existed, and refusal automatically tagged an enemy. The networking between these trade clubs and societies was more like a web. They came with offers a citizen wasn't wise to refuse. Not only did unethical deals and practices prevail, but sexual immorality was also rampant. Somehow extramarital sexual expression got twisted up in the concept of liberation. Of course, nothing provokes more bondage than sexual immorality, but Satan is ever the liar, isn't he?

The Revelation 2 Jezebel was very powerful in Thyatira. She did everything she could to infiltrate the church with secret guilds and societies. Lydia was also powerful in Thyatira. Together they provide a lesson on abuse versus the wise use of authority. Let's perform a character sketch of Jezebel and invite Lydia to hold up her lamp of contrast to the insidious darkness. We live in a culture where women can be very successful and can hold many authoritative positions. Many women have strong gifts that rise to the top in various professions. That's wonderful—as long as they know what to do with their position. Unless we women actively submit to the true liberation of Christ's authority, we can be terrifying. If God gifts us professionally, we want to be Lydias. The following characteristics describing Jezebel will help shed light on any traits we may share.

If God gifts us professionally, we want to be Lydias.

Jezebel assumed places of authority God did not assign her.

Fill in the following blanks, based on Revelation 2:20: " 'You tolerate that

woman Jezebel, who_____**.' "**

Before you conclude that her infraction was assuming a role that could belong only to men, look up the following Scriptures and describe the nature of each association between women and the gift of prophecy.

Luke 2:36-38 _____

Acts 2:17-18 _____

Acts 21:8-9 _____

The New Testament records the viability of a woman's having the God-given gift of prophecy, what we might generalize as speaking forth. Jezebel had no such gift. She wasn't called. She was controlling! She wasn't wisely authoritative. She was bossy! Oh, that none of us—male or female—would confuse the two!

Certainly, God calls women into places of leadership, but in the spirit of 1 Corinthians 11:5, I believe our heads must be covered by higher authority. I cannot express how strongly I feel about this. As women we enjoy wonderful protection as the biblical proverbial buck stops with the men of our households and churches. If God calls a woman to assume a leadership role, I believe with all my heart that she is safe and operating in God's authentic anointing only under that umbrella!

I'd be in disobedience to God if I let disapproval stop me.

Given my past and my lack of credentials, I will never understand the sovereignty of God to appoint me to an area of leadership. At the same time, I know what He has called me to, and I'd be in direct disobedience to God if I let someone's disapproval dissuade me. I cannot describe, however, the terror that shoots through me over finding myself in an area of leadership. How anyone can have an intimate relationship with God and be arrogant and fearless in a position of authority is beyond me.

What do you think James 3:1 means? _____

_____

Why would anyone ask for stricter judgment? Get a load of Revelation 2:22-23! Jezebel was asking for it, whether she knew it or not. Please don't miss that Jezebel's most serious infraction was not her sin but her unwillingness to repent! Lydia stands in stark contrast to Jezebel as a woman of success. She was a worshiper of God—not herself or position. She opened her heart to Paul's message rather than pull rank on him. Both professionally and spiritually, the tone of Scripture suggests that she was a servant-leader.

Jezebel abused her feminine gift of influence.

" 'By her teaching she _____ my servants' " (v. 20).

Women have a unique, God-given gift of influence. Notice that the serpent came to Eve rather than Adam. I think perhaps he suspected that Eve could talk Adam into anything. I am married to a very strong man. He no doubt wears the cowboy boots in our family, but if I used my feminine wiles just right (or just wrong), I fear I could talk him into almost anything. I have to be very careful, because he loves me and wants to please me. You see, in some ways I am his weakness.

Do you understand? If so, describe the concept from your own experience.

_____

_____

_____

Many accounts in Scripture attest to the power of a woman's influence. Eve and Sarai represent some biblical blights, but thankfully, we can find more scriptural examples of positive womanly influence than negative. Lydia is certainly one of them.

Carefully search Acts 16:15. Note Lydia's powerful influence and describe

how she used it. _____

_____

_____

Jezebel misused her sexuality (see Rev. 2:21). Sister, I'm not sure our culture has taught us to use anything more powerfully than our sexuality. Don't think for a moment that seducing someone into fornication is the only way a woman can use her sexuality to manipulate. We can be completely clothed and in broad, public daylight and still misuse our sexuality.

What are some ways that we women can misuse our sexuality?

_____

_____

God gave sexuality as a gift, not a tool.

I might have a sister in Christ who is horrified by our discussion of this tawdry topic. True, she may never have dreamed of using her sexuality seductively or manipulatively. Then again, this same woman may wield it like a massive weapon in her marriage. God gave sexuality as a gift, not a tool. Married women sometimes horrifically misuse sexuality to get what they want. Routine withholding is just one example.

Recently, my precious firstborn and I had a very intimate talk. I wasn't silly enough to think she didn't know the facts of life, but I wanted to make sure she knew the etiquette of the godly marriage bed and the misuse of sexuality as a weapon. We were both a bit uncomfortable but loved each other even more and laughed all the harder in the wake of our talk. Perhaps your mother had a different kind of talk with you—or none at all. I'm still waiting for my mother to have the talk with me. Sweet, sweet sister, I'm not your mother, but I am honored to be your friend. God created us to be women complete with all our gifts, contributions, and influences. Let's be women well.

1R. Alan Culpepper, *John, the Son of Zebedee: The Life of a Legend* (Minneapolis: First Fortress Press, 2000), 139.

2Tertullian, *On Prescription Against Heretics*, as quoted in Culpepper, *John,* 140.

3Oswald Chambers, *My Utmost for His Highest* (New York: Dodd, Mead & Company, 1963), 211.

4Edward Mote, "The Solid Rock," in *The Baptist Hymnal* (Nashville: Convention Press, 1991), 406.

5Spiros Zodhiates, "Lexical Aids to the New Testament," 918, in Spiros Zodhiates, Warren Baker, and David Kemp, *The Hebrew-Greek Key Study Bible* (Chattanooga, TN: AMG Publishers, 1996), 1596.

6Timothy Trammell, "Smyrna," *Biblical Illustrator,* spring 1992, 3.

7Ronald F. Youngblood, ed., *Nelson's New Illustrated Bible Dictionary* (Nashville: Thomas Nelson, 1995), s.v. "Smyrna."

8E. Glenn Hinson, "Smyrna," *Bible Illustrator,* winter 1980, 72.

9Youngblood, *Nelson's New Illustrated Bible Dictionary,* s.v. "Smyrna."

10W. Grinton Berry, ed., *Foxe's Book of Martyrs* (Grand Rapids: Baker House Books, 1992), 21–24.

11Frank E. Gaebelein and J. D. Douglas, *The Expositor's Bible Commentary* (Grand Rapids: Zondervan Publishing, 1981), 440.

12Ibid.

13A. T. Robertson, *Word Pictures in the New Testament,* vol. 5 (Nashville: Broadman Press, 1960), 307.

14Larry E. McKinney, "Thyatira," *Biblical Illustrator,* spring 1992, 70.

15Youngblood, *Nelson's New Illustrated Bible Dictionary,* s.v. "Jezebel."

VIDEO RESPONSE SHEET

Group Session 8

In the midst of many symbols and shrouds, the Book of Revelation frames several visions of such startling clarity and detail that we could stand before them for hours and continue to discover something new. **Revelation 7:9-17** encases one of those.

As we study these Scriptures, let your imagination play like a videotape. We'll push the pause button on several different elements in the scene and see what we can glean.

1. A great _____ that can't be counted standing before the _____

   and in front of the _____

   This multitude is …

   • Every _____: *ethnos*—set apart by location, customs, and laws

   • Every _____: *phule*—set apart by blood lines tracing to common ancestors

   • Every _____: *laos*—set apart by various common bonds of a society

   • Every _____: *glossa*—set apart by dialects or languages

   These four descriptions represent every means of division between the inhabitants of earth.

2. Those who have come out of (the) _____ _____ (v. 14). Carefully note that scholars are divided about the exact meaning of this phrase. Some believe the masses of people pictured have come out of "great tribulation" (as may be implied in the KJV and could simply imply Acts 14:22), while others believe they have come out of "*the* great tribulation" (as *may* be implied in the NIV and NASB). *If* Scripture means *the* great tribulation, this gathering suggests that the most profound evangelical movement in church history will occur during the most dreadful days of human history.

Compare Revelation 6:9-11. Many scholars believe these martyrs are among those gathered in Revelation 7:9.

3. The consummation of _____ _____ in glorious _____. Please don't

   miss the fact that these "nations, tribes, and peoples" are gathered as one, but—at least in this vision

   and for this time—retain some level of distinction.

4. The _____ of the _____ (vv. 11-12). "Amen!"

5. The _____ of God (vv. 15-17)

FROM A THRONE'S EYE VIEW

Day 1
The Church in Sardis

Day 2
The Church in Philadelphia

Day 3
The Church in Laodicea

Day 4
The Throne Room

Day 5
The Lamb

Second only to the sense of Christ's presence in my life, I crave His voice. I want to hear Him speak more than I want my next breath. Christ's words are life to me, even when they must hit hard to plunge to the depths He desires. As we continue our study of Christ's messages to the seven churches, we stand to learn as much from the rebukes as from the commendations. Christ left His church to be a blazing torch in the darkness of a desperate world. When He uncovers our weaknesses, His motivation is always to uncover the light He has placed within us. Our week concludes with an earthly glimpse of a heavenly throne room, followed by a Lamb worthy to open the sealed scroll. Let's ask God to help us discover hidden treasures in the mines of Revelation.

Principal Questions

Day 1: How could a chronic fear of death inhibit a believer's entire life and ministry? What does Hebrews 2:14 say about the subject?

Day 2: For what did Christ commend the church in Philadelphia after acknowledging its " 'little strength' " in Revelation 3:8?

Day 3: How did the church at Laodicea describe itself (see Rev. 3:17)?

Day 4: Where is the Lamb depicted as standing in Revelation 5:6?

Day 5: How did John respond when no one was found to open the scroll in Revelation 5:4?

Day 1 THE CHURCH IN SARDIS

TODAY'S TREASURE
" 'Wake up! Strengthen what remains and is about to die, for I have not found your deeds complete in the sight of my God.' "—Revelation 3:2

With the winds of Thyatira at our backs, let's set our sights about 30 miles southeast toward the ancient city of Sardis. As we travel together, I wonder if you are as sobered as I am by Christ's meticulous attention to all who gather in His name. We, the people of His churches, carry the reputation of Christ in our cities like those holding banners in a town parade. What do our banners say about Him? Christ isn't looking for perfect churches, because He knows they are composed of imperfect people. He is looking for churches that glorify God and lift up Christ.

Like you, I do not attend a flawless church. In the wake of difficult times caused by the departure of key personnel, I've watched it develop a strangely purer kind of beauty. A beauty that comes from desperation. With the loss of five ministers, we no longer had a person's name from which to draw our reputation. Days turned into months, and months turned into several years with no permanent replacements. We had to find out who we were as a church without a man's name. I believe we have. Our church stands for many things but none more strongly than missions. The banner of our church might read, Take Your Faith to the Streets and the Nations.

I would not dare encourage you to think critically of your church, but every one of us should consider Christ's reputation that our church carries. If the church you attend and serve carried a banner representing Christ, what positive statement would it make?

These appropriate thoughts prepare us for today's visit to ancient Sardis. Please read Revelation 3:1-6 and fill in the pertinent information.

- **Christ's self-identification coinciding with the Revelation 1 vision:**

  _____

- **Christ's commendation based on intimate acquaintance:** _____

  _____

- **Christ's rebuke:**_____

- **Christ's exhortation:**_____

- **Christ's specific encouragement to overcome:** _____

The personalities and moral attitudes of every city permeate its churches unless we deliberately overcome them. For instance, churches in wealthy areas with upper-crust attitudes must overcome misguided superiority to keep from portraying that attitude. Likewise, churches in cities with deeply ingrained prejudice will carry the same banner unless they deliberately risk being different.

A city's attitudes permeate the churches unless we overcome them.

I can think of few indictments more serious than " 'you are dead' " (Rev. 3:1). Perhaps you'll be as interested as I was to learn that Sardis was best known for a necropolis called the cemetery of the thousand hills. Sardis looked on a distant skyline of burial mounds. Can you imagine a city known for its cemetery? The city was preoccupied with death.

Can you see any bearing of your town's reputation on your church? Explain briefly and vaguely if it's not affirming. Keep in mind that we are each a part of the church where we serve.

_____

_____

Christ is a master of words. His wordplays are most concentrated in His letter to the seven churches. The church in Sardis could not miss Christ's parallel to their necropolis when He confronted their deadness. He also said, " 'You have a reputation of being alive' " (Rev. 3:1). Christ may have made a wordplay on the name of the bishop of Sardis. His name, Zosimus or Zotikus, comes from the Greek word _zoe_, meaning _life_. Whether or not Christ implied the irony of the bishop's name, He was incensed over the church's deadness. No church can blame its deadness entirely on leaders. The lively prayers of saints can do more to resurrect a church than any leader could do to kill it.

> The lively prayers of saints can resurrect a church.

Dead churches must be a confounding mystery to the hosts of heaven. The ministering spirits that invisibly flood the atmosphere must look on the radiance of Jesus Christ and wonder how anything that carries His name could be dead. Above all things, Christ is life! I am convinced that few things mar the cause of Christ like lifeless churches. Before we all shout "Amen!" let's keep in mind that lifeless churches are made up of lifeless Christians. Thankfully, Christ still raises the dead, but His serious warning was to wake up and respond without delay! Like an athlete who let his muscles atrophy, the church needed spiritual rehab—beginning by strengthening the little that remained.

What invaded the church in Sardis with such deadness? The history of this ancient city suggests three permeating contributors.

First, the people of Sardis fixated on death rather than life. Where burial mounds become idols, thoughts of death overtake thoughts of life. In a previous study I received a letter from a sister in Christ who was alarmed that I mentioned visiting a friend's gravesite. She was not unkind. She was simply surprised that anyone who believed so strongly in heaven would esteem meaningless remains by visiting a grave. Though I didn't agree with her philosophy, if I were more focused on my believing friend's death than on her life, my sister would have had a point.

Some might ask, "Why would any of us be more fixated on death than life?" We don't have to idolize burial mounds like the Sardians (not to be confused with sardines) to focus on death more than life. Worship in its simplest essence is attentiveness. One way we can focus on death more than life is to possess a life-inhibiting fear of it. I have known people who were so scared of death that they could hardly live. You might say they were worshiping burial mounds much like the Sardians—whether or not they realized it.

How could a chronic fear of death inhibit a believer's entire life and ministry? What does Hebrews 2:14 have to say about the subject?

_____

My beloved grandmother was petrified of death. Perhaps she had good reason after losing three children and her husband. Having been greatly affected, my mother also had a troubling fear of death. I witnessed the adverse effects of such fears on both of their lives and determined that I did not want to follow suit. I have had to be very deliberate about not allowing the attitudes of those around me to permeate my belief system.

One way we can focus on death more than life is to possess a life-inhibiting fear of it.

How about you? In the margin list any attitudes toward death that have surrounded you. Are they attitudes you wish to keep?

The people of Sardis not only fixated on death but also relied on their past achievements. Commentator William M. Ramsay wrote, " 'No city of Asia at that time showed such a melancholy contrast between past splendor and present decay as Sardis.' "[1] Sardis was like a leading lady in a Greek tragedy who waltzed around town in riches turned to rags thinking everyone still saw her as she was 30 years ago. In essence, Christ wrote the church of Sardis to hand this self-deceived woman a mirror—just as He's handed one to me again and again. However, Christ does not hand someone a mirror to destroy. He hands her the mirror to wake her up!

Last year I attended special homecoming festivities at my college alma mater. I greatly enjoyed renewing friendships and acquaintances. I was mystified and somewhat amused as I watched other people caught in a time warp. They were still hanging on with a death grip to their beer rather than having relationships with people. They dated the same brand of beer they drank 25 years ago and still tried to pull off the same smooth lines that didn't work back then. Some even attempted to comb their few remaining hairs the same old way. May I simply say that the '70s weren't a great time for hair?

If a time warp weren't so pitiful, it would be hilarious. Sardis was warped by time. She lived off her past fame, and the results were tragic. Unfortunately, the church within its walls followed suit. The apostle Paul spoke a powerful testimony on the subject.

Read Philippians 3:4-15 and summarize Paul's life philosophy.

_____

_____

Sardis lost its bid to build a temple to Caesar in A.D. 26. Smyrna won instead. I wonder whether the people of Sardis knew they needed fresh life and vitality when they appealed to Rome for the honor of building the new temple. When they were rejected in favor of a rival city much too close, I wonder whether they took on an all-too-common attitude: "Why should we even try? Who cares anymore?"

Unless good reason exists to respond otherwise, rejection can cause people to lose heart faster than almost anything else. Though the church of Sardis had nothing but disdain for pagan practices and temples, my hypothesis is that the people of the church unknowingly wore the same cloak of dejected identity as their surroundings.

Have you ever seen yourself or someone you love interpret rejection as a deathblow? ❑ Yes ❑ No If so, explain.

_____

_____

Perhaps this best sums up the deadness of Sardis: "Sardis was a city of peace, not the peace won through battle, but 'the peace of a man whose dreams are dead and whose mind is asleep, the peace of lethargy and evasion.' "[2] The statement stuns us, not because it speaks so perfectly to an ancient city's decay but because it speaks to many of us today.

What has happened in our lives to take the wind out of our sails? To cause us to drop arms and cease defending ourselves against our enemy? To leave works incomplete? Have we grown lethargic? What would we rather evade than face? If Christ has given us life, who has the right to impose deadness on us through rejection?

Christ's identity to the church in Sardis is also the key to its resurgence. He holds the " 'seven spirits of God' " (Rev. 3:1). Life infiltrates our churches when God pours out His Holy Spirit. Spirit-flooded churches are built one way: through Spirit-flooded people.

Who has the right to impose deadness on us through rejection?

Day 2 THE CHURCH IN PHILADELPHIA

TODAY'S TREASURE

" 'I know your deeds. See, I have placed before you an open door that no one can shut. I know that you have little strength, yet you have kept my word and have not denied my name.' "—Revelation 3:8

After learning hard lessons from our travels to Pergamum, Thyatira, and Sardis, I could use a breather, couldn't you? Our next destination should provide one. Our travel time is briefer today. We have only about 28 miles to travel southeast of Sardis to find Philadelphia, a high plateau city. About that breather: I should mention that the city was built on a dangerous volcanic area. Barring an eruption, our visit should be refreshing.

Very few ruins are visible today because the modern Alasehir perches on top of them. Interestingly, "the most prominent ruin is that of an ancient church dedicated to John."[3] What ruins cannot tell us, the Word of God can.

Please read Revelation 3:7-13 and fill in the pertinent information.

• **Christ's self-identification coinciding with John's Revelation 1 vision:**

_____

• **Christ's commendation based on intimate acquaintance:** _____

_____

• **Christ's rebuke:** _____

• **Christ's exhortation:** _____

• **Christ's specific encouragement to overcome:** _____

_____

Pergamum's King Attalus II (159–138 B.C.) established Philadelphia. I was astounded by the many times the city's name changed. At one time it was renamed Neocaesarea (New Caesar) and another time, Flavia. Later, due to the establishment of the emperor cult in the city, it earned the title Neokoros, or Temple Warden. Little Athens became its nickname in the fifth century. Verse 12 may hint at the ever-changing identity of the city.

What did Christ promise to write on those who overcome?

_____

Living in a city with an ever-changing identity wasn't the only challenge the church in Philadelphia faced. Christ said, " 'I know that you have little strength' " (Rev. 3:8). Scholars almost unanimously agree that He did not mean spiritual strength, or He would not have commended them. Christ never commends spiritual weakness. Rather, He views weakness as an opportunity to discover His strength (see 2 Cor. 12:9-10).

Bible commentators believe that Christ's reference to the little strength of Philadelphia's church referred to its diminutive size and small visible impact. Poorer, less influential people composed that church; yet they endured patiently (Rev. 3:10). In our numbers-oriented society, we can hardly overestimate the discouragement that comes from perceived ineffectiveness. Don't think for a moment the enemy won't do everything he can to convince you that your efforts in Christ's name are in vain. He preys on feelings of uselessness and worthlessness. That's precisely why the enemy seeks every avenue to fuel and perpetuate them. We all have a God-given need to matter.

Each of us has a God-given need to matter.

Why do you think the need to matter is sacred?

_____

Needing to matter does not mean you are self-centered and vain. It means that you are human. What you and I do with the need can become extremely vain and self-centered, but the need itself is sacred. Fragrant flowers don't need someone to smell them to keep blooming. Lions don't kill their prey for significance. They're simply hungry. Only humans yearn to matter. God acknowledged the need immediately following our creation and, significantly, before our fall into sin.

How did God give us purpose in each of the following Scriptures?

Genesis 1:28 _____

Genesis 2:15 _____

Genesis 2:19 _____

God could have created the beasts of the field naturally subservient to us. Instead, He acknowledged our need to matter by telling us to rule over and subdue them. God could have made the garden of Eden self-maintaining. Instead, He appointed Adam to work and take care of it. God knew that Adam could use the challenge and the satisfaction responsibility would bring. Eve's entire purpose for existence was to matter. No one else was a suitable helper to Adam. God formed us to seek lives of purpose and, for those who follow His lead, to find them ultimately in Him alone.

One of the most important concepts we learned in week 6 was that the Father desires for each of our lives to bring forth much fruit. I desperately want you to flourish in the ministry God has for you, and I think the church in Philadelphia offers a few pointers in that process.

First, Christ alone is the judge of what matters. The small, seemingly insignificant band of believers in Philadelphia may have been blind to the fruit of their own efforts, but Christ found them beyond rebuke. I think the key word in His commendation is the description He used for the way they endured: patiently. Often we are tempted to give up before the harvest comes.

Ecclesiastes 3:1 tells us "there is a time for everything and a season for every activity under heaven." In Genesis 8:22 God promised that " 'as long as the earth endures, seedtime and harvest, cold and heat, summer and winter, day and night will never cease.' " Though far less predictable, we experience seasons of spirit as well as climate. The church in Philadelphia had probably been in the seedtime season without a large harvest longer than they wished—yet they continued to endure patiently.

> **According to the parable of the sower in Luke 8:11, what is the seed?**
>
> _____ _____ _____ _____

> **For what did Christ commend the church in Philadelphia after acknowledging its " 'little strength' " in Revelation 3:8?**
>
> _____

Unashamed of Christ's name against a bitter majority, the church kept Christ's word, thereby faithfully planting seeds. They did not give up, though the harvest seemed dreadfully distant. Remember, a landowner doesn't judge a harvest by the quantity of fruit alone. Diseased fruit means nothing but loss to him. He looks for quality.

> **Are you frustrated by what appears to be a small return on much effort in a ministry opportunity? If so, explain.**
>
> _____
>
> _____

Remember that God not only allows long seasons of seedtime but also sometimes appoints them to enhance the quality of the eventual harvest. At times He actively tests our faithfulness in smaller things to see whether we can handle bigger things. I hesitate to make this point, because big is not the goal. Christ revealed is the goal. However, if a high-volume ministry is one way God chooses to reveal His Son, those to whom He temporarily appoints them by His grace (see 1 Pet. 4:10) could undoubtedly describe countless appointments to small and frustrating opportunities along the way. In retrospect, most now recognize those small tasks as crucial tests.

I remember pouring my heart into several discipleship courses when only two or three persons showed up. I sensed God asking, "What are you going to do now? Cancel the class? Or give them no less than you would give 25 and finish the semester?" I am certain those were precious opportunities and also tests. I believe He tested me to see whether I would esteem the opportunity to teach Mother's Day Out and four-year-olds in Sunday School. Both extended the profound opportunity to mark young lives for eternity; yet some would be foolish enough to deem them unimportant. Thankfully, you obviously don't have to be a genius or particularly gifted to pass God's tests. I certainly would have failed. God is primarily looking for faithfulness to fulfill whatever duty He places before us. He guards our hearts by dissuading us from feeding our egos with result-oriented service.

Second, Christ is the door opener. One reason for so much frustration in ministry is our determination to open our own doors—in Jesus' name, of course. Some of our fists are bloody from beating down doors that we believe were supposed to open for ministry.

What does Revelation 3:8 tell us about doors Christ opens and shuts?

_____

I imagine God saying, "Did I tell you that was the right door? And if it were, would I not have opened it for you?" I often think of Peter's prison gate automatically opening for his escape because God appointed it (see Acts 12). I picture God with an invisible remote control in His hand controlling every door of opportunity on earth. As a rule of thumb but not without exceptions, I usually conclude that if the door requires beating, it's probably not the right one. And if God has shut a door, forget trying to open it! Remember, for a true harvest to result, the Holy Spirit has to prepare the way and go before us through the door. That's how it opens! Otherwise, it's either the wrong door or the wrong time.

Because the church of Philadelphia endured patiently, Christ placed before it an open door that no one can shut. Many scholars believe that open door was for missions directed farther east to other parts of Asia. Therefore, some commentators call the church of Philadelphia the missionary church.

How do the following verses support a high probability that the idea of an open door often implies missions opportunities?

Acts 16:6-7_____

1 Corinthians 16:9 _____

Each of us is called to missions. As we seek to keep Christ's Word and stay unashamed of His name (see Rev. 3:8), He will open doors of opportunity for us in His own time. If we faithfully sow seed, the harvest will come one day. Some missionaries never viewed their harvests from the fields of earth, but what better seat than heaven to get the full picture?

Has the account of the church of Philadelphia spoken to you today about your own ministry? If so, how?

_____

In closing, I want you to see two more jewels in the crown of the Philadelphians. Refresh your memory about Christ's promise to them (see Rev. 3:9). One of the meanest tricks Satan ever plays is to try to convince us that God doesn't love us and that we're exerting all this energy and exercising all this faith for nothing: "Look at all you've done, and He doesn't even care! It's all a big joke!" Satan used the Jews in Philadelphia to demoralize the small church, and he uses countless puppets to demoralize us today.

One of Satan's meanest tricks is to try to convince us that God doesn't love us.

Christ promised that one day the very people who sneered at the church in Philadelphia would acknowledge how much He loves them. We are not to be motivated by spite, but Jesus wants you to know that one day everyone will know how much He loves you. You have been unashamed of Him, and He most assuredly will prove unashamed of you.

Finally, Christ promised to make the overcomers pillars in the temple of His God. What significance this terminology had to the Philadelphians! The city was under the constant threat of earthquakes. The threat was especially vivid after a devastating earthquake in A.D. 17. Some historians say that the church had to rebuild their small sanctuary several times in only a few decades because of tremors. Often the only sign of life in a city left to ruins is the pillars.

What kind of kingdom are we receiving (see Heb. 12:26-29)?

_____

Christ's promise to the overcomers was that they would be kept from the hour of trial coming on the whole world and that they would stand like pillars in a kingdom that can never be shaken. Why? Because they mattered and, in spite of popular opinion, they chose to believe it. Dear One, let no one take your crown by convincing you otherwise.

Day 3 THE CHURCH IN LAODICEA

TODAY'S TREASURE

" 'You say, "I am rich; I have acquired wealth and do not need a thing." But you do not realize that you are wretched, pitiful, poor, blind and naked.' "—Revelation 3:17

Today we have quite a trip before us. Our next and final stop in our discovery of the seven churches is Laodicea. We'll find the city 45 miles southeast of Philadelphia and about 100 miles due east of our first stop in Ephesus. As we walk through the gates of our last destination in this segment of Revelation, we will have come virtually full circle. By the way, you might want to fill up your canteen in Philadelphia before we leave. I hear the water in Laodicea isn't worth drinking.

Please read Revelation 3:14-22 and fill in the pertinent information.

• **Christ's self-identification coinciding with the Revelation 1 vision:**

_____

• **Christ's commendation based on intimate acquaintance:** _____

_____

• **Christ's rebuke:** _____

- Christ's exhortation: _____

- Christ's specific encouragement to overcome: _____

_____

This segment contains so many wordplays and inferences that I am frantically asking God to help me choose what to teach and what to leave behind. I want to excavate the whole city! Many adjectives could apply to Laodicea, but let's consider three.

The church in Laodicea was indifferent. No one could accuse Christ of being luke-warm in His rebuke. Center on the impassioned statements " 'You are neither cold nor hot. I wish you were either one or the other!' " (v. 15). I agree with scholars who resist the interpretation that Christ wanted the Laodiceans to be either hot or cold spiritually. Though such figures of speech are common in our era, terming someone hot or cold in the faith wasn't part of the vernacular then. Furthermore, I hope we could safely conclude that Christ—who never desires for anyone to perish—would also not prefer anyone to be cold toward Him rather than lukewarm. I believe Christ meant, "For crying out loud, be of one use or the other!" We have much to learn about this distinct city that will shed light on Christ's rebuke and exhortation.

> No one could accuse Christ of being lukewarm in His rebuke.

Carefully read Colossians 4:12-14. Paul spoke of Epaphras as being one of them. To whom was the Letter of Colossians written (see Col. 1:2)?

_____

What two other cities are also mentioned in Colossians 4:13?

_____   _____

Epaphras was probably somewhat of a circuit preacher from Colosse. He divided his time between the church in his hometown and churches in Laodicea and Hierapolis. Laodicea lay directly between the other two cities, 7 miles southeast of Hierapolis and less than 10 miles north of Colosse. Ancient Hierapolis was famous for therapeutic hot springs, and ancient Colosse was known for sparkling cold waters. As we'll soon see, Laodicea could boast just about everything except an independent water supply. Ruins reveal a sophisticated, six-mile-long aqueduct that drew water from other sources.

In 1961–63 a team of French archaeologists excavated a structure called a *nymphaeum* located practically in the center of the city. The square water basin had stone columns on two sides and two semicircular fountains attached to it. The ornate fountains likely stood as beautiful centerpieces in the city square.[4] Characteristic of Laodicea, their beauty vastly exceeded their usefulness. You see, by the time the water was piped to the city from miles away, it was neither cold nor hot. You might easily imagine someone cupping her hands under the enticing waters to take a refreshing sip, only to spit it out in disgust. Sound familiar? Hot water has therapeutic value, and cold water refreshes, but lukewarm? If only I knew the Greek word for *yuck!*

Christ's vehement frustration with the church of Laodicea was that it would be of some use! The last thing I want to tout is a works-centered faith, but we have been called to faith-centered works. Christ intends for us to be useful! Churches are meant to be viable, active forces in their communities and not just where they have vested interests. Churches have doors not only for the world to come in but also for the church to go out.

In our previous lesson we talked about each person's innate need to matter. We need to discover how our gifts and contributions can be useful. If where we matter highly matters, we have slipped from innate need to ego feed. Anyone can be useful. In the spirit of Christ's exhortation to Laodicea, anyone can offer a cold glass of water to the thirsty or a hot cup of tea to the hurting. Or how about a frozen casserole? Or a warm pound cake? At times in my life nothing has ministered to me more than those two things! Christ exhorts His bride, "Be of use to my world!" At times therapeutic. At other times refreshing. Each of us can be hot and cold.

> Christ exhorts His bride, "Be of use to my world!"

 How do you most make yourself useful? _____

_____

The church in Laodicea was independent. What in the world happened to this church? Where was its need to be useful? The Laodiceans did what many people in our culture do today. They filled their gaping need to matter with possessions, then gauged their usefulness by their wealth. Praise God, neither then nor now can wealth indicate worth. Save your breath trying to convince Laodicea, however. When Christ drafted His letter to John, Laodicea was the capital of financial wizardry in Asia Minor—a marvel of prosperity.

How did the church describe itself (see Rev. 3:17)? _____

_____

Mind you, Christ's letter isn't addressed to the *city* of Laodicea. It is addressed to the *church* in Laodicea. How does that hit you? I can almost imagine the preacher glancing at the order of service during worship and saying, "Skip the offertory! After all, we're rich! We do not need a thing!" We'd die of shock in our church. I can't remember a time when we've had more money than needs. If we can't think of a thing to do with our surplus, I fear we've lost touch. The needs out there are endless.

I discovered some interesting pieces of information that help explain the Laodicean church. In A.D. 26 the city placed a bid with the Roman senate to build a temple to the Emperor Tiberius. It was denied on the basis of inadequate resources. The city's wealth so vastly increased during the next several decades that by A.D. 60, after the devastation of an earthquake, it didn't accept aid from Nero. It had plentiful resources to rebuild itself. (Do you hear the hints of independence?) In a nutshell, Laodicea thanked Rome but assured them that the city did not need a thing. Strangely, much of its original fortunes in the first century came from the fertile river valley that supplied lavish grazing for nice, fat sheep. The Laodiceans specialized in a tightly woven, black wool fabric that sold for a pretty penny. Behind their fortune, frankly, were farm animals that smelled.

I grin as I recall Keith's glib comment many years ago over a sudden outburst of superiority by one of his beloved sisters, a college student at the time. He looked over at me and said, "I wonder if now would be a good time to remind her that our family 'fortune' was made in other people's toilets." (His father owned a large plumbing company.) With much glee Keith and I have occasionally reminded our own daughters of the same profession that butters their bread.

New money. The Laodiceans had it. Certainly not all those with sudden wealth invest it in their ego accounts and disconnect their servers from the unfortunate. Furthermore, not all those with old money are charitable. My point is that the Laodiceans were in the lap of luxury and didn't think they had a care in the world. Little did they know that Christ was walking beside their lampstand.

The last portion of Psalm 62:10 speaks a good word to the Laodiceans and to us. What does it say?

_____

_____

I live in a city that never expected to be known for the collapse of one of the biggest financial empires in America. We learned the sobering lesson that billions of dollars can be lost as instantly as hundreds. We cannot set our hearts securely on riches, no matter how vast.

We cannot set our hearts securely on riches, no matter how vast.

Christ addressed another wealth-related issue in Matthew 13:22 that is readily recognizable in Laodicea. List a few ways wealth can be deceitful.

_____

_____

_____

Beloved, wealth alone is not the issue. We serve a God who can distribute the world's riches any way He sees fit. Few things can be more useful in our troubled world than resources in the hands of wise people. The problem is wealth's undependability and deceitfulness.

Two of my precious friends have not been deceived by wealth. Frankly, I never knew they were wealthy until someone told me. I've served in the same church with them for several decades and have never met less pretentious, more generous people. They are constantly involved in both inner-city and international missions. I'm convinced that their only attitude toward their resources is that of stewards over a trust. While others in their position might have locked themselves behind gates and pretended that much of the world wasn't starving to death, they threw themselves right into the middle of it.

The Laodicean church could have used my friends! Somehow it didn't grasp the principle "Unto whomsoever much is given, of him shall be much required" (Luke 12:48, KJV).

Do you know someone who has been faithful to this principle? If so, share. Be sensitive about any discomfort that using names might cause.

_____

This brings us to our final point: _the Laodicean church was self-deceived._ Its worth was so ingrained in its wealth that the people honestly saw themselves as utterly independent. We " 'do not need a thing' " (Rev. 3:17). Famous last words. Beloved, I'm not sure any of us get away with not needing a thing for long. Certainly, the kinds and intensities of our needs differ from season to season, but I don't expect God to risk our growing an independent spirit through sustained sufficiency. Of course, I don't know this for a fact because I can't remember having such a spirit. The older I get and the more my eyes open to the facts of life and ministry, the more my list of needs exceeds my list of wants. For instance, I need to have an active, effervescent, daily relationship with Jesus Christ, or I'm sunk. I need my husband's blessing. I need my coworkers. I need my church family. I need a friend I can trust. These are just a few necessities of life to me right now.

MY REAL NEEDS

What about you? In the margin list a few of your very real needs.

_____

_____

_____

_____

_____

_____

_____

_____

_____

You see, one reason we readily give (through lives that matter) is that we too need. That's how God planted the concept of give-and-take into true humanitarianism. Taking stock of both our contributions and our needs helps guard us against self-deception. Sadly, the Laodiceans had needs, too. They just didn't recognize them.

Fill in Christ's stunning response to the Laodicean deception: " 'You say, "I am rich" ... but you do not realize that you are ...

_____ ' " (Rev. 3: 17).

One of my worst nightmares is to think I'm rich when Christ knows I'm poor and my estimation of myself is higher than His.

How does Christ's address to Smyrna (see Rev. 2:9) starkly contrast with Laodicea's?

_____

How grateful I am that Christ had a remedy for the Laodiceans! Their self-deceived indifference had not deemed them castaways. Christ wrote the Laodiceans a three-part prescription. His first prescription was gold refined in fire.

What did Jesus mean? (First Peter 1:6-7 is a great hint if you need it.)

_____

His second prescription was " 'white clothes to wear' " (Rev. 3:18). The black wool fabric for which Laodicea was famous was the fashion rage all over that part of the world. Jesus suggested that they trade their fashions for purity. Ouch!

His final prescription was salve to put on their eyes. Not only was the city a marketing center and financial capital, but it also housed a well-known medical center best known for Phrygian powder, which was used to make salve for eye conditions. All the while, they were blind as bats and poor as beggars. I've been both.

One thing I've learned about God is that He is faithful in every way. He is faithful to forgive, redeem, bless, and provide. He is also faithful to chastise when His child won't readily turn from sin. Yes, the Laodiceans had a prescription, but Christ had no intention of letting them wait a month of Sundays to get it filled without consequences.

My head is spinning from all we've learned through our tour of the seven churches. Take a moment to review. What one truth stands out most to you?

_____

_____

I wish I could hear yours. I offer mine in closing: Christ has invested everything on earth in His church. He willingly fills her, frees her, purifies her, and restores her, but He never takes His eyes off her. Lives are at stake. Church matters. Bride, make yourself ready!

Day 4 THE THRONE ROOM

TODAY'S TREASURE

"Day and night they never stop saying: 'Holy, holy, holy is the Lord God Almighty, who was, and is, and is to come.' " —Revelation 4:8

Today we approach the very throne of God through the vision extended to John in the fourth chapter of Revelation. If we had any idea who and what we approach when we go to the throne of grace (see Heb. 4:16) through prayer and communion with God, our lives would change dramatically. I am convinced that we would fall on our faces far more often and that we'd pray with far more substance and certainty.

My deepest longing for today's lesson is that God would use our time in a magnificent chapter of Revelation to markedly adjust our perception of Him. No matter how far we move from our former misconceptions and small calculations, we will never fully comprehend the wonder of God's throne with our human minds. We can be profoundly affected, however, by the mere pursuit.

Read all of Revelation 4. Then on a separate sheet of paper draw an illustration of the heavenly scene. Stick figures are fine. As elementary as the assignment may seem, it will help us draw some critical conclusions.

Christ's revelation to John shifts dramatically as chapter 4 unfolds. In chapters 2—3 the earth-turned-spotlight of the Spirit cut through religious appearances, revealing the best and the worst about the seven churches in Asia Minor. In Revelation 4 the spotlight swung back to the origin of all illumination as Christ summoned John heavenward in spirit to behold the divine. Heaven was awhirl with activity; yet all attention centered on Someone sitting on a throne. Notice that the absence of detailed description jealously guards God's majesty. John simply described the splendor of the throne as being like brilliant gems.

The jasper known to John's world can be pictured as something like a diamond in ours. I wonder whether John saw something like light reflecting in spectacular displays off the prisms of a diamondlike object. The carnelian stone was a blood-red form of quartz that could symbolize access to the throne the one and only way: through the shed blood of Christ. The emerald green of the encircling rainbow could easily symbolize God's eternal covenant with those who receive His life. When the scales of humanity peel away from our eyes and we behold heaven, I believe we will see colors as never before. Perhaps only the crystal sea will be clear. Oh, how I praise God for the crystal sea!

Aren't you thankful that God included a vision of His throne room in Scripture? Actually, the Bible records several visions of His throne room in beautiful consistency.

I'd like for you to read two other similar revelations in Isaiah 6:1-5 and Ezekiel 1:22-28. Record the basic similarities and additional descriptions.

_____

_____

God never vacates His throne. He is never off duty.

What a relief to know that the throne is never depicted without Someone sitting on it! God never vacates His throne. He is never off duty. His sovereignty is never usurped. He is unceasingly praised. The threefold acclamation of God's holiness or perfect otherness occurs, significantly, only in the visions of the throne room.

Look at Exodus 26:33. What two rooms in the Old Testament tabernacle are distinguished in this verse?

The original term translated *holy place* employs only once the use of the word translated *holy*. The holy place was the room where the priests ministered before the Lord on a daily basis. It was the location of the table of showbread, the lamps, and the altar of incense. Behind the veil was the most holy place, which the high priest entered only once a year and with fear and trembling. God's presence, which extended earthward, dwelled between the cherubim on the atonement cover, or mercy seat. The original rendering of the term *most holy place* actually repeats the original word for *holy* for emphasis. The original wording for the holy place could be translated *the holy* and the most holy place, *the holy holy*.

Scripture characterizes some things as holy; others as holy, holy; and yet another as holy, holy, holy. I wonder whether the following explanation could be plausible. The places where God's people serve and minister before their God might biblically be characterized as once holy. As saints we are set apart in our service to Him as holy, but an even holier interaction exists. The places God agrees to meet with His people on earth through reverence and genuine worship might be characterized as twice-holy. True worship is the most holy experience we can have on this earth. But one day, when our feet leave their last prints in this soil and we approach God in His glorious heavenly abode, we will stand before the three-times-holy. We will join the seraphim who cry " 'Holy, holy, holy is the Lord God Almighty' " (Rev. 4:8)! The word *seraph* means *to burn*. Surely the closer we come to God's true presence, the more we will burn with passion!

Perhaps like me, you try to distinguish between members of the holy Trinity. Whom did John depict on the throne in these three revelations?

Before we immediately assume God the Father as the occupant or no distinction at all, please read Revelation 5:6. Where is the Lamb (Christ) depicted as standing?

I don't believe the revelator meant us to picture Christ standing up on a chair. Our familiarity with a throne is entirely related to a piece of furniture. The word *throne* seems to encompass the center, from which Christ presides with all authority. I am very intrigued that Ezekiel's vision describes "a figure like that of a man" (Ezek. 1:26) on the throne, and according to John 12:41, Isaiah saw Jesus' glory when he beheld the vision in Isaiah 6. Ordinarily, the manlike descriptions of God are attributed by most scholars to Christ. According to comparisons with Daniel 7 and Revelation 5, both the Father and the Son inhabit the throne room. Could it be that in the Old Testament God wanted most to reveal Christ and in the New Testament Christ wanted most to reveal God? I think it's quite possible and very like each of Them to shed light on the Other.

Return your focus to Revelation 4. The reference point for locating the elements described in this heavenly scene is critical.

Where was the rainbow? _____

Where were the 24 "other thrones"? _____

Where did the lightning and peals of thunder originate? _____

Where were the seven blazing lamps? _____

Where was the sea of glass? _____

Where were the four living creatures centered? _____

Where did the elders lay their crowns? _____

What conclusion could you draw from the reference point of every element in the Revelation 4 vision?

_____

Beloved, all existence centers on God on His throne. John had the perspective-changing opportunity to do something all of us secretly wish we could do. For a little while recorded in Revelation 4 and onward, he got to see life from heaven's perspective. His description implies something tremendously profound: everything else in existence is most accurately described only in its relationship to the throne of God.

Before we discuss our nearsighted vision (see 2 Pet. 1:9), never lose sight of the fact that God looked on His prize creation and liked us very much. Carefully look at Revelation 4:11, which implies much about God's creating us by His will. God's *thelema* is "an expression or inclination of pleasure; a want or desire which pleases and creates joy."[5] In other words, He created us because it pleased Him. Our attitudes and actions don't always please Him, but creating us, loving us, and redeeming us give Him great joy.

Much of humanity's trouble stems from our naturally insatiable self-centeredness. We often see ourselves as the center of the universe and tend to describe everything else in reference to ourselves rather than God. The human psyche almost invariably processes incoming information in relationship to its own ego. For example, if the news forecasts an economic slump, the natural hearer automatically processes what it could mean to self.

Although this response is natural, in perpetual practice self-absorption makes us miserable. In some ways humanity's egocentrism shows our lust for omnipotence. We want to be our own god and have all power. Our first reaction might be to deny we've ever had such a desire. Meanwhile, many of us take immediate responsibility for handling most of the problems in our midst, changing most of the people we know, and feeding our control addiction with the drug of manipulation. Simply put, we try to play God, and frankly, it's exhausting. No wonder God never sleeps, nor does He slumber (see Ps. 121:3)!

God gives those of us who are redeemed what 1 Corinthians 2:16 calls the "mind of Christ." We view life far more accurately when we learn to view it increasingly through the vantage point of the One who spoke it into existence.

In the margin list three of your greatest challenges or concerns.

THE HEART OF THE BELOVED

John had the perspective-changing opportunity to do something all of us secretly wish we could do. For a little while recorded in Revelation 4 and onward, he got to see life from heaven's perspective.

MY GREATEST CHALLENGES

1. _____

_____

_____

2. _____

_____

_____

3. _____

_____

_____

Now go back and write the words *Before the throne* before each of those challenges. The heart of prayer is moving such challenges from the insecurities and uncertainties of earth to the throne of God. Only then can they be viewed with dependable accuracy and boundless hope.

Go back to your original drawing of the elements in the throne room of God. Insert every one of the challenges you mentioned earlier in that diagram. In other words, write the phrases in your drawing. Carefully look at the drawing; then close your eyes and do your best to picture the glorious seraphim never ceasing to cry "Holy, holy, holy!" Imagine the lightning emitting from the throne and hear the rumblings of the thunder. Picture the elders overwhelmed by God's worthiness, casting their crowns before the throne. Read 1 Timothy 6:11-16 and add these thoughts to everything we've just pictured. I ask you the following question under my own tremendous personal conviction: Do we think God, the blessed and only Ruler, the King of kings and Lord of lords, who alone is immortal and lives in unapproachable light, can manage our lives and our problems?

Oh, Beloved, approach the throne of grace with confidence! Our God is huge.

Day 5 THE LAMB

> **TODAY'S TREASURE**
>
> *"I wept and wept because no one was found who was worthy. ... Then I saw a Lamb."—Revelation 5:6*

I want to cry over Today's Treasure, and we haven't even begun the lesson. Oh, how I long for the day when we will sit at the feet of the true Rabboni and hear Him expound on His own Word, just as the two on the road to Emmaus did: "Beginning with Moses and all the Prophets, he explained to them what was said in all the Scriptures concerning himself" (Luke 24:27). I cannot help but weep! If we could only grasp the perfections of Scripture, holding up the Word like a large, brilliant diamond. Only in the spray of colors cast by the prisms of the Old Covenant can we tilt the diamond to see the New. The Bible is a divine masterpiece, dear student! A progressive unveiling of marveling mystery and astounding consistency. Find a good seat in the auditorium today. Our study takes us before a stage to see the most profoundly consistent concept in Scripture fully unveiled.

> Only in the spray of colors cast by the prisms of the Old Covenant can we tilt the diamond to see the New.

Do more than simply read Revelation 5. Ask God to help you hear the events with spiritual ears and picture them to the farthest reaches of your imagination. After reading the entire chapter, describe the scroll.

_____

_____

We can't be certain what the scroll represents. One possibility is that it is like the one in Ezekiel's vision (see Ezek. 2:9-10). What was on this scroll?

_____

Some see the scroll as containing woes. Certainly the coming chapters of Revelation contain woes, so the interpretation is plausible for the Revelation 5:1 scroll. Eruptions of praise when Christ victoriously claimed the scroll, however, cause me to wonder how it can be associated with woes and laments alone. I tend to think the seals themselves involve wrath, but the words within unfold something ultimately glorious.

Another possibility is that the scroll represents God's will or testament for the completion of all things on earth and the transition to all things in heaven. In ancient Rome wills or testaments were sealed with six seals. A slight variation of this view refers to the Roman law of *mancipatio.* Under this law an heir received either an inheritance at the death of the deceased or the use of an inheritance. Thus, some scholars believe that the scroll is the title deed to earth.

Though I'm curious, I'm comfortable not knowing the exact identity of the scroll because—whatever it is—it is in the hands of Christ, but concentrate on verses 2-3. These events may not have happened over a simple matter of seconds. The verb tense of the Greek word for *proclaiming* may suggest that the mighty angel could have repeated the question several times, scattering glances to and fro for someone who was worthy. The deafening silence left by no answers then heightened the anxiety of the listener.

How did John respond, according to Revelation 5:4?

_____

By now surely you have some picture of John in your mind and affection for him in your heart. Keep in mind that the power and presence of the Holy Spirit doesn't make us feel less. The Spirit brings life. Every one of John's senses was surely quickened. His response to the sight of the throne must have been indescribable awe. A tidal wave of grief crashed against the backdrop of awe. The word used for *weep* usually implies accompanying demonstrations of grief.

In our previous lesson we stood transfixed with John as witnesses to the vision of the throne room of God. Something dramatic happened in the transition of the scene in chapter 5. Suddenly John was no longer watching revelation. He was part of the scene. Previously a bystander to the elders who cast their crowns before the throne, he was then approached by one as he wept.

How did the elder comfort John? Look very carefully at the terminology in verses 5-6 and fill in the blanks.

One of the elders said to John, " 'See, the _____ of the

tribe of Judah, ... has _____.' "

John must have gazed expecting to "see" ("behold," KJV) a Lion. Instead, John wrote, "Then I saw a Lamb, looking as if it had been slain" (v. 6). Look at the verbs "has triumphed" and "had been slain." You see, the Lion of the tribe of Judah has triumphed the one and only way possible, according to the plan probably written within that scroll: as a Lamb that had been slain. Simply put, the Lion triumphed as the Lamb slain.

The Lion triumphed as the Lamb slain.

Briefly summarize what happened after the Lamb took the scroll.

_____

In our previous lesson the elders sang to God the Father. Several hymns appear in this chapter. To whom is each addressed (see vv. 9-10,12-13)?

_____

Notice that the hymn in verses 9-10 is addressed to the Lamb and called "a new song." I wonder if the reason may be that praises like those described in Revelation 4 have been sung appropriately throughout eternity. The word _new_ is a time-related word. Words such as _new_ and _old_ have to refer to something involving—or in relationship to—earth or created beings. They have no reference in that which pertains to heaven alone. Obviously, something glorious happened involving earth and those bound by time that releases a new song.

The song itself tells what happened. In essence, what was it?

_____

_____

The new song proclaimed the one and only hope of earth: the Lamb slain!

Beloved, not only did the new song have to do with the earth, but it also proclaimed the one and only hope of earth: the Lamb slain! The primary picture of Christ in Revelation is undoubtedly Jesus as the Lamb. The title repeatedly bursts forth like fireworks in the grande finale of Holy Writ. And for good reason. No concept in the Word of God has been more consistent.

Though we will only touch the surface, let's take a quick look at the place occupied by the Lamb throughout Scripture. Please look up each reference even if you can quote it from memory. Don't let familiarity cheat you on this exercise!

Genesis presents the account of creation. Look at the interesting terminology surrounding the Lamb in Revelation 13:8. "The Lamb that was slain ...

_____ _____ _____ __ _____ _____."

How do you feel about the fact that the plan of redemption was obviously already set in motion before humans were created?

_____

You see, Beloved, humanity's fall did not take God by surprise. Before He said, " 'Let there be light' " (Gen. 1:3), He basically said, "Let there be a plan." And there was. A Lamb slain from the creation of the world.

What happened on the sixth day of creation in Genesis 1:24-25?

_____

In the midst of countless creatures, hoofed and not, God created the lamb. I happen to think God is the sentimental type. It shows throughout Scripture, and we, a sentimental people, were created in His image. I don't think He created the lamb with little notice. He knew the profound significance He would assign to the small, helpless creature.

Notice that Adam wasn't created until after the animals. God saved what He considered His best for last. I think the fact that a lamb was created before a person is quite fitting. Throughout the Old Testament, people would require a heap of them.

What first appears in Genesis 3:21? _____

This is the first reference to a sacrificial death. Because God dressed them with a skin, we know that an animal perished for them to be covered. We have no way of knowing whether the animal was a lamb, but I can hardly picture it any other way.

What is recorded in Genesis 4:3-4? _____

Not coincidentally, from the moment in Scripture that life appears outside the garden, we see sacrificial offerings. God wasn't partial to Abel. He was partial to Abel's offering. Abel presented God an offering from his flock. When not distinguished otherwise, a flock almost always refers to sheep in Scripture. Notice that the Lord looked with favor on Abel. From the Old Testament to the New, the Lord looks with favor on those who are symbolically covered by the blood of the Lamb. Verse 7 intimates that Cain knew the right thing to do and had the same chance to bring a sacrificial offering. The basic tenet of all biblical rebellion is refusing the blood of the Lamb.

Far from coincidence, the first time in Scripture the word *lamb* is used is in Genesis 22. Fittingly, the words *sacrifice* and *worship* are introduced in the same chapter, and the word *love* appears for only the second time. Read Genesis 22:7-8 and then glance over this unparalleled Old Testament chapter. The event it describes is the heart of what Galatians calls the gospel preached in advance to Abraham (see Gal. 3:8; Rom. 9:7). Glory!

What happened just as Abraham was about to slay his beloved son (see v. 13)?

_____

The ram, a male sheep, was secured for Abraham's use by horns caught in the thicket. Horns remained very significant throughout the Old Testament and were positioned on the corners of the altar of sacrifice so that a lamb could be secured to them with ties.

Glance back at Revelation 5:6. How are horns associated with the Lamb?

_____

We don't have to fear that Christ is going to look like some frightening monstrosity. John's language is figurative. In the prophecies of both Daniel and Revelation, horns represent authority and power. The Lamb's power and authority to redeem on earth came through His willingness to be slain.

The Lamb's power to redeem came through His willingness to be slain.

We cannot find a more perfect Old Testament picture of the blood of the sacrificial lamb than the one recorded in Exodus 12:1-14. What do these verses describe?

_____

What is this lamb called in Exodus 12:21? _____

The concept that unfolded outside the garden, echoed from Isaac's Mount Moriah, and dripped from the doorposts of captive Israel remained constant throughout the Old Testament. Numberless animals were sacrificed throughout the centuries at the altars of the tabernacle and the temple. God's wonders in behalf of Israel were astounding; as long as they followed Him, He fought for them. Then they repeatedly fell into idolatry. After God sent the prophets with warnings, Old Testament Scripture comes to an abrupt halt—but not without a promise. Malachi 4:5 promises that Elijah will come "before the great and dreadful day of the Lord."

As in many other prophecies, God spoke symbolically. Who fulfilled this prophecy, according to Matthew 11:12-14? _____

Look at John 1:29. What did John the Baptist first say when he first saw Jesus coming toward him?

_____

Luke 22 records the last supper Christ shared with His disciples. Because a Jewish day begins just after sundown and lasts until the next, Christ was actually crucified on the very same day they ate their final meal together.

What day was it, according to Luke 22:13-14? _____

Oh, do you realize we've only seen a glimpse? Yet look at the consistency! A lamb, the lamb, the Lamb! So we wouldn't miss the woolen thread, Revelation, the book of the Bible that brings all things to completion, shouts this title like triumphant blasts from a ram's horn. Not once. Not twice. But 28 times! The Lamb slain from the foundation of the world for the salvation of the world.

Humans can shake an arrogant fist all they want, but they will never shake God. The plan is firm. No plan B exists. All things are going just as He knew they would. We look around us and hang our heads over the miserable estate of this lost, depraved world. And all the while, God sits on His throne. I can imagine Him saying, "As long as man has breath, I have a Lamb."

> "Then I looked and heard the voice of many angels, numbering thousands upon thousands, and ten thousand times ten thousand. They encircled the throne and the living creatures and the elders. In a loud voice they sang:
>
> "Worthy is the Lamb, who was slain,
> to receive power and wealth and wisdom and strength
> and honor and glory and praise!" (Rev. 5:11-12).

"As long as man has breath, I have a Lamb."

[1]William M. Ramsay, *The Letters to the Seven Churches of Asia* (London: Hodder & Stoughton, 1904), 375, as quoted in Frank E. Gaebelein and J. D. Douglas, *The Expositor's Bible Commentary*, vol. 12 (Grand Rapids: Zondervan Publishing, 1981), 448.

[2]William Barclay, *Letters to the Seven Churches* (New York: Abingdon, 1957), 71, as cited in Gaebelein and Douglas, *The Expositor's Bible Commentary*, 448.

[3]Joseph F. Green, "The Seven Churches of Revelation," *Biblical Illustrator*, spring 1980, 49.

[4]Henry L. Peterson, "The Church at Laodicea," *Biblical Illustrator*, spring 1982, 74–75.

[5]Spiros Zodhiates, "Lexical Aids to the New Testament," 2525, in Spiros Zodhiates, Warren Baker, and David Kemp, *The Hebrew-Greek Key Study Bible* (Chattanooga, TN: AMG Publishers, 1996), 1631.

VIDEO RESPONSE SHEET

Group Session 9

Read Revelation 12:7-12. Revelation 12:9 calls the enemy of our souls by five names:

• The _____ _____

• That _____ _____

• The _____

• _____

• _____

Primary defenses against the accuser:

1. "By the _____ of the _____." Once we are covered by the blood of the Lamb,

   Satan can do nothing to "uncover" us. So what's a devil to do? Try to make us "feel" uncovered.

2. "By the _____ of their testimony"

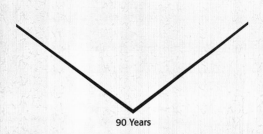

90 Years

THE ACCUSER'S FORMULA

Your ____
- Your _____
+ Your _____

GOD'S FORMULA

_____ was
+ _____ is

BLESSED BENEDICTION

Day 1
A Song No One Else Can Sing

Day 2
The Wrath of God

Day 3
The Devil's Doom

Day 4
The New Jerusalem

Day 5
Seeing His Face

Though we've reached our final chapter, don't wind down too quickly. Many sights await us in our journey's final miles. Some will thrill us. Others may horrify us. All of them are meant to change us and prepare us for the future. No book of the Bible will make us more thankful to belong to Jesus Christ than the Book of Revelation. Never lose sight of the fact that "there is now no condemnation for those who are in Christ Jesus" (Rom. 8:1). Though we have walked side by side with many who are lost, our futures will literally be worlds apart. May God increase our desire to pray for unbelievers and to more willingly share not our fears but our faith. In the meantime, we can trust the wisdom and eternal plan of the One " 'who is, and who was, and who is to come, the Almighty' " (Rev. 1:8). Study hard this week, Dear One.

Principle Questions

Day 1: How were the 144,000 marked, according to Revelation 14:1?
Day 2: Why will people refuse God (see Rom. 2:5)?
Day 3: Exactly how will Christ strike down His foes (see Rev 19:15,21)?
Day 4: In Revelation 21:14 what did John see on the 12 foundations of the city wall?
Day 5: How had John lived the essence of John 15:12-17?

Day 1 A SONG NO ONE ELSE CAN SING

TODAY'S TREASURE

"No one could learn the song except the 144,000 who had been redeemed from the earth."—Revelation 14:3

Today we begin the last week of our journey together. We've come to such an exciting part of our study that it hardly seems to be winding down. In only a few days, though, we will embrace and say farewell, at least for a season. You've been the perfect traveling companion, and I am grateful for the privilege to walk these last few miles with you.

Our focus is on ideas in the Book of Revelation that we believe John most wanted us to grasp. I've had to make difficult decisions about what to prioritize in our overview of the final book of Scripture. I love the study of Last Things, and I am fascinated by all the symbols and interpretations of this intriguing benediction to God's Word. Yet our time constraints and goals convince me to draw out a few key ideas from the many truths we can discover in the book.

I will be approaching this portion of our study from the perspective that primarily looks at the passages as describing future events. Be aware that Bible scholars have many different interpretations of these passages. Please take my study as just one student's understanding of the meaning of some very complex passages of Scripture and ask God to reveal what He wants you to learn. Today our thoughts will center on Revelation 14.

> **Please read the whole chapter and organize its concepts. Write in the margin a very basic three- or four-statement outline. Keep in mind that John often introduced new segments of the vision by the words "Then I looked" or "Then I saw."**

You can certainly tell from the tone of this chapter that the pulse of the book just escalated. If you listen closely, you can almost hear the hiss of the sickle cutting through air thick with looming judgment. The long prophesied Day of the Lord, when He will settle all accounts, draws nearer and nearer. The mere thought leaves me with a strange mingling of anticipation and dread. I desperately desire the coming of His kingdom; yet I yearn for all to confess Christ before judgment comes. Our next lesson will be difficult because we are going to discuss God's wrath. Today's Scriptures provide a prelude to prepare us for that lesson and also remind us of our God's perfect plan and provision.

The vision of the 144,000 purposely follows the harrowing prophesies about the two beasts described in Revelation 13. One of the first principles I learned in Bible study about the kingdom of darkness is that anything God does, Satan attempts to counterfeit. We shouldn't be surprised.

> **Please read Isaiah 14:14. I'm convinced that these words can apply only to Satan, the morning star "fallen from heaven" (Isa. 14:12). What is Satan's blasphemous goal?**

MY OUTLINE OF REVELATION 14

_____

_____

_____

_____

_____

_____

_____

_____

_____

_____

203

Now read Revelation 13 and record every way the kingdom of darkness imitates the works of God but with a twisted, evil intent. Don't be intimidated. Some students will find a few and others many. Even if this is the first Bible study you've ever done, you will undoubtedly discover several counterfeits based on what we've already covered.

_____

_____

The light of God is incomparably brighter than the darkness of Satan.

We can hardly comprehend why God's plan for the ages makes room for the full expression of such evil, but let's try to understand that Revelation records events that bring both light and darkness earthward. Never lose sight of the fact that the light of God is incomparably brighter than the darkness of Satan. God and Satan are not equal-though-opposite powers. God allows Satan to exist and act only in ways that ultimately satisfy certain critical elements in God's kingdom agenda for planet Earth. Before Satan meets his inevitable doom, God will allow him to drop many of his ancient masquerades, as well as reveal himself in some respects. Revelation centers on the ultimate unveiling of Jesus Christ, but the Bible's benediction also appropriately pictures all things revealed—whether good or evil, pure or defiled, heaven or hell.

In the wake of the inconceivable massacre of Revelation 13, God refreshed the beloved disciple with the vision of a remnant marked for survival and the sounds of rushing waters, thunder, and harps. Review Revelation 14:1-5 again. Capture its emotions and sip its healing tonic after the bitterness of the preceding chapter. Scholars disagree about whether these are the same 144,000 mentioned in Revelation 7:1-8. I believe verses 3-4 suggest that likelihood.

What do these verses tell us? _____

_____

I believe very possibly this seal is described further in Revelation 14:1. How were the 144,000 of Revelation 14 marked, according to the first verse?

_____

Glory! The name of the Lamb and the Father! On their foreheads! I don't think we should naturally assume that these names were visible to earthly eyes. Remember, John was seeing a vision far exceeding the natural realm. I believe that John more likely saw the marks on the 144,000 as they were visible in the supernatural realm just as the hosts of heaven and the demons of hell viewed them. Why do I make this point? Because I believe we share some similarities with these 144,000. They won't be the only ones who are sealed.

Who else is sealed, according to Ephesians 1:13? _____

The Greek words for _seal_ in reference to the 144,000 and to all believers in Jesus Christ in Ephesians 1:13 are the same. Granted, the seal of the 144,000 had a different purpose as it rendered them off limits, in effect, to the enemy until God completed His purposes. I am not suggesting that our seal is exactly the same or that it includes the name of the

Lamb and the Father, although I think the possibility is viable. On the other hand, I do think we very likely bear a mark or seal that identifies us in the supernatural world as God's own. The concepts in the Word of God are very consistent from the Old Testament to the New. Under the order of the original priesthood during the time of the tabernacle, God instructed the priests to wear a turban, described in Exodus 28:36-38.

What did the seal say, and where was it positioned on Aaron?

Principles God applied to Israel in the visible realm are often true of New Testament believers in the invisible realm. Notice the parallel between the inscriptions on the foreheads. According to 1 Peter 2:9, we are a priesthood of believers. Ephesians 1:13 tells us we also bear a seal. If we are the New Testament priesthood and we also have a seal, could it possibly be on our foreheads as well? We can only imagine.

I believe one thing is certain: we are marked, and in all probability this seal is visible in the supernatural realm. Beloved, you may struggle with doubts over whether you are saved, but I don't believe that a single angel or demon in the unseen world has any doubt. We who are saved bear the seal of our Father. As 2 Timothy 2:19 says, "God's solid foundation stands firm, sealed with this inscription: 'The Lord knows those who are His.'" Hallelujah!

> We who are saved bear the seal of our Father.

How do you feel about having a seal marking you as Christ's for all the supernatural world to see?

Scholars are very divided as to who makes up the 144,000 and whether the Mount Zion in this vision is on earth or in heaven. Where the latter is concerned, the Bible clearly refers to both. The tragedy for any student of this chapter would be to get caught up in the symbolism and miss the song.

What song? Take another look at verse 3. The song no one could learn—except the 144,000 who had been redeemed from the earth. Please don't miss that John heard the song, but he could not learn it. Notice that it was a new song. I am not a singer, but I dearly love to sing praise songs to my God. We have a wonderful praise team at our church. I enjoy learning a new song every week or two, but I must admit that I get frustrated on occasion when most of what we sing is unfamiliar. I often think how silly I am, because every song I love was once unknown to me.

Name a praise and worship song you at first found difficult and unfamiliar but over time came to love as a favorite.

My favorite songs are the ones that become mine over time as I sing them to God through the filter of my own experience and affection. Though such preferences may seem self-centered and self-absorbed, praise and worship are very personal to me. In fact, as long as our feet are planted in the soil of earth, I know of few more intimate encounters than raising our voices in worship to the God of heaven. When I am most involved in worship, I may as well be completely alone in the sanctuary with Him.

Nothing provokes a new song in my heart like a fresh surge of hope in a wilderness season. The song "Shout to the Lord" will forever be special to me because I first heard it at a time of deep personal suffering. The words came to my soul from God as hope that I would survive—and even thrive once again. First I heard the new song; then I learned it. My motivation to learn it came through its voice to my experience in that difficult but strangely beautiful season with God.

Who could learn the song John heard? _____

Why do you think no one else could learn the song? None of us have the definitive answer to the question. Just offer your thoughts.

_____

_____

The Greek word for *new* in reference to the new song in Revelation 14:3 implies new in quality as opposed to number. In other words, the song wasn't new in terms of a new release in Christian contemporary music. The song of the 144,000 was new because it had an entirely different quality from anything they'd sung before. It meant something to them that no other song had ever meant. I think no one else could learn the song because no one else had ever lived it. From their unique experience God gave them a song that only they could learn.

Under what circumstances did David too receive a "new song" (Ps. 40:1-3)?

_____

_____

We can also receive a new song from God that arises from hardship's victories.

If we are willing, we can also receive a new song from God that arises from hardship's victories, not necessarily in musical notes but in fresh truths engraved on the heart. These are precious gifts that eventually come to those who keep the faith and wait to see God redeem great difficulty. These songs can be heard by others, but they cannot be learned secondhand.

This concept is both the life and near-death of me at times. I love the gift of new songs that finally emerge like frolicking whales from the deep waters of trial or suffering. At the same time, I am frustrated when I cannot talk someone into loving and trusting God. They just don't seem to realize that His Son is the greatest adventure in life. I want each member of the body of Christ to love Jesus passionately and to live the excitement of His abundant life so badly that I could sob. I practically jump up and down in ministry, insisting, "If He will do this for me, He will do this for anyone!"

Until individuals let Jesus redeem their personal lives, hurts, losses, and failures, they can hear the song but cannot learn it. Songs of the heart are learned only through personal faith experience. Once we learn the songs, however, no one can take them from us.

Do you have a testimony about a time when God gave you a new song or a new hope in a virtually hopeless situation? If so, please share.

_____

_____

Day 2 THE WRATH OF GOD

TODAY'S TREASURE

"I saw in heaven another great and marvelous sign: seven angels with the seven last plagues—last, because with them God's wrath is completed."—Revelation 15:1

I deeply hope that our previous lesson prepared us to some extent for today's focus. Unfortunately, we cannot be serious students of what John most wanted us to know and avoid the subject of God's wrath. If Revelation were a movie, the images we'll study today would undoubtedly send me out for a refill of popcorn. However, Revelation is no movie. Nor is it fiction. I'm not glad.

Perhaps the truest words that ever fall from tainted human lips are these: God is faithful. Indeed He is. What may trouble us today is that He is always faithful. In other words, God always does what He insists He will do, whether we like it or not. The idealist in me wishes the wrath of God didn't even exist and would never be unleashed. Then the realist in me—

- reads accounts of unspeakable cruelties and abuses to children;
- reviews another part of human history blighted by war crimes and bloody crusades spearheaded by those claiming to act in God's name;
- hears God's name publicly mocked, profaned, and derided through various forms of media;
- listens to the arrogant who have convinced themselves they are gods;
- sees the violence bred by hatred, ignorance, and prejudice;
- stands by while princes of the earth lay their bricks on an unseen but very present Tower of Babel.

Like you, I look around me and shudder with horror over and over again, asking, "Where is the fear of God?" Then I shake my head and wonder what kind of power God must use to restrain Himself.

What makes you shudder and know in your heart that God's wrath must come?

_____

I don't even have to look as far as the world. At times I've looked no farther than my own mirror or my own church and wondered at the words of Lamentations 3:22, "Because of the Lord's great love we are not consumed." I have said to Him more times than I can count, "Lord, why You do not rend this earth and swallow up Your own people, not to mention this godless world, is beyond me." Of course, I know that God spares believers because He did not spare His own Son (see Rom. 8:32). For all of time the most succinct answer to those questions can be found in 2 Peter 3:9.

God spares believers because He did not spare His own Son.

Write a paraphrase of 2 Peter 3:9.

_____

_____

Sometimes I have to check and make sure it's still there. Praise God, His Word never changes. I might warn you, we have lots of it to read today, but the subject matter is critical and should no doubt hold our attention. Before we turn our attention to several chapters in Revelation, I'd like for you to read the context of the verse you just noted.

Please read all of 2 Peter 3:1-15 and write three facts you reap.

_____

_____

In some ways God's wrath will simply finish off what humans started. I am convinced that we will do a pretty good job of destroying ourselves and our planet. The Book of Daniel talks of wars and conflicts that many interpreters believe apply to the end of the age. God's Word promises a new heaven and a new earth but not until this one is destroyed.

Matthew 24 prophesies increasing wickedness and destruction with a mounting strength and frequency of birth pains. Toward the very end of this age God will allow the full measure of permissible wrath to be poured out on this earth: the wrath of human beings (never underestimate it), the unholy wrath of Satan, and the holy wrath of God. No wonder this time of great tribulation will be like no other. The wrath described in the Book of Revelation unfolds in a mysterious sequence of seals, trumpets, and bowls.

Read these passages and note the descriptions that stand out most to you.

The seals: Revelation 6; 8:1-5 _____

_____

_____

The trumpets: Revelation 8:6-13; 9 _____

_____

_____

The bowls: Revelation 16 _____

_____

_____

I feel enormous horror for those who refuse to believe. In your own words, what does God's Word say to believers in 1 Thessalonians 1:10?

_____

The wrath of God described in the Book of Revelation is not toward the redeemed.

I am not implying that believers won't go through terrible times. The Word clearly states that we will (see 2 Tim. 3:1), and many Christians already are. My point is that the wrath of God described in the Book of Revelation is not toward the redeemed. They will be delivered either from it or through it. I believe the greatest evangelism explosion of all times will occur during the end times. The inoculation against the coming wrath of God is confessing His Son as Savior and repenting of sin. No one who comes to Him with a sincere heart of reception and repentance will be refused—unless they wait too late. I so badly did not want to write that last phrase.

As the end of time approaches, God will reveal Himself in countless ways, pouring out His Spirit, His wonders, and His mercies. Those mercies, however, are dealt according to demand. In other words, some people respond to tender mercies. Others don't respond until God shows severe mercies. Others don't respond at all. Never forget that God wants to save people and not destroy them. During the last days the heavens will show so many signs and evangelists will preach so powerfully that I am convinced people will practically have to work at refusing Him. Tragically, many will.

Why will people refuse God (see Rom. 2:5)? _____

_____

People will not refuse God because He didn't love them or make provision for them. Beloved, please hear my heart. God's wrath cannot be separated from His character and person. Even in His unleashed wrath God cannot be less than who He is. God is holy. He is good. He is love. God is righteous, and God is right. The Judge will judge, but unlike ours, His judgments are always based on truth (see Rom. 2:2).

God is also inconceivable compassion, forgiveness, and mercy. I need look no farther than my hands on this keyboard for proof. How He has forgiven me! When others might have left me for dead and said I got what I deserved, He tended my filthy, self-inflicted wounds and pulled me from the ditch. See for yourself that God's mercy far exceeds that of human beings.

Turn to Jonah 4. Why was Jonah angry with God?

_____

How did God respond to him?

❑ **Squashed him like a bug**   ❑ **Demanded an immediate apology**
❑ **Patiently instructed him**   ❑ **Gave him 30 days to repent**

God is neither mean nor unjust. He is holy. Beloved, God will judge this world. The Day of the Lord will come, and none will doubt that He is God. He will not be mocked. He would have to be untrue to His own character to do otherwise. Read Revelation 15:1-5.

I love the reference to the song of Moses and the song of the Lamb. You see, God will bring perfect order and completion from a season that will seem the ultimate in chaos and destruction. The end of times will culminate in the brilliant plan of God rising from the smoldering tomb of earth. From the back this resurrected life looks like the old covenant. From the front it looks like the new covenant. But when all is said and done, the two will be seen as they were always intended: as one perfect whole. As one perfect life: Christ's. All will make sense.

God is neither mean nor unjust. He is holy.

Read Revelation 15:3-4 in your Bible to end today's study.

Day 3 THE DEVIL'S DOOM

TODAY'S TREASURE

"The devil, who deceived them, was thrown into the lake of burning sulfur, where the beast and the false prophet had been thrown. They will be tormented day and night for ever and ever."—Revelation 20:10

Today's study will not require as much reading as our previous lesson, but our subject matter is still very intense. All things—both good and evil—will intensify like the crescendo of a shofar hailing the King of kings and a government with no end. We cannot comprehend the ways and means by which God will work out "everything in conformity with the purpose of his will" (Eph. 1:11), but we can trust in the all-wise sovereign and supreme God who can do no wrong.

One of the Scriptures on my personal set of index cards right now is Daniel 4:37. I insert my name rather than Nebuchadnezzar's when I read it aloud over my own life. Why don't you begin by reading this Scripture aloud and inserting your own name?

" 'I, _____, praise and exalt and glorify the King
of heaven, because everything he does is right and all his ways are just.
And those who walk in pride he is able to humble' " (Dan. 4:37).

Don't miss our final video session together. We will focus on Revelation 19:5-16 and celebrate the wedding supper of the Lamb in advance. This passage will be included in today's reading, but I want you to understand why we won't center on these marvelous Scriptures at this time. We are saving the best for last. Our reading assignment today will take place in four parts, with brief discussions following each one.

Part 1: Give Revelation 19:11-21 a title as if it appeared in a newsmagazine.

_____

> People probably reject God because they are unwilling to bow to authority.

To the astonishment of all that is reasonable, masses of people still gather with the beast to make war against the Rider on the horse and His army. After unprecedented signs and wonders and mercies of God, ranging from tender to severe, many refuse to repent. Why do they exercise the foolish audacity to stand as a foe against the blazing Son of God? One reason probably exceeds all others when people reject God in the face of over-whelming evidence: unwillingness to bow to authority.

Notice the wording in Revelation 19:19 and fill in the blank.

**"Then I saw the beast and the _____
and their armies gather together to make war against the rider."**

Based on glorious Scriptures like Revelation 7:9, I believe that innumerable people will turn to Jesus Christ and be saved in the last days. Revelation 19—20 also tells us that many will perish in their arrogant refusal to turn to truth.

I can't help but focus on the reference to the "kings of the earth." The Word intimates that some of those who refuse to bow will be the reputed power brokers of the earth. Their lust for dominance will literally be the death of them. How foolish! In their refusal to bow to a righteous God, they will bow to the prince of hell.

Satan's scheme is as old as his first appearance in the garden. He tries to convince humans that they can be their own bosses, their own gods. It's a sham. We were created to worship and bow down. (Perhaps that's why God gave us legs with knees.) He fashioned us to serve under a greater rule. We cannot be our own bosses, no matter how insistently we deny our purpose. Yes, God ordains human government and places people in high positions—but always under His divine dominion. Nebuchadnezzar could teach us the life principle in Daniel 4:37 as few others can. He learned the hard way that those who take credit for the kingdoms of the earth pay a hefty price.

Exactly how will Christ strike down His foes (see Rev. 19:15,21)?

_____

_____

I believe a sword symbolizes Christ's tongue because He will strike down His foes by His words. His is the same mouth that spoke the universe into existence and whirled the earth into orbit. Unlike me, Christ doesn't have to use His hands to speak or to strike His foe. He speaks, and His will is accomplished. How fitting that God assigned John the revelator the privilege of announcing Christ's returning title, as stated in Revelation 19:13.

What is that title? _____

No other inspired writer was given insight into the *Logos*. The same Word made flesh to dwell among us will also return with a shout of victory as His foes fall at His feet. Every knee will bow—one way or the other.

> The Word made flesh will return with a shout of victory as His foes fall at His feet.

Part 2: Assign Revelation 20:1-6 a title.

_____

What irony that references to a "great chain" and being "set free" are right here in passages prophesying the devil's future. Scripture tells us that Satan will be bound for a thousand years before he is thrown into the lake of burning sulfur (see Rev. 20:10). Scholars are very much divided over when the thousand years takes place. No matter the time frame, Satan will be bound for a season.

I couldn't be happier that the means is a great chain. How appropriate! As far as I'm concerned, the last days are high time for Satan to be bound in chains! Perhaps for all of us who have cried "How long, O Sovereign Lord, until You avenge our bondage?" I can't wait for him to know how chains feel. In fact, I hope the great chain is made from all the ones that have fallen off our ankles!

I want Satan to experience the same sense of powerlessness with which he deceived many of us. Praise God for truth that sets us free! Satan tried his hardest to keep me bound and to destroy my life, my family, my testimony, and my ministry, but God defeated him by the power of His outstretched arm. The future will show not only Satan defeated but also his wickedness toward us avenged.

> The future will show Satan defeated and his wickedness toward us avenged.

How about you? What are you anxious for God to avenge on your behalf?

_____

_____

A serious set of chains will quite sufficiently avenge the wrongs Satan dealt us. What will the world be like while Satan is in chains? Based on my own personal study, I tend to think the period of Satan's bondage in the abyss coincides with the kingdom of Christ on earth, a kingdom characterized by peace, righteousness, and security. Keep in mind, however, that brilliant scholars stand both for and against this interpretation. God will accomplish His will in His own way, regardless of human opinion.

Revelation 20:3 offers what may be the ultimate irony. After a season of bondage Satan will be set free by God for a short time. May I say somewhat tongue-in-cheek that this example could suggest that God can set anyone free! Of course, Satan's freedom will not be liberty from sin and rebellion but freedom to rise up once again in rebellion against God. Our next reading tells us what will happen.

Part 3: Write a title for Revelation 20:7-10.

_____

I suppose we need not worry about whether Satan will learn his lesson while chained in the abyss. He is the embodiment of evil. He will return to his old tricks the moment he is released, exceedingly empowered by ever-increasing rage.

In the final rebellion masses of people will choose to stand in defiance against the holy Son of God. Mind you, by this time Christ will be fully revealed. We can only imagine what schemes of deception the evil one will use to convince people that he can promise them more than God their Maker. My guess is that they will be deluded into thinking that they are choosing their own lusts and greeds rather than an eternity of holiness in the presence of God. They will know the truth; yet they will choose a lie. Thinking they are choosing themselves, they will choose the devil.

Unlike the boastful and crude philosophies, hell will not be one big party. Hell will be eternal bondage to torment. I cannot bear the thought of it and want no one to go there.

Let's take a look at the last segment of Scripture in today's lesson.

Part 4: Give Revelation 20:11-15 a title.

_____

Based on my understanding of Scripture and the final judgments, only the lost will stand at the great white throne.

How does this seat of judgment seem to differ from the one described in 1 Corinthians 3:10-15 and 2 Corinthians 5:1-10?

_____

_____

Those who know Christ will stand before the judgment seat of Christ, where those who have lovingly and obediently served Him will receive rewards. The judgment seat for the saved will not be a place of condemnation (see Rom. 8:1).

Our passages in Revelation describe a very different scene. The great white throne appears to be a seat on which only condemnation takes place. Every person who has refused God will stand before Him that dreadful day. Though the earth and sky will try to flee His awesome presence, those who have refused God will have no place to run.

Those who have refused God will have no place to run.

Carefully look at Revelation 20:13. How will each person who stands before the great white throne be judged?

_____

_____

Perhaps you noticed the one similarity between our judgments. Reward will be given according to the deeds of those saved by the blood of the Lamb. Likewise, punishment will be given according to the deeds of those who refused it. I am convinced that Revelation 20:13 intimates differing levels of punishment according to the depths and lengths of the evil accomplished by each person. Why would I have ever thought otherwise? Is God not just? Doesn't He look on the individual hearts and deeds of every responsible person?

The lake of fire will be a place of torment for every inhabitant, but I believe Scripture teaches that punishment will vary according to each person's deeds. The righteous Judge knows every thought and rightly discerns every motive of our hearts. As we learned in Romans 2:2, His judgments are based on truth.

God began His magnificent creation of humankind with one man. Though the plains of planet Earth now bulge with six billion people, God still breathes life into each being one at a time. We were fashioned for God and were designed to seek Him. He created a universe and an order with the divine purpose of bearing constant witness to His existence. Heaven unceasingly declares His glory, and all who truly seek Him find Him.

Not one person's absence from heaven will go unnoticed by God. Not one will get past God haphazardly. Not one will accidentally get swept away in a sea of nameless souls. God is not careless. He intimately knows every soul that will refuse to know Him. Because He created us for fellowship, God's judgments cannot be rendered with cold, sterile detachment. God so loved the world that He sent His Son to seek and to save the lost. Though none can refuse to be seen, many will refuse to be found.

God's passionate plea from Ezekiel 33:11 rises in volume as the day draws nearer. "As surely as I live, declares the Sovereign Lord, I take no pleasure in the death of the wicked, but rather that they turn from their ways and live. Turn! Turn from your evil ways! Why will you die?"

Day 4 THE NEW JERUSALEM

TODAY'S TREASURE

"I saw the Holy City, the new Jerusalem, coming down out of heaven from God, prepared as a bride beautifully dressed for her husband."—Revelation 21:2

I have grown to love John through our weeks of study. I enjoy imagining that he could have been nothing more than a teenager when Christ bade him follow. The possibility that John was the youngest disciple also propels my imagination. Did the others pick on him yet favor him? These men shared deep interpersonal relationships. They worked together, traveled together, ate together, and slept under the stars together. They saw wonders and horrors together. They grieved and hoped together. I'm not sure many of us could boast the kinds of relationships these men shared.

Years passed, and that small band of apostles scattered like seed cast from the hand of the Gardener. His sovereign fingers cast some of the seed into soil not far from their homeland, but at the flick of His wrist others sailed seas. John was one of those. His exile invited many unwelcome opportunities, but one the bittersweet gifts of the desolate island surely was remembrance. Like the sun reflecting off the briny waters, John must have reflected on all the twists and turns of divine destiny that brought him to the mounds of rock rising from the sea. Patmos.

> John must have reflected on the divine destiny that brought him back to Patmos.

Reflect on yesterday's lesson and glance once again at Revelation 20. List a few things John saw and recorded in that part of the vision.

Now imagine having been the one to see those sights! Do you realize that John saw Satan? Like us, he had seen his activity in thousands of ways, but he had never seen his visible and unholy essence. In the Revelation 20 vision, John saw him bound, loosed, then doomed. Keep in mind that John probably survived his stay on Patmos. Writings of the early church fathers return him to Ephesus.

We have no idea how long John lived, but how do you think his vision of Satan affected how he thought and taught from that time forward?

Now imagine John seeing the final judgment of the lost at the great white throne. Don't separate his sights from his personality and emotional makeup. Think about the tender heart of this disciple. Perhaps no one wanted to see people shun the love of God and perish less than John. Before his very eyes the sea, death, and Hades gave up their unbelieving dead, and they were judged for their deeds. After death and Hades were thrown in the lake of fire, the unbelieving were cast there, as well. John saw all of this!

How do you think the sight of the judgment affected the way John thought and taught from that time forward?

_____

Today our thoughts will center on the sights John beheld in Revelation 21. Look only at the first word of Revelation 21:1: "then." Oh, Beloved, how I thank God for *then*. Your life may be excruciating right now. Your challenges may be more than you can stand. Your strength may be sapped. Your health may be terrible. No matter how difficult this present season, Dear One, God has a *then* on your time line of faith. Every believer has a new chapter ahead that is filled with dreams come true. Whatever you are facing is not the end of the story.

> Whatever you are facing is not the end of the story.

Please read all of Revelation 21. Contrast its hopes with the horrors of the chapter preceding it. Record various ways Revelation 21 contrasts with Revelation 20. Give this exercise deep thought. No two chapters of New Testament Scripture provide a more profound side-by-side contrast of eternal destiny for the lost and the saved.

_____

_____

_____

_____

Now let's look at the elements in Revelation 21 that may have meant the most to the apostle John. According to Revelation 21:1, what was different in the new heaven and the new earth?

"There was no longer any _____."

Some historians claim that the coast a few miles from Ephesus could be seen from the tip of Patmos on a crystal-clear day. Imagine how John longed for those he served, aching to see them and tearfully pleading that they return to their first love.

What might the sea between them have represented to John?

_____

I long for the day when seas will no longer separate brothers and sisters in the family of God. I want to know my faithful brothers in Sudan, Iran, and all over the world. My dear coworker Sabrina loves the ocean the way I love the mountains. She would hardly be able to imagine heaven with no sea. We know for a fact that heaven will have at least two bodies of water, because Revelation records rivers and a crystal sea. Remember, much of the terminology in the final book of the Bible is figurative. I believe the reference in Revelation 21:1 to no sea means that nothing else will ever separate us. We will be one just as Christ asked the Father (see John 17:20-23). We will have all the beauty of the oceans without the separation.

After telling us that the new heavens and earth will not be disjointed by seas, John described the new Jerusalem. Meditate on his words: "I saw the Holy City" (v. 2). I am convinced that most of us Gentiles cannot relate to the attachment many Jews through the centuries have felt toward their homeland. Even those whose feet never touched the Holy Land yearned for it as a lost child longs for her mother.

I saw this peculiar bond just weeks ago in the face of my Hebrew friend and ancient lands' guide, Arie. He and his family are now residents of Tel Aviv, but his heart never departs Jerusalem. The turmoil erupting within and around Jerusalem doesn't just concern or upset him. It brings him pain. I asked him how he felt about the ongoing crisis in the Holy Land. As I witnessed the agony in his face, I sorrowed that I had asked something so obviously intimate. I consider myself very patriotic; yet I had to acknowledge that I knew nothing of Arie's attachment to his homeland.

How does Psalm 137:5-6 describe many Jews' attachment to Jerusalem?

Arie told me that the deeply heartfelt commitment to keep Jerusalem ever before them is restated at every Orthodox Jewish wedding. In the midst of joy they always remember Jerusalem and the tragic loss of the temple. If Arie and other Jews through the ages have experienced an indescribable attachment to the holy city and a sense of grief over the temple, try to imagine the strength of John's ties. He grew up on the shores of Galilee at the highest peak of Jerusalem's splendor since the days of Solomon's temple. Herod's temple was one of the greatest wonders of John's world. No Jew could behold its splendor without marveling. Even weeping.

John knew every wall and gate of the holy city. He had walked the lengths and breadths with the Savior Himself. He had sat near Him on the Mount of Olives overlooking its beauty. John was also part of the generation who saw the city's destruction in A.D. 70. By the time Jerusalem fell, John was probably already stationed in Ephesus, but the news traveled fast, and the sobs echoed louder with every mile. The grief of the diaspora, mixed with the unreasonable guilt of not having died with the city, surely shook their homesick souls.

Then John "saw the Holy City, the new Jerusalem, coming down out of heaven from God, prepared as a bride beautifully dressed for her husband" (Rev. 21:2). How his heart must have leapt with unspeakable joy! There it was! Not just restored but created anew with splendor beyond compare. " 'He will wipe every tear from their eyes' " (Rev. 21:4). I wonder if John was weeping at the sight.

Some people say that we won't be able to cry in the new heaven and earth. Clearly, we get at least one last good cry, since God will wipe away every tear! I cannot imagine that I am going to see my Christ and my God and their heavenly kingdom and not weep.

Our last tears, however, will no longer be those shed in mourning:
" 'There will be no more death or mourning or crying or pain, for the

_____ _____ _____ _____ has passed away' " (Rev. 21:4).

We are shocked by pain again and again; yet it characterizes our existence.

Since Adam and Eve grieved over the loss of intimate fellowship with God and the agony of one son murdered by the other, life has been characterized as the old order. We are shocked by pain again and again; yet it characterizes our existence. None of us can avoid it. We can anesthetize pain, but we will neither fully experience this life nor celebrate the next without it.

To what part of this old order will you be happiest to bid farewell?

_____

The new order will bring all things to completion and will prepare the heaven and the earth for eternal bliss. " 'Now the dwelling of God is with men' " (Rev. 21:3). Hallelujah! The sorrow of man's expulsion from the garden will be exceeded only by the unquenchable joy of God's dwelling with men. You may have noticed that John did not see a temple, sun, or moon in this new Jerusalem.

The sorrow of expulsion from the garden will be exceeded only by the joy of God's dwelling with us.

Why will these elements be absent in the new holy city (see Rev. 21:22-23)?

_____

Perhaps you also noticed another reference to "the kings of the earth" (v. 24). These kings stand in stark contrast to the kings of the earth in Revelation 19:19 who will rise against the Rider called Faithful and True. I believe "the kings of the earth" who will bring splendor into the new holy city may be the redeemed described in Revelation 20:4 and others like them.

Who are these redeemed, and what specifically will they do?

_____

When God creates the new heaven and the new earth, I think quite possibly those who reign with Him in the kingdom—not as equals but under His authority—will be among those bringing "their splendor into" the new holy city. I also believe that prior to the end of time kings of many nations will bow their knees in adoration and confession of Jesus Christ, the Son of God. Indeed, "the glory and honor of the nations will be brought into it" (Rev. 21:26). Our future is beyond the words and imaginations of scholars, poets, and Hollywood movie producers. We will bask in the brilliance of our God when He proclaims a new beginning and creates a heaven and an earth from the ideal of His imagination.

As we conclude today's lesson, let's take one last glimpse at a detail in the new Jerusalem that might have had a fairly profound impact on John.

What did John see on the 12 foundations of the city wall (see Rev. 21:14)?

_____

Beloved, do you realize that among them John saw his own name? This was the John who refused to write his own name in the Gospel he penned. Can you imagine what kinds of thoughts he had as he saw his name on a foundation of the New Jerusalem?

I have no idea what being one of Jesus' disciples was like, but I don't think they felt superhuman or vaguely worthy of their calling. I'm not even sure those original disciples ever grasped that what they were doing would change the world. I can't picture them thinking, *What I'm doing this moment will go down in history and will be recorded in the eternal annals of glory.* I think they probably got down on themselves just as you and I do. I also think they were terribly overwhelmed at the prospect of reaching their world with the gospel of Christ and sometimes seeing only handfuls of converts.

Days and months later, when John stared at that wall and its foundations again in his memory, can't you imagine he was overcome that God esteemed them? And marveled that the plan had worked, considering the mortal agents He had chosen to use?

Every day I deal with a measure of low self-esteem in ministry. I never feel up to the task. Never smart enough. Never strong enough. Never prayed up enough. Never prepared enough. Do you feel the same way? Then perhaps you also feel the same flood of emotions when this truth washes over you: God loves us. He prepares an inconceivable place for those who receive His love and highly esteems those who choose to believe His call over the paralyzing screams of their own insecurities. No, our names won't be written on the foundations of the New Jerusalem, but they are engraved in the palm of His hands (see Isa. 49:16).

> God loves us. He prepares an inconceivable place for those who receive His love.

Day 5 SEEING HIS FACE

TODAY'S TREASURE
"They will see his face, and his name will be on their foreheads."—Revelation 22:4

I can hardly believe my eyes. How can our time together have passed so quickly? The last day of study is always the most difficult for me to write, primarily because I hate good-byes. Years ago in my broken state I begged God to completely consume my imagination, because I knew I would never be free until He transformed my thinking. In answer to that prayer, God has granted me an imagination to picture spiritual realities almost as vividly as the physical. The journey you and I have taken for the past 10 weeks is as real to me as anything we could have experienced face-to-face. Even though I may never have seen your face, I have pictured you hundreds of times, esteemed your place in the body of Christ, and grown very fond of your company. We have walked side by side. I do not want to be someone others follow. My deepest desire has been to journey beside you, opening God's Word together and conversing over its truths.

Another reason the last day of study is difficult to write is that I want to say so much before we part. I felt the same way when I left Amanda at college for the first time. As the tears welled in our eyes, I said, "Baby, I had so much I wanted to say, and right now I am so overcome, I'm at a loss for words." I'll never forget her response. "Mom, you said it all yesterday … and the day before that." We both laughed. That's what I get for talking so much. I've already used up all my good words by the time a really profound moment rolls around. You've heard far too many words from me as it is.

I grin as I remember a letter I received from a woman who tried to do one of my Bible studies. She described my approach like this: "So many words. So little said." I laughed my head off and added a hearty "Amen!" I say too much. Talk too long. Get too involved. I'm passionate to the point of looking foolish to my critics. I am over my head and underqualified, but this I can assure you: I love. It's real. And I have loved you.

We've come to a Y in the road, but before we say good-bye, let's sit down for a little while and open our Bibles together. A river happens to be in our reading today. Why don't we go sit on a rock on its shore, take off our sandals, and put our feet in? Please read the last chapter in the inspired Word of God, Revelation 22. Fill in pertinent information in the following categories.

Additional descriptions of the new heaven and earth:_____

_____

John's personal responses:_____

_____

Warnings: _____

_____

Invitations: _____

_____

Twice toward the end of the Revelation John became so overwhelmed at the sight of such glorious visions that he fell at the feet of the angel (see Rev. 19:10; 22:8-9). Both times John received a swift rebuke and a reminder that the angel was nothing more than a " 'fellow servant' " (v. 10). Amazing, isn't it? We work side by side with the angels from glory. They are our fellow servants! Remember that next time you feel alone in your task.

I'd also like to draw another application from John's untimely buckling of the knees. He did not make the mistake of falling down at the feet of the angel when the visions were difficult and frightening to behold. He fell over the good news. God has performed the phenomenal through the past several years of Bible studies. We have increasingly heard from members of every denomination and segment in the body of Christ. Nothing could be more thrilling to me, because my call to interdenominational ministry is deep. At the same time, please let me issue a warning. Satan's primary objective is to entice us to bow to anything and anyone other than God. I believe Christians will be most tempted to fall down and worship spokespersons who tell us what we want to hear. In the words of the angel, " 'Do not do it!' " (v. 10). Worship God alone.

Now let's camp on Revelation 22:2 for a moment.

What lessons can you draw from comparing Revelation 22:2 with Psalm 1:1-3?

_____

_____

During our stay on this earth we are meant to be like trees of life bringing forth fruit in our seasons so that others can taste and see that the Lord is good (see Ps. 34:8). In order to bear much fruit, we've got to stay by the river. Perhaps even in it! I can hardly wait for you to compare this verse with Ezekiel 47:1-12.

We are meant to bring forth fruit so others can taste and see that the Lord is good.

What might the river represent, according to these verses? _____

_____

The river in both visions seems to represent the outpouring of God's power and anointing. As we conclude our journey together, I pray that we've progressed in our walk with

God, taken off our rationalizing seat belts, and thrown ourselves into His great adventure. In the introduction we considered the first words of Christ John penned.

What was the question in John 1:38? _____

_____

In the introductory video segment I asked you to write a letter of response to Christ, sharing with Him what you were seeking most at that present season of your life. I asked you to tape your letter on the inside of the back cover. After you conclude this lesson, if you're ready, you may read your letter and, if you wish, share its insights with your group.

Based on Ezekiel 47:3-6, how deeply do you see yourself in the figurative river of Christ's power and activity?
❑ Still on the bank   ❑ Ankle deep   ❑ Knee deep
❑ Waist deep   ❑ Swimming!
Reflect on where you were when we began this journey. Underline the choice above that characterized you best at that time.

We will not be completely
healed until we see Christ
face-to-face.

Beloved, I don't want you to be discouraged if you're not waist deep or swimming. I am only asking whether we are more deeply immersed in Christ than when we began. Are we progressing? That's one of the most important questions of all. Mind you, we can swim one season and crawl our way right back onto the bank and even into the desert the next. We will not be completely healed of our inconsistencies, infirmities, and weaknesses until we see Christ face-to-face.

Face-to-face. I can't think of a more fitting focus for our last few moments together. I hope you didn't miss the most beautiful statement in the final chapter of Scripture: "They will see his face" (Rev. 22:4). For many of us the very sight of His face will be heaven enough. Everything else is the river overflowing its banks. Until then, we who are redeemed are like spirit-people wrapped in prison walls of flesh. Our view is impaired by the steel bars of mortal vision. We are not unlike Moses, who experienced God's presence but could not see His face. To him and to all confined momentarily by mortality, God has said, " 'You cannot see my face, for no one may see me and live' " (Ex. 33:20).

When all is said and done, we who are alive in Christ will indeed see His face and live. Happily ever after. I can hardly wait—yet right this moment I am absorbed by the thought of someone else seeing that face. Someone I've grown to love and appreciate so deeply over the past 10 weeks. Several of the early church fathers plant the apostle John back in Ephesus again after the conclusion of his exile on the island of Patmos. I wonder what kinds of thoughts swirled through his mind as he returned to Asia Minor. I've made this trip by sea and, though it is beautiful, it is not brief. As his thinning gray hair blew across his face, he had time to experience a host of emotions. We have gotten to know him well.

List the kinds of things you imagine John thought and felt on the ride back to Ephesus.

_____

_____

John lived to be a very old man. We have no idea how many years he lived beyond his exile. The earliest historians indicate, however, that the vitality of his spirit far exceeded the strength of his frame. His passionate heart continued to beat for the Savior he loved for so long. In closing, please read some of the words obviously inscribed on his heart as deeply as on his pages.

How had John lived the essence of John 15:12-17? _____

_____

John ended his life a true friend of Christ, for he took on His interests as surely as Elisha took on the cloak of Elijah. Early church fathers reported that long after John lacked the strength to walk, the beloved disciple was carried in a chair through crowds gathered for worship. John's final sermons were short and sweet: "My little children, love one another!" He poured his life into love. Christ's love. The focus of his final days captures the two concepts I've learned above all others in this 10-week journey.

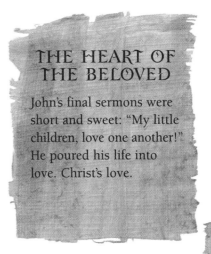

THE HEART OF THE BELOVED

John's final sermons were short and sweet: "My little children, love one another!" He poured his life into love. Christ's love.

- Christ calls His beloved disciples to forsake ambition for affection. John moved from his pillar position in the Jerusalem church to relative obscurity. Better to pour out our lives in places unknown than to become dry bones in the places we've always been.
- Only disciples who are convinced they are beloved will in turn love beyond themselves. Actively embracing the lavish love of God is our only means of extending divine love to injured hearts. We simply cannot give what we do not have.

Our Abba seems to have made a practice of telling us almost nothing about the actual deaths of His saints. According to Psalm 116:15, we know that their deaths were precious to Him. In fact, we might surmise that the exclusion of details is precisely because they were so precious to Him. Intimate. And none of our business. But don't think for a moment the Savior wasn't nearby when the sounds of an old Son of Thunder grew faint and then silent. After all, John was among the very few who stood nearby when the incarnate Word fell silent.

John's death marked the close of the most critical era of human history. He was the single remaining apostle who could make the claims with his own pen: "That which was from the beginning, which we have heard, which we have seen with our eyes, which we have looked at and our hands have touched—this we proclaim concerning the Word of life" (1 John 1:1). *We* had turned to *I*, and soon *I* would turn to *they*.

At his age John's fragile body probably showed symptoms of failing some hours or even days before he breathed his last. If loved ones gathered around him, they likely did what most of us would do. They tried to make him as comfortable as possible. They may have gently slipped a pillow under his head to help support him as his lungs heaved for air. That's what we did when my mother's fragile frame could no longer sustain the strength to house her soul.

However, I'm not sure John needed a pillow. Somehow I picture him in his death much the way he had been in his life. To me, the scene that most vividly captures the beloved disciple appears in John 13:23 at a certain table decades earlier. The *Amplified Bible* says it best: "One of His disciples whom Jesus loved [whom He esteemed and delighted in], was reclining [next to Him] on Jesus' bosom" (John 13:23). Yes, perhaps John died just as he had lived. Nestled close. Reclining on the breast of an unseen but very present Savior, John's weary head in His tender arms. "The Spirit and the bride say, 'Come!'" (Rev. 22:17). And in the distance could be heard gentle thunder.

BELOVED DISCIPLE

My eyes grow dim.
   My strength grows faint.
I wonder, Lord,
   why do You wait?

That day with John
   when You walked past,
I was so young—
   could follow fast!

We lived, it seemed,
   at whirlwind's pace.
Whirling wonders
   place to place.

So far removed,
   sometimes I dream
I'm there again,
   so real it seems.

I laugh with You.
   I see You walk.
On waters mad
   I hear You talk.

I lean against
   Your shoulder there.
I hear You breathe
   away my cares.

Dream's rooster crows.
   I jerk to wake.
Tears stain my face.
   Why do You wait?

My thunder's gone.
   The young have come
their place to take
   and fast to run.

My passions stilled,
   I have no taste
for all but You.
   Why do You wait?

My skin wraps bone.
   My bones, they ache.
I reach for You!
   Why do You wait?

An answer comes,
   though none can hear.
While old man weeps,
   the Lamb draws near.

"Son of Thunder,
   if you knew
hell's angry rumble
   over you!

My faithful son,
   'tis easier still
to jump the cliff
   than climb the hill.

You stayed the course
   when days wore on.
Love burned white hot
   while life grew long.

Long after faith
   of friends sparked sight,
and victor's crowns
   replaced their plight,

You yet remained
   and loved again.
Why do I wait,
   My faithful friend?

Because the sight
   prepared for you
is beyond white
   and beyond blue.

I dim your eyes
   like stage grows dark.
Anticipate!
   Till curtains part."

The old man sobbed,
   heard not a word,
rose from rock bed,
   pained joints stirred.

"Let's see," he mused,
   "What day is this?
Ah, Sabbath's passed.
   Lord's Day it is."

He groaned deep prayers.
   He thundered praise.
A man in Spirit
   on his Lord's Day.

Then startling came
   a voice behind,
like trumpet talking,
   voice divine!

John whirled around,
   and there He was:
the One who is,
   the One who was.

His body froze,
   his soul afret.
A sight too much,
   he fell as dead.

Then healing voice
   spoke life to lung,
"Take scroll and write
   the vision, Son.

Am I not still
   the God of time?
Make I mistakes?
   Have I no mind?

If sovereign I
   should choose to wait,
while you yet live—
   anticipate!"

Prepare, O bride.
   Let eyes grow dim.
Die, lesser sights.
   Cast eyes on Him.

Spend yourself
   till stage is set.
Beloved Disciple,
   love still yet.

VIDEO RESPONSE SHEET

Group Session 10

1. The one-word call to worship probably has great significance (v. 7). The word *hallelujah* (NIV) or *alleluia* (KJV) comes from the original Hebrew *halelu,* meaning to _____, and *Yah,* the shortened form of _____ or _____. With one exception (Ps. 135:3), *allellouia* is always found at the beginning or end of psalms, suggesting that it was a _____ call to praise in the _____ _____. This may suggest that, although every nation, tribe, and tongue will be part of this glorious wedding, the ceremony itself may be decidedly _____.

In ancient Hebrew tradition ...

2. The actual wedding arrangements were the responsibility of the _____ and _____ _____. (See Judg. 14:10-11.)

3. The chief responsibility of the bride was to _____ _____ (v. 7):

   • The bride prioritized _____.

   • The bride took special baths of _____ _____ and _____ _____.

   • The bride chose _____ jewelry to wear on her wedding day.

4. During the ceremony, held under the _____ _____ or *huppah,* the bride traditionally _____ the groom (Jer. 31:22).

5. _____ _____ were pronounced during the ceremony (Rev. 21:1-3,22-23).

6. Although deep repentance and personal cleansing took place in preparation, the actual wedding day was marked by great _____ of _____ (Song of Songs 3:11).

   • Custom prohibited anyone from _____ or _____ on the day of the wedding (Rev. 19:7).

   • The original word for "be glad" is *agalliao,* which means "to _____, rejoice with exuberance; often to _____ for _____, show one's joy by _____, _____, or _____, denoting _____ or ecstatic joy and delight."

Personalize Isaiah 62:5: "As a bridegroom rejoices over his bride, so will [my] _____ _____ over ____."

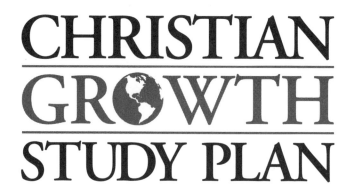

CHRISTIAN GROWTH STUDY PLAN

In the **Christian Growth Study Plan (formerly the Church Study Course)**, this book *Beloved Disciple* is a resource for course credit in the subject area Personal Life in the Christian Growth category of plans. To receive credit, read the book; complete the learning activities; attend group sessions; show your work to your pastor, a staff member, or a church leader, then complete the information on this page. The form may be duplicated. Send the completed page to:

Christian Growth Study Plan
One LifeWay Plaza, Nashville, TN 37234-0117
Fax: (615) 251-5067, email: *cgspnet@lifeway.com*
For information about the Christian Growth Study Plan, refer to the *Christian Growth Study Plan Catalog*. It is located online at *www.lifeway.com/cgsp*. If you do not have access to the Internet, contact the Christian Growth Study Plan office, 1-800-968-5519, for the specific plan you need for your ministry.

Beloved Disciple
COURSE NUMBER: CG-0707

PARTICIPANT INFORMATION

Social Security Number (USA ONLY-optional)	Personal CGSP Number*	Date of Birth (MONTH, DAY, YEAR)
– –	– –	– –

Name (First, Middle, Last)		Home Phone
		– –

Address (Street, Route, or P.O. Box)	City, State, or Province	Zip/Postal Code

Please check appropriate box: ❑ Resource purchased by self   ❑ Resource purchased by church   ❑ Other

CHURCH INFORMATION

Church Name

Address (Street, Route, or P.O. Box)	City, State, or Province	Zip/Postal Code

CHANGE REQUEST ONLY

☐ Former Name		
☐ Former Address	City, State, or Province	Zip/Postal Code
☐ Former Church	City, State, or Province	Zip/Postal Code

Signature of Pastor, Conference Leader, or Other Church Leader	Date

*New participants are requested but not required to give SS# and date of birth. Existing participants, please give CGSP# when using SS# for the first time. Thereafter, only one ID# is required. **Mail to:** Christian Growth Study Plan, One LifeWay Plaza, Nashville, TN 37234-0117. Fax: (615)251-5067.

Rev. 3-03